MAKING GENDER WORK

MANAGING WORK AND ORGANIZATIONS SERIES

Edited by Graeme Salaman, Reader in Sociology in the Faculty of Social Sciences and the Open Business School, the Open University

Current and forthcoming titles include:

MAKING GENDER
WORK
MANAGING EQUAL OPPORTUNITIES

Edited by
Jenny Shaw and
Diane Perrons

Open University Press
Buckingham · Philadelphia

Open University Press
Celtic Court
22 Ballmoor
Buckingham
MK18 1XW

and
1900 Frost Road, Suite 101
Bristol, PA 19007, USA

First Published 1995

A catalogue record of this book is available from the British Library

ISBN   0 335 19365 X (pb)   0 335 19366 8 (hb)

Library of Congress Cataloging-in-Publication Data
Making gender work: managing equal opportunities / [edited by] Jenny
    Shaw and Diane Perrons.
       p.   cm.
    Includes bibliographical references and index.
    ISBN 0-335-19366-8 (hb). — ISBN 0-335-19365-X (pb)
    1. Sex discrimination in employment. 2. Sex discrimination against
women. 3. Sex discrimination in employment—Great Britain. 4. Sex
discrimination against women—Great Britain. I. Shaw, Jenny, II.
Perrons, Diane C.
HD6060.M35   1995
658.3′042—dc20   95-15678
                                                                         CIP

Typeset by Type Study, Scarborough
Printed in Great Britain by St Edmundsbury Press Ltd,
Bury St Edmunds, Suffolk

CONTENTS

Contents

CONTRIBUTORS

Helen Brown is Head of Women's Development at the Office for Public Management. She is author of *Women Organising* (Routledge 1992), as well as numerous articles on gender issues in organizations. Currently she is concerned with developing new approaches to women which are effective across organizations and cultures within a context of social responsibility.

Paul Burnett is employed by East Sussex County Council. He has interests in education and has had responsibility for overseeing the Equal Opportunities Policy for the Council.

Linda Clarke studied law at Sussex University and Trinity Hall, Cambridge. She qualified as a barrister and is currently a lecturer in the Centre for Legal Studies at Sussex University. She is an Associate Adviser to the Industrial Society and writes regularly on employment law.

Rita Donaghy is on the National Executive Council of UNISON (Public Service Union), member of the Trades Union Congress (TUC) General Council and member of the Executive of the European TUC. She was an international observer at the first democratic elections in South Africa. She is permanent secretary for the Student Union, Institute of Education, London University.

Contributors

Lisa Harker is currently Research and Information Officer at the Child Poverty Action Group. Formerly she worked as a researcher specializing in family-friendly policies at the Daycare Trust. She is co-author of *The Family-friendly Employer: Examples From Europe* (Daycare Trust 1992) and co-editor of *Making Family-friendly Policies Work* (Daycare Trust 1993).

Margaret Hodge has been MP for Barking since June 1994. She was elected councillor for the London Borough of Islington 1973–94. During that time she chaired the Housing Committee from 1975–8 and was Leader of Islington Council from 1982–92. She founded and chaired the Association of London Authorities from 1984–92 and was Vice Chair of the Association of Metropolitan Authorities from 1990–1. Between 1992 and 1994 she worked as a public sector consultant with Price Waterhouse and as Visiting Fellow at the Institute of Public Policy Research.

Sally Holtermann is an independent research economist and formerly a Senior Economic Adviser in the Department of Health and Social Security. In recent years she has specialized in issues around women's employment, child care and equal opportunities.

Carole Pemberton is a research consultant at the Sundridge Park Management Centre, Bromley. She specializes in career management from the perspectives of the individual and the organization. She is co-author (with Peter Herriot) of *Competitive Advantage Through Adversity* (Sage 1994) and *New Deals: The Revolution in Managerial Careers* (Wiley 1995).

Diane Perrons taught for many years in the School of Business Studies at London Guildhall University. Recently she has moved to the Department of Geography at the London School of Economics and Political Science. Her research interests include equal opportunities policies and employment change, and more generally economic and social cohesion in Europe. She is a coordinator of the European Science Foundation Network on gender inequality in Europe.

Jenny Shaw is a sociologist in the School of Cultural and Community Studies at the University of Sussex. Her current research interests include the pace of life, time negotiation in families and shopping. She is the author of *Education, Gender and Anxiety* (Taylor and Francis 1995) and *Why the Rush?* (Routledge 1996).

Gillian Stamp is Director of the Institute of Organization and Social Studies at Brunel University. She is currently involved in the continued developments emerging from the Career Path Appreciation (CPA) approach to evaluating the potential of individuals and helping to design organizations. The work is especially pertinent to societies and economies in rapid change, and a current project involves collaboration with non-governmental organizations (NGOs) and commercial banks in South Africa to research, design and implement the best lending and borrowing practices for micro- and medium-scale entrepreneurs.

Ruth Valentine has worked for over twenty years in the voluntary sector, initially as a manager and trainer, and for the past four years as a freelance consultant. She is also a poet and fiction writer, teaches creative writing and is training as a psychotherapist.

INTRODUCTION – GENDER WORK

Jenny Shaw and Diane Perrons

For some people gender *is* their work, whilst for others it is the reason why they get more or less pay, training and recognition *at* work. This book is a response to both the rise of jobs or careers in equal opportunities and the conditions which make such jobs necessary a quarter of a century after legislation outlawing unequal pay was introduced in Great Britain. A key trend is the rising one of sex discrimination cases going to tribunal which, at the rate of over 25 per cent more cases each year, is striking. Whilst it can indicate either a growth in discrimination or confidence that cases can be successfully pursued, whatever interpretation is offered it is clear that work which demands a gender expertise is growing.

Some of this gender work is specialist professional knowledge in the fields of industrial relations, law or personnel management, and some of it is more academic. Courses in women's or gender studies and in feminism have had a dramatic growth in higher and further education for two decades, during which time it has been possible for a minority to build academic careers out of an interest in and commitment to develop feminist and gender theory. Although equal opportunities, or what we call gender work, means different things to different people, it is also clearly the by-product of two distinct revolutions: feminism and the rise of the service sector, itself a function of a shift towards knowledge-based production in modern societies. The first provided the moral justification for the push towards equal opportunities in the workplace, whilst the second provided the grounds for transforming that moral justification into an economic service. As a consequence, gender work is set to expand.

However, the new, paid, gender work is a long way from being a recognized occupation, like social work, with formal qualifications and a professional training, though it is moving in that direction. It is the aim of this book to plot that direction, collect and assemble the expertise of practitioners and academics working in the field, provide some practical guidelines and anticipate new forms of exploitation and gender divisions. As a 'toolkit' book it is intended to help those involved in gender work to come up with practical suggestions, design policies and give good advice; and as a review of contemporary issues concerned with gender and work, it is designed to provide an analysis of the context within which those policies will be enacted.

Ten to fifteen years ago, there were relatively few jobs in equal opportunities in Great Britain, and relatively few graduates entering the labour force with degrees which included, in all or part, courses in feminism, gender or women's studies. Today there are many such jobs and thousands of such graduates keen to turn an academic knowledge of gender into a vocational skill. In Australia such people are sometimes called 'femocrats', feminists who have chosen to pursue their politics and the goal of gender equality from inside state bureaucracies. There are, of course, many others who may not think of themselves as feminists, but who bear responsibility for managing equal opportunity, and still more, often freelance, who offer practical courses in assertiveness training, presentational skills, anti-sexism and women's rights. However, the catch to this development is that it comes as part of the employment revolution which is said to spell the end of the secure 'career' and to enjoin workers, instead, to 'go portfolio' (Kanter 1990; Handy 1994).

Celebrants of the trend see a more nimble, up-to-date and responsive labour force and claim that it may even be gender-progressive as it is women who have centuries' experience of flexible working and related survival strategies which they might turn to competitive advantage. Others, less optimistic, see a need for vigilance and for specialists who can identify new trends and modes of exploitation and explain why old ones reappear. Either way, the freelance equal opportunities consultant is the arche-typal new worker and product of several combined trends – a feminized labour force, service sector growth, greater insecurity and self-employment – the analysis of which is their stock-in-trade.

Whilst fed by changing employment conditions, the growth of gender work marks a significant shift in feminist politics. Of the many changes that second wave feminism has undergone since 1970, mainstreaming as well as diversification, it is clearly no longer a sect pursuing marginal politics and strategies. The next stage on from 'the personal is political' is to make politics work and this has extended the debate beyond family life, personal relations and work into questions of rights and citizenship, as well as to the establishment of institutions such as the Equal Opportunities Commission (EOC) and Opportunity 2000. Never-theless, for many years most practical gender work was of the unpaid, voluntary or directly political variety. In the early 1970s female academics were often resented as exploiting feminist activists, and there may be a similar suspicion surrounding the equal opportunities industry of today. Professionals are often viewed as self-serving, and some scepticism about expertise is usually healthy, but the hostility towards making a career out of gender indicates something else too. Founded in part, quite honourably, on a commitment to grass-roots politics and a desire to avoid the risk of being compromised by payment, it also draws on the traditional view that the purity of women's commitment derives from their sense of 'vocation' and willingness to work for no money. Making gender work cuts through some of these hitherto hidden forms of exploitation.

As university teachers we had begun to feel uneasy about the fates of our students who went into gender work and responsible for those who might follow them. We feared their entering the workplace relatively unprepared and guessed that, as juniors in their organizations, they might face overwhelming tasks and political minefields. Many would, and did, retire bruised by the experience, determined to plough easier furrows. For pursuing a career in equal opportunities is no easy option. Of course, pioneers in any field tend to bear heavy personal costs. However, the results of a survey of equal opportunity personnel are somewhat shocking (Kandola *et al*. 1991). Not only was turnover high and training negligible, but three-quarters of those surveyed were determined to move out of both their job and the organization; and 90 per cent showed higher than average symptoms of physical illness. Measures of mental health problems and stress on the home/work front were almost as high. Even more depressingly, a number of these pioneers have themselves become subjects of internal or legal actions. The Equal Opportunities Commission has faced legal action for sex discrimination and the first equal opportunities officer to work in higher education has similarly been involved in legal action with her employer over equal opportunities. It is a risky business.

Intending gender workers need to take time to understand both organizational cultures and the culture of equality if they are to escape feelings of incompetence or dented self-esteem which can mark those working in the field, especially if they enter it unprepared. They must expect conscious resistance to their efforts and be aware of how hard it is to change basic assumptions; but they also need to be alert to unconscious sources of resistance in themselves and in the organizations which are even harder to deal with (Obholzer and Roberts 1994). Social identity clearly makes a difference to the strategies that can be pursued, as well as to the outcomes. So being male, female, an insider or outsider (e.g. consultant) are as important as place in the formal hierarchy – especially as they make a difference at the unconscious level. In particular there are gender-specific phantasies of omnipotence underlying the concerted effort to bring about change (Ernst 1989). Male phantasies, for example, tend towards feelings based on mastery of the environment whilst women's tend towards an unconscious image of a nurturing, but equally powerful, mother. Both versions are misleading and if not recognized lead to disappointment and rejection, of the job, of oneself, or of the very possibility of equal opportunities work. The saving up of impossible tasks for one person to sort out, the consultant, the new appointment or a senior manager, for example, display how in the face of difficulty phantasies can be projected on to and into another person.

The original idea behind this book, therefore, was to make available a number of realistic, first-hand accounts and to contextualize them so that students thinking about working in this area would enter with their eyes open, knowing what needed to be done and carry with them a set of skills with which to start work. Such an aim is clearly a reflection of another gap, that between the optimism of youth and the disenchantment of seasoned feminists such as ourselves who both feared depressing our students with accounts of persistent discrimination, yet also found their reluctance to believe such accounts naive. The problem is partly a generational one, but it is also that the situation is confusing. In 1994 Kate Figes, daughter of a prominent second wave feminist, Eva Figes, published a book decrying the 'myth' that women were now equal to men in Britain (Figes 1994). However, in the same year, another feminist of the younger generation, Helen Wilkinson (1994), published a report showing that British values had become feminized, that younger women felt equal to young men and did not expect to face discrimination. The same time and the same country, but opposite interpretations. This is not so surprising, for the world is a complex place and there is no single, dominant theory of gender or even dominant account of what governs gender relations within the workplace with which to make sense of this complexity.

However, all the contributions to this book imply some theoretical perspective: for effective intervention always depends on knowing something about the processes one wants to influence. Whilst they may not seem to relate directly to contemporary discussions, say, of the relationship between sex and gender or whether the aim of reform should be to start from an assumption that men and women are different or the same, there are theoretical distinctions which inform all the forms of intervention discussed here and they fall broadly into three categories: structural ones, organizational ones and individual ones.

Structuralist explanations focus on institutions such as the labour market (Scott 1994; Sally Holtermann, Chapter 3). Although sometimes they may focus more broadly on patriarchal (i.e. male-dominated) systems (Walby 1988), the important point is that they lead to action only at the most macro, party-political level which, for most people, is not where they see themselves as change agents. Nevertheless, recognizing the scope for change in gender relations at this level is terribly important, as Rita Donaghy, Margaret Hodge and Diane Perrons counsel, for there are some things that only governments, or changes to governments, can do.

Meanwhile, many people yearn for more immediate returns to their efforts and find the idea of change at the organizational level more attractive: though this too may require patience and the long view, as suggested in Paul Burnett's chapter describing the second round of a local authority equal opportunities policy and Carole Pemberton's on culture as a management tool to engineer organizational change. By contrast, other contributors are more optimistic about the speed of change at the organizational level. The policies described by Lisa Harker are practical examples of strategies that a firm determined to make itself family-friendly can adopt within existing structures. Similarly, Diane Perrons gives practical advice on monitoring techniques, Carole Pemberton a blueprint for a gender audit and Gillian Stamp describes both a technique for identifying and releasing hidden potential and the benefits a radical reshaping of an organization's hierarchy can bring.

Legislative frameworks, which are part of the structural level, still require implementation at the level of the organization and committed personnel. Key individuals can be decisive, as Margaret Hodge and Paul Burnett illustrate. Individualistic explanations underpin those strategies which promote change by raising self-esteem, establishing mentoring systems or encouraging role-modelling. All imply that individuals alone, or with a little help, can change either their own or their organization's position. This will not always be possible. Of course, instant success is not an everyday experience with any of these strategies at any level, but if individuals are not to burn themselves out they may sometimes need to content themselves with arguing for a form of consciousness-raising at the individual level, by putting the equalities issue on the agenda.

To avoid despair, identifying the context in which any equal opportunities or gender work is undertaken is crucial. Individuals may be able to exert some influence on the culture of an organization, the shape of the hierarchy or the methods of recruitment and promotion, but they cannot, alone, affect the political, welfare or economic contexts in which we all live; only organized collective action can achieve change at this level. Similarly, if, as some now argue, the gap between men and women's pay is determined by the overall dispersion of wage rates, then effective intervention may need to be two-pronged: that is, aimed both at the unregulated labour markets which produce wide wage differentials as well as at the concentration of women in the lower echelons of that distribution (Blau 1993; Sloane 1994). Knowledge of such broad framing conditions, as well as local variations, is therefore crucial to understanding what can be done. In Part 1 of this volume this socio-economic and legal context is discussed in more detail. Some of our readers, either now or in the future, may be asked to conduct research at the local level and they need to know how their findings relate to the larger, national picture: that is, whether they are typical or subject to certain unique local conditions.

Effective intervention at any level, individual, organizational, structural or political, means recognizing differences between the public, private and voluntary sectors, between firms or organizations within them, and within each sex, between individuals. Gender distinctions can take a somewhat different form in different contexts. For example, gender segregation may run more or less along vertical or horizontal lines (Hakim 1981). Service sector work differs from manufacturing in the form of gender segregation, in the spread of pay differentials and in its overall willingness to adopt equal opportunity policies. In general, local authorities have gone further and faster down the road towards equal opportunities than has the private sector, but the picture is by no means clear cut. Banking has been a front runner in equal opportunities for several years and the public sector is far from uniform. Whilst the NHS was the first organization to join Opportunity 2000, higher education, where gender has become a legitimate research and teaching area, is distinctly backward, as Helen Brown points out in her chapter. This uneven development and sequence of formulation and re-formulation demonstrates that an equal opportunity policy is not a once-and-for-all end in itself, but a continuing process. Circumstances change, new problems arise, backlash has to be dealt with, additional claims become apparent and have to be balanced, while conflicts with other policies have to be negotiated. The different experiences of activists and consultants working in these different sectors are explored in Part 2.

Clearly some sectors have been slower to face up to the problem, or may be less susceptible to the good practice made available by Opportunity 2000. Conflict over priorities and tactics embroils many organizations: for gender work has to compete with other forms of equal opportunities and redefine itself, its aims and objectives, in terms of 'diversity' which looks set to supersede equal opportunity as an acceptable definition. In the conclusion we return to the issue of the changing language and realities of equal opportunities, but note here that interpretations vary. There are broader and narrower definitions of gender (it is sometimes used as a synonym for women) and broader and narrower definitions of equal opportunities. Accordingly, it may no longer be possible to focus on gender matters without making reference also to ethnicity, religion, age, disability and sexual orientation.

To make the picture more complex gender, or masculinity and femininity, is not forged only in the context of woman-to-man relations but out of man-to-man relations or woman-to-woman relations too (Connell 1987; Kandyotti 1994). Consequently, a concern with the fate of a large proportion of women workers may need to be focused on the mechanisms which lead to a polarization in pay and quality of employment between different groups of women workers. For the success of some women may be tied to the continued or growing disadvantage of others, as in the case of a predominantly informal system of childcare where middling or well-paid women depend on other, much lower-paid, female child-minders (Folbre 1994). The 'Nannygate' scandals which blighted President Clinton's attempt to appoint women to senior posts in his administration and discredited the women in question when it was found that they relied on illegal, low-paid immigrant women to look after their children demonstrate both how much women exploit other women and how far childcare costs (economic, personal and political) are still perceived as the exclusive responsibility of mothers and not of fathers.

Advancing equal opportunities is never an easy task and simple solutions rarely work. When Oxford University proposed to establish forty new professorships, opposition to the plan was mounted on the grounds that men would, inevitably, get most of the new posts. It was argued that if the university was serious about improving the career chances of female academics it might be better to increase the number of readerships which, given female academics' current place within the hierarchy and prevailing practices, would be more within their reach. Collusion or realism? Oxbridge, of course, is unique, though it may demonstrate particularly clearly the principles and strategies of closure and exclusion which characterize gender relations at work and the need to develop local strategies for local conditions.

Although economic circumstances change and limit the scope open to employers as much as employees, employers are nowhere near as powerless as they sometimes claim, which is why the role of trade unions as the legitimate and most experienced campaigners for pay and conditions of work remains important. The voluntary sector too can play an important role, though it raises a rather different set of challenges for equal opportunities work. These are tied to highly gendered notions of public duty and the history of voluntary organizations as female-dominated institutions heavily dependent on unpaid work. The media attention given to the female ex-director of Shelter when she moved to become director of the Consumers Association focused equally on her previous success in changing Shelter and at the shock and horror that this had produced within that organization. Women were still not expected to be effective managers.

Yet in other respects voluntary organizations are similar to many other occupations. As career structures have been created they have been seized by men. A male management stratum develops and masculine values begin to dominate the ground rules and practices of the organization under the guise of 'professionalism', which may be little more than the creation of a career ladder which men then climb to the position of chairman, director, etc., leaving women doing the background, voluntary work. But, as Ruth Valentine points out, there is a degree of collusion in all this. Failing to speak out, perhaps because of a fear of being dubbed selfish or a whinger, is tantamount to assent. Though, of course, speaking out when the explicit rationale of the organization is the needs of some other disadvantaged group risks falling foul of what Ruth Valentine calls a puritan tendency to make a hierarchy out of oppression and which, in turn, leads to competition for the status of 'most oppressed'.

One of the perennial problems which cannot be solved by legislation aimed at combating discrimination is the fact that different people want different things out of life. This turns the issue into the much broader one of what sorts of choices should a society support and who should bear the costs of making them? There is a particular notion of the good life underpinning any equal opportunity programme and the danger is that because multiple goals make it hard if not impossible to ensure justice and equity, a model of the good life based on men's careers and lifestyles is erected as a unisex standard. Objecting to this form of patriarchy has, after all, been a main plank of feminism and it would be a shame if the pragmatic day-to-day demands on gender workers led them to lose sight of it. Sally Holtermann addresses this issue through the distinction between choice and chance and Linda Clarke through that between sameness and difference. While monitoring equal opportunities is necessary and increasingly complex in the present deregularized context, as Diane Perrons argues, the measure of women's success should not be confined to how much like men they have become.

With all these levels of difference to be held in mind, skills to be acquired and claims to be balanced, it is clear that both the practice of gender work and the knowledge on which it is based are becoming complex. This collection will not turn each and every reader into a labour lawyer or an economist, or fast forward them into contemporary gender theory. But it will familiarize them with the vocabulary and forms of argument currently in use, and with the terrain to be covered. It has a strong practical focus and is intended to complement the growing academic literature on gender inequality in the workplace (for example, Scott 1994; Humphries and Rubery 1995).

Our division of this book into two parts, one dealing with the context and the other with case studies and more practical measures, cannot, of course, be watertight. Several of the chapters in Part 1 are rich with practical suggestions for changing the distribution of personnel, techniques of monitoring, family-friendly policies and conducting gender audits. All the chapters in Part 2 relate to broad contextual constraints, even if analysing them is not their prime purpose. Our reason for dividing the book in this way was to highlight the difference between situations where effective intervention is possible within organizations and those where more fundamental change at the political level is required. We recognize that because of the macro scope of Part 1 it is easy to be pessimistic about the prospects for change, but this would be a false conclusion, as the contributions in the second part demonstrate.

Part 1

THE SOCIO-ECONOMIC, LEGAL AND CULTURAL CONTEXTS OF GENDER WORK

Diane Perrons

Gender workers work in a context set by the socio-economic and legal framework, by national cultures and by the culture prevailing within their specific organizations. These macro and micro characteristics provide the environment within which the goal of equal opportunities has to be pursued. In Part 1 different levels of this framework are explored.

In Britain a liberal market regime exists in which the determination of wages and working conditions is essentially left to the market. Within this framework equal opportunities are formally supported; it is believed that all individuals should have the opportunity to compete freely with each other and legislation exists to prevent discrimination against individuals on the basis of gender or race. However, there is no commitment to equality of outcome. Thus policies which might protect or support groups

13

of workers, such as women, who for structural reasons, face unequal starting positions have been strongly resisted; an example being the resistance of the British government to the social policies of the European Union (EU). Indeed, since 1979, Britain has become an increasingly market-oriented society with emphasis being placed on deregulation, privatization and the creation of a flexible labour market. Yet comparative evidence indicates that employment conditions for women as a whole are better where regulation is stronger (Rubery 1992a; Whitehouse 1992). So, despite the government's formal commitment to equal opportunities and support for business initiatives such as Opportunity 2000, in reality neither its economic policies nor the changes to employment legislation have been favourable to women. Some of the implications of this liberal market framework for the attainment of equal opportunities are discussed in Chapter 2 which deals with recent changes in the position of women in the British economy.

Given the current popularity of market ideologies and the importance placed on the efficacy of the market as a means of resource allocation, including the determination of economic rewards, such as earnings, it is essential to have some understanding of theories of market behaviour so that the logical foundations of this perspective can be critically evaluated. Sally Holtermann provides such an understanding by examining in more detail the economic processes that operate in a market economy. She reviews a number of theories within mainstream economics that try to explain women's lower levels of participation and earnings. Some of these explanations rest on the characteristics of women themselves such as their level of qualifications or work experience; some refer to the existence of gender-differentiated tastes and preferences for different kinds of jobs; some to the preference of employers for different types of labour; while others examine the interrelationships between these factors and the gender division of labour more generally.

Whether the fundamental causes of this inequality lie in discrimination within the workplace, an unequal gender division of labour in the home, or the different preferences of women and men for differently rewarded forms of work, women presently pay high costs for their unequal role in terms of earnings foregone over their lifetimes. Improving their employment situation would clearly bring them financial gains. However, gains for both organizations and the wider economy could also arise from a more equal treatment for women in employment. Firms would make savings on recruitment and training costs (see also Harker in Chapter 6) and the economy would gain from the additional output and skills. Nevertheless, despite the economic rationale and the strong ethical case for equality, existing legislation is often ineffective and recent legislative changes are moving away from those necessary to create a supportive environment for the enhancement of women's role in the economy.

Both Linda Clarke and Sally Holtermann point to the way existing legislation permits employers to specify conditions, provided they can be 'reasonably justified' by the nature of the work, that systematically discriminate against women. European rulings have tightened this loophole a little, but existing practice in employment tribunals suggests that the quality of the evidence required to justify discrimination varies significantly; and more-over before compensation can be awarded, which in the past has in any case been fairly minimal, the discrimination has to be shown to be intentional.

Legislation in the UK has some way to go before it will be able to tackle issues now taken up in Europe. Indeed, while individuals will often find recourse to the law slow, the essence of law is a stick rather than a carrot, and so in the longer run, and for those not actually pursuing a case, it is fear of prosecution that produces the fastest change. In this sense the membership of the EU has been effective in that it has forced progressive legislative change upon a reluctant government in the UK in relation to both the Sex Discrimination and Equal Pay Acts. By referring to these developments in the legal framework and to specific cases Linda Clarke, in Chapter 4, provides an insight into the workings of the law and the kinds of issues an equal opportunities officer would have to deal with. Although the law is intricate, and effective use of it impossible without specialist knowledge, the chapter provides an elementary grasp of the law that is essential for modern gender work.

A further issue raised by both these authors, although in rather different ways, is the concept of equality and what exactly this means. Within the liberal conception of justice, equality requires that similarly situated individuals should be treated alike and this leads to the formulation of measures to tackle individual cases of discrimination. However, when the cause of unequal treatment arises from deep-seated gender divisions that, for example, severely constrain women's ability to enter the labour force in the first place, it is questionable whether equal treatment in employment for unequally situated individuals is sufficient to create equality of outcome, if indeed this is the goal. Thus Linda Clarke raises the question of whether women's rather different position requires different treatment to obtain equality. Sally Holtermann suggests, however, that equality, in the sense of sameness, may not be what is desired if women and men have genuinely different tastes and preferences, and inequality, or at least differences in outcome, may in some circumstances be compatible with distributive justice. Perhaps in this case what is required is equivalence rather than equality and for the reward structures associated with gender-differentiated occupations to be re-evaluated.

When the goals of equality are not transparent and when the employment framework itself is undergoing rapid change, the question of monitoring outcomes also becomes more complex. These issues are raised in Chapter 5 which provides a more detailed account of how the moves towards increasing deregulation and employment flexibility have made both the pursuit of equal opportunities policies and forms of monitoring more difficult. Indeed, there can be conflict rather than complementarity between equal opportunities and other government policies. Similarly, while most large organizations have equal opportunities in place, their relationship with other aspects of company policy is rarely explored. In reality few organizations actually monitor the outcomes of their equal opportunities policies and those that do only do so at a basic level which fails to encapsulate the full extent of the unequal position of women in employment, both objectively and in terms of how women feel they are treated. In view of this complexity a technique for monitoring equality which goes beyond assessing the extent to which women have colonized key positions within the employment hierarchy is proposed.

Having established the general framework at the social level within which equal opportunities workers operate, organizations themselves can vary in the extent to which they facilitate the attainment of equal opportunities. One way is to introduce family-friendly policies including flexible working arrangements, forms of leave and childcare facilities. Historically, as Lisa Harker points out in Chapter 6, these policies have been directed at mothers rather than fathers and provide women with a means of reconciling the competing demands of domestic and paid work, although the extent of provision in the past seems to have varied more with the needs of business and the economy rather than with the needs of women themselves. In the late twentieth century, with changing family and employment structures, and in particular the expansion in the numbers of lone mothers, these policies are even more necessary and should be directed at parents rather than women.

However, as with other issues, such as training, there is a case of the 'prisoners' dilemma' – many organizations might have some kind of social conscience and belief system that supports equal opportunities and indeed have recognized that they may benefit from cost savings. However, without compulsion, they remain unwilling to take measures on their own for fear that providing childcare etc. might incur unreasonable costs not shared by other, less progressive organizations, or that having facilitated women's advance within their own organizations these well-trained women will be poached by less progressive employers seeking to improve their equal opportunities position without committing resources to this goal themselves. Organizations will be unwilling in many cases to take these risks unless they are obliged to do so by legal means. Thus individual businesses cannot be relied upon to introduce more general equality policies and a national policy is required to set a base level of conditions to which all employers must conform. Indeed where such legislation exists experience from other countries indicates that employers themselves then do more and, as Lisa Harker argues, the ultimate responsibility for creating an employee-friendly atmosphere must rest with the government.

A further potential obstacle and opposition to the realization of equal opportunities arises at the micro level from the culture of the organizations. In Chapter 7 Carole Pemberton illustrates how this many-layered concept can be used analytically for exploring gender in organizations. Sometimes viewed as a social structural factor which limits change, it can also be viewed as a local variable to be manipulated. Whilst her chapter is not optimistic (she shows that the most sophisticated use of the concept explains the failure rather than the success of equal opportunities initiatives) her schematic representation of culture helps explain the paradoxical quality of many firms' responses to equal opportunities.

While each of the three levels of organizational culture – the national and social context, the explicitly created internal culture, and the more subtle culture, reflecting the assumptions, values and beliefs of the members of the organization – all have effects, Carole Pemberton argues that it is at this last level that the obstacles and impediments to the pursuit of equality issues are often found. Although it is often difficult to uncover these deep-seated value systems that may impede equality, a series of questions are proposed which, together with others relating to the organizations' capacity to effect change, are used to construct a gender audit. This gender audit could be used by potential employees, equal opportunities workers and consultants to assess the extent to which the culture of any particular organization will facilitate or resist change. It could also be used to assess comparative company performance in relation to the pursuit of equal opportunities.

This understanding is necessary for both equal opportunities workers and others seeking change. Both need to recognize that although there may be an economic case for equal opportunities which could be supported by the law, and although some family-friendly provisions may be in place, there may still be barriers within their own organizations. This awareness will enable those seeking change to identify the specific challenges they face in their own places of work. The effectiveness of policies operating within organizations is examined more fully in Part 2.

2

RECENT CHANGES IN WOMEN'S EMPLOYMENT IN BRITAIN

Diane Perrons and Jenny Shaw

In the 1990s women's participation in the formal economy increased to an unprecedented degree, while that of men declined. On this basis, if present trends continue, it is conceivable that employment rates of women and men will converge to the point of 75 per cent employment for each sex. At the moment, however, the employment rate of women is around 67 per cent, whilst that of men is around 83 per cent (Gregg and Wadsworth 1994). Nevertheless, the quality of women's employment, in terms of earnings and occupations, leaves much to be desired.

Women are under-represented in all the top jobs; for example, in 1992 only 5 out of 1,370 managing directors or chief executives were women, and in 1994 only 5 per cent of judges were women. Some 9 per cent of MPs and less than 6 per cent of university professors were women and, despite some notable exceptions, women are under-represented in the upper echelons of the civil service (Gregg and Machin 1993; Clement 1994; El-Faizy 1994). At the same time, women are over-represented in low-paid, low-status, part-time jobs with few prospects for upward mobility. Despite the existence of equal pay policies for over twenty years, earnings-related inequalities between women and men have been slow to narrow. On the most favourable measure, namely hourly earnings, women have not yet attained 80 per cent of male earnings. On the basis of weekly earnings for either manual or non-manual workers the proportion scarcely rises above 70 per cent (see Holtermann pp. 34–5). However, in the last twenty years earnings differences between women, although smaller than differences between men, have also increased, although not to the same extent as earnings inequalities between men, reflecting the fact that women overall are concentrated in a much smaller range of jobs than men.[1] Indeed, many are concentrated in an economic ghetto from which their chances of escape are minimal (Organisation for Economic Cooperation and Development (OECD 1994)).

There are a variety of explanations for these developments. There has been a profound change in the structure of the British economy. In common with many other countries the service sector has expanded and manufacturing has declined. However, the form of these developments has been rather different in Britain. The decline of manufacturing has been both more prolonged and severe, leading to a fall in employment, especially of low-skilled men, which has generated increases in the rates of both male unemployment and economic inactivity (Schmitt and Wadsworth 1994). At the same time, the expansion of employment in the service sector, where women are disproportionately represented, has taken an increasingly flexible and part-time form. Indeed, the stock of full-time jobs has fallen from 77 per cent to 67 per cent for all employees and from 57 per cent to 47 per cent for women between 1979 and 1993. The net result has been that only 20 per cent of those entering work have become full-time permanent employees (Gregg and Wadsworth 1994).

The development of the service sector in Britain bears similarities to trends in the USA but less so in relation to the rest of Europe which is now its major trading partner. It is characterized by a wide dispersion of employment opportunities and earnings (Michie and Wilkinson 1994) and also by its highly gendered form, two features which may be fundamentally linked. At one pole there are high-status, highly paid jobs in sectors such as financial services which are disproportionately taken up by men. At the other pole there are flexible, often part-time jobs in sectors such as retail and more personal services which are dispropor- tionately taken up by women. The wages paid at the lower pole, even for full-time work, are about one-third lower than would have been the case for low-skilled work in manufacturing (Schmitt and Wadsworth 1994) and, by any stretch of the imagination, do not constitute a living wage. As a consequence, the jobs are unattractive both to many men and to women without a working partner and are taken up by those whose existence does not depend entirely on their own earning capabili- ties or who take up a number of such jobs.

These developments are crucial to the understanding of gender in the workplace and to the various recommendations put forward to remedy inequalities. Concern has been growing about a tendency for households to polarize between those who have two earners and are thus 'work rich' and those which have no earners, where both husbands and wives are unemployed and where the household is thus 'work poor' (Morris 1990; Gregg and Wadsworth 1994; Miliband 1994). Members of the first type of household are exhausted, especially the women, as there is little evidence of real change in the domestic division of labour (Harman 1993) despite a change in beliefs and the rise of what is now sometimes called the 'newish' rather than new man (Kier- nan 1992; Wharton 1994). Indeed a recent survey found that 80 per cent of women say that they prepare every meal in their household while only 22 per cent of men make a similar claim (Nicolaas 1995). Members of the second type of household suffer loss of financial independence, self-esteem and a social role, and experience poor health.

Over a relatively short time the British economy has been transformed by changes in employment legislation and a general policy of deregulation and privatization into one of the most flexible in Europe (Michie and Wilkinson 1994). These changes, from an employer's perspective, are generally deemed desirable, though, increasingly, doubts are raised about the 'short termism' of this assumption. What is clear is that they have catapulted

Britain towards an under-trained and low-wage economy and an ever more divided social structure (Hutton 1995) which, in turn, affects the prospects of making progress on equal opportunities.

Thus many new forms of employment have flexible hours or are carried out on a part-time basis which enables employees to combine paid work with childcare and other caring responsibilities. From the employees' point of view it must also be noted that flexible hours and part-time work are not synonymous. It is often a matter of one or the other, and women's reported preference for part-time work (Hakim 1991) may be deceptive as women take the least bad option when combining work with caring and other domestic responsibilities. Given the relatively low provision of childcare by the state or by employers in Britain, many employees welcome these, less than optimum, changes. For example, there are only 14,105 places in employer-subsidized nurseries, or less than one place for every 250 children (Maruani 1992; Working for Childcare 1994). And, whilst there are currently four million children under 5 years old in Britain, only half have a state nursery place as compared to 95 per cent of under-5-year-olds in France. Moreover, where state nurseries places exist they are only available for a very limited number of hours per day.

Over 42 per cent of women's jobs are part-time, and part-time work is accounting for a growing stock of employment – amounting to 23 per cent of all jobs (Rubery et al. 1994). Moreover, part-time work is the fastest expanding sector of all work. Within some organizations efforts have been made to equalize conditions between part-time and full-time workers in line with the human resources philosophy of all workers being equally valued. However, attaining this equivalence between workers may occur through a reduction in the overall quality of employment conditions and, indeed, the very existence of full-time workers. For example, the Burton Group obtained equivalence for part-time and full-time workers essentially by replacing 1,000 full-time jobs by 3,000 part-time ones – obtaining parity for the workers, but at the same time increasing the flexibility of the workforce (Cowe 1993).

Part-time work is not just a question of hours of work. The range of jobs which are organized in this way are highly segregated and confined primarily to feminized sectors of the labour force. Although many of these jobs are secure, the opportunities for career advancement are limited (Simkin and Hillage 1992) and pay is in general significantly lower. Whether or not women work as part-timers seems to be associated more with the stage in their life-cycle than with their qualifications or skills. However, having entered the part-time sphere, women often remain there permanently, which has detrimental implications for their continuing employment status and financial security (Rubery *et al*. 1994). This expansion and feminization of part-time work requires that equal opportunity initiatives need to consider the question of parity for part-time workers.

To enhance the position of women workers overall, even with the existing domestic division of labour and childcare provision, equal opportunities policies need to focus on the content and structure of employment and consider whether all jobs could be organized on a part-time basis such that by working part-time women are doing exactly that, i.e. choosing their working hours rather than choosing an inferior job with inferior prospects. To avoid the downward occupational mobility associated with working part-time, policy initiatives should focus on promoting increases in the quality of part-time work so that it can be better integrated into career ladders and promotional chains (Rubery *et al*. 1994). Otherwise the extent of polarization between continuously working women and those who take career breaks will probably widen. Although some organizations do provide assistance with childcare (see Harker, Chapter 6) and allow some workers to work shorter hours, it seems that little attention has been given so far to the question of the restructuring of work overall: that is, to enable all jobs to be organized on a part-time basis, ensure that the skills and talents of women and men are not wasted and that people have the opportunity to develop careers while not forsaking all caring and other responsibilities or interests.

Most of the much vaunted flexible work is employer- rather than employee-friendly. Employers benefit from flexibility because it enables them to vary the quantity of employment offered with changing demands for their services. Sophisticated analysis of till receipts in supermarkets, for example, enables the number of checkout workers to be matched closely to changing demand throughout the day. Thus highly flexible contracts, including zero hours, have been introduced. In this case employees are committed to work for a given employer but the quantity of work offered can vary considerably in any period, including no work being offered at all. Indeed, the extent of the flexibility is such that it would be extremely difficult to be able to plan either working times or incomes (Hewitt 1993b). Thus, while providing employment, these new forms of work do not contribute either to women's career development or their financial independence. Indeed, while the new flexibility can be of mutual benefit to employers and employees it can have negative effects for women in the sense that it constrains their choice of occupation and limits their career development (Simkin and Hillage 1992). Part-time employment, for example, is often not available higher up the career ladder and is frequently associated with little or no training. Similarly, flexible work can lead to long and unsocial hours being worked (Wharton 1994).

For many women, however, the road to paid employment lies through part-time work in the service sector – in sales or clerical and secretarial work where promotional ladders are few and far between. For example, in the Industrial Society's report on secretaries a contrast was drawn between predominantly female graduates who entered as secretaries, and for whom little further training was envisaged, and the predominantly male graduate entries who entered into specific managerial training programmes where all aspects of the companies' work would be viewed. While many of the secretaries looked for, and obtained, greater variety in their work by initiating and suggesting projects of their own, the idea of progression into administration or management was not taken seriously by their employers. Moreover, despite the fact that their contributions to the organizations were regarded as invaluable by their employers, 44 per cent of organizations were paying these often well-qualified people less than the European decency threshold (Allcock 1993).

Evidence from elsewhere in Europe, in particular the Netherlands, suggests that the form of part-time work can vary enormously. The very short hours, poor working conditions and limited prospects for advancement experienced by part-timers seems to be a feature fairly specific to Britain, where many women end up by taking two or three such jobs to make ends meet. In both the Netherlands and France, part-time work can mean a four-day week and it is not automatically associated with poor working conditions. These countries indicate that employment can be organized to give both women and men more choice over their working hours (Platenga 1994).

A further source of inequality arises from the pervasive nature of gender segregation. Women and men still do profoundly different jobs, even when in the same sectors and occupations. A growing literature has developed on measuring the extent of employment segregation, but the consensus still seems to be that, despite some changes at the margin, with some women entering previously male spheres (though more often it is the reverse), both horizontal and vertical segregation by gender in the labour force remains extensive (Hakim 1992). Segregation exists both in traditional sectors such as retailing, where even at the occupational level women and men tend to sell different products (Scott 1994), and in the new high tech and service sectors (Crompton and Sanderson 1994; Lovering 1994), where women are confined to specific tasks and at the lower end of the employment hierarchy.

Segregation in itself is not inevitably inequitable, especially if it is the product of unconstrained choice. However, the problem arises because of the different rewards received and different possibilities for career development experienced by men and women in their different spheres. Muscular strength and dealing with money, stereotypically linked with men, are still valued more highly than dexterity and dealing with people, more usually associated with women. Thus equal opportunities policies need to be concerned with the reward structure, although attempts to do so have not always been successful. For example, in 1987 a national review of manual workers' pay in local authorities was carried out and a new wages scheme was introduced on the basis of equal pay for work of equal value. However, the new scheme related solely to basic rates, and for male workers this only amounted to about 60 per cent of total pay, the difference arising from a whole series of bonus payments for which women did not seem to be eligible. Thus, despite the formal erosion of unequal opportunities, the more insidious forms of inequality remain even in organizations strongly committed to equal opportunities, even before the effects of deregulation and privatization are considered (Bruegel 1994, see also Donaghy Chapter 12).

Attention also needs to be paid to the entry structure of different occupations within organizations. Referring to the differences in opportunities for women in the banks as compared with the building societies, Crompton and Sanderson found that greater opportunities for women existed in the building societies, where there were multi-tiered entry systems based on qualifications, rather than in the banks, where a uni-portal system was more common and career progression was assumed to take a linear form within the organization (Crompton and Sanderson 1994). However, changing technology can have important if paradoxical effects. The development of a centralized computer system and consequent decentralization of decision making gave rise to branches entirely run by women. But the managers, in fact, had less total control over the branch: they could manage staffing levels but not lending or budget decisions which were computerized. Their role was equivalent to an assistant branch manager in a larger unit, a predominantly female stratum, but where there was little progression from assistant to manager, except in the case of male management trainees (Crompton and Sanderson 1994). So, even in the case of the building societies where women's position was slightly better, it was still restricted in scope to fairly routine decision making and to limited control over a small and predominantly female workforce.

While organizations can think about the structure of work and the reorganization of all jobs on a part-time basis, for change to be more fundamental and concern the size of rewards given to different activities, action at the national or international level would be required. It is interesting to note how far the gains made in the last year for part-time workers through the extension of redundancy and maternity arrangements are the consequence of having to conform to European initiatives. They are not the result of either company initiatives or those from the national state, despite there being a strong case that overall benefits accrue from a more highly skilled and highly paid labour force. Whilst women are perceived as, and in reality are, low-paid workers, the chances are high that they will continue to be used in ways which have negative implications both for themselves and for the economy in terms of levels of investment and degree of competitiveness. For by not fully utilizing people's skills, not only does society condemn them to a dull existence, but it traps the economy as a whole into a low skills equilibrium (Bruegel and Perrons 1995).

Indeed, if the economic scenario which predicts Britain's descent into a low wage, low skill based economy proves correct, it would be wise and timely to heed the evidence from Third World economies which show just how much women are forced into bearing the costs and consequences of structural adjustment (Moser 1989). The economic and cultural implications of these structural changes cannot be overestimated. The more divided or polarized the society or the economy, the greater the chances that gender divisions will flow along them (Hofstede 1980). All the more reason to pursue 'family-friendly policies' which do not inadvertently deepen gender divisions by assuming that caring is women's work (see Harker, Chapter 6).

While stressing that, for the lack of women- or family-friendly policies as well as for reasons of prejudice, women are still under-represented, nevertheless, there has been expansion in the higher echelons of employment. The proportion of women in professional and managerial occupations rose from 12–14 per cent at the start of the decade to 21–24 per cent by 1990 (Hakim 1992; Humphries and Rubery 1992; Gregg and Machin 1993). Some of this increase may be attributable to the increased use of the word managerial in predominantly caring occupations, especially in the public sector (Coyle 1989). For example, some nursing grades have been reclassified as middle managers, but the other side of this regrading process has been a loss of pay for nurses left on the wards and, very often, new forms of discrimination or inequality within the managerial category. In universities, for example, there is a process whereby as a few more women get senior lectureships, men holding such posts suddenly become readers. This is not to deny that in both the public and private sectors a small number of women have moved into genuinely managerial positions.

Diane Perrons and Jenny Shaw

Still, according to the Institute of Management and Remuneration Economics survey the proportion of management jobs held by women fell from 10.2 per cent in 1993 to 9.5 per cent in 1994 and the proportion of directors has remained at 2.8 per cent. There is some variation in the proportion of managers between sectors. In distribution it is relatively high at 15 per cent and banking and finance is best of all at 18.1 per cent, whilst in the high technology areas it is as low as 7.5 per cent (Trapp 1994). These findings are supported by another survey carried out by the British Institute of Management of 29,000 top executives working in 533 UK-based companies between the years 1989–92 (Gregg and Machin 1993). This survey found that only 8 per cent of the top executives were women, and that within this group not only did women's share fall in the higher levels of the hierarchy, but even when women were in the same category as men their pay was lower.

The story of promotion and appraisal is much the same. Promotion rates among top executives show that the rate of promotion is lower for women and, more disconcertingly, is focused on younger people, with those less than 40 years old being more likely to be promoted (Gregg and Machin 1993). Clearly this is disadvantageous to women who take career breaks as their age, at any given level in the hierarchy, is likely to be higher than an otherwise equivalent male and will be held against them. Studies of appraisal and performance-related pay show that women do not fare well because what they do within organizations tends not to figure in the formal criteria for appraisal (Bevan and Thompson 1992). The view that promise will show early is based on a masculine view of the world: it is part of work-based sexism which Jean Lipman-Blumen (1976) calls the homo-social theory of roles and which leads men, narcissistically, to promote only those who look like themselves.

Where women have advanced into management it has often been in specific spheres involving either individual skills or qualifications as, for example, in finance, law or medicine where more objective criteria for advancement exist, or in areas such as personnel which are linked with women's stereotypical expertise in caring responsibilities (Crompton 1994). But within these categories there is also an organizational effect. The larger and

28

more bureaucratic (and therefore more hierarchical) the organization, the more concentrated women will be at the lower levels. Women lawyers or doctors do best in entrepreneurial settings where they can set up firms and they do less well in bureaucratic ones where they are dependent on seniors picking them out and promoting them (Keller 1984). The most celebrated British businesswoman at present is Anita Roddick, founder of The Body Shop, whose career encapsulates this process. Creating their own businesses enables women not to be excluded from certain areas such as general management which involves control over people, as they tend to be, at least in the private sector. In relation to earnings, the pay levels of women are significantly less than men, being 69 per cent of men's earnings for those in managerial positions and 75 per cent for those in professional occupations (Roos and Reskin 1992; Gregg and Machin 1993). Moreover, even when allowances are made for the kind of company and the precise occupation, differences of between 6–8 per cent were found to exist between women and men executives doing the same kind of job (Gregg and Machin 1993).

A variety of explanations for these patterns may be advanced, some of which are discussed in more detail by Sally Holtermann in the next chapter. On the one hand, women's level of training and education may, at least in the past, have been lower and it is possible that women who have spent time out of the labour market have actually lost skills. On the other hand, girls now surpass boys at GCSE and A-level and women match men in admission to higher education. Only in postgraduate qualifications do men still outnumber women, but these educational gains are devalued if qualifications have a different impact on men's and women's careers or, indeed, count for very little in any career after the first job. Roberts et al's. (1993) study of the British civil service showed that whereas women needed educational qualifications to get on at all, such qualifications made much less difference to men's progress. Another popular explanation for the persistence of inequalities is the recession and its consequences. Downsizing and delayering have become facts of life which have taken out a whole stratum of middle management, often exactly those positions which women might have aspired to and got. The lack of grades, especially those next-to-senior ones, certainly seems to be part of the explanation of why the proportion of women managers is actually falling, but women's greater propensity to resign is also clearly discernible (Trapp 1994).

The position of women who obtain top appointments is not easy and in many cases they feel under constant scrutiny and strain, needing to dress and behave in very particular ways in order to be accepted. As a minority within the managerial tiers women may often have to tolerate forms of behaviour from their male colleagues, including sexual harassment, which they find unacceptable because these same individuals may have powerful roles in the organization and form part of an important set of contacts (Hearn 1989; Schein 1994). The higher they rise, the harder they fall, and with more people eager to witness and crow at their demise.

The failure of 'successful' women to support other women, or their propensity to betray them, has often been noted and explained in terms of isolation. Women are not the same as men and if they pretend to be or act 'like men' they render themselves hostages to fortune. Individual solutions to an unequal and gendered world, i.e. to a structural problem, are rarely possible. In this situation what is required is a fundamental rethink about the scheduling of paid work and the organization of caring if any form of equality is to be achieved. The Nordic countries' attempt to promote 'Time to Care' and a six-hour day to facilitate it (Esping-Anderson 1990) is an example worth noting; though so too is Norway's experience of parental leave provision which had to be amended so that it could not be taken predominantly by mothers rather than by both parents equally.

However, for effective rethinking to get off the ground, patient and piecemeal persuasion of hundreds and thousands of individuals, firms and organizations is necessary in the context of a supportive legislative framework. This is bound to be a laborious and uneven process. There is no single solution to equal opportunities and no single point of entry. Change agents have to be acutely aware of the limits and constraints within which they operate. A personnel officer or a union representative alike knows that they cannot change the prevailing law, the current government or the state of the labour market, but that they have to work within the context made up of them all. Of course, many organizations describe themselves as equal opportunity employers and circulate papers to appointing and promotion committees which are promptly filed. The next stage on from announcing the intention to be an equal opportunity employer is to show that you really are by monitoring procedures and collecting data. But while initiatives at the organizational level secured by a monitoring procedure are a step forward, unless they are accompanied by sanctions for failure to act, the 'policy' will be effort wasted. Just as the declaration of a commitment to equal opportunities is only a start, the policy does not stop at tabulation. Procedures have to be established which produce different outcomes.

Although the moral case for equal opportunities has largely been won, over the last decade and a half the influence of neo-liberal ideologies and institutions such as internal markets has grown and may represent a countervailing force. So whilst many will accept the moral case for equality they will, at the same time, stress the overriding importance of the 'bottom line' and the value of market discipline. This means that economic arguments have to be met with economic facts. This is the climate in which the arguments have to be made, but it does not follow that egalitarian policies are wholly incompatible with business success. As Sally Holtermann shows in the next chapter, the economic case is just as capable of supporting progressive practices as it is of regressive and inegalitarian ones. The case for equal opportunities is not wholly economic, though 'winning' on these grounds is clearly advantageous.

Note

1 Figures from the 1995 Social Trends find that the gap between the highest and lowest decile of male workers grew from £203 a week in 1971 to £402 in 1994, while for women the equivalent gap grew from £118 to £279 (figures in constant 1994 prices) (*Social Trends* 1995).

3

THE ECONOMICS OF EQUAL OPPORTUNITIES

Sally Holtermann

The purpose of this chapter is to examine the economic basis for the justification of equal opportunities policies. In so doing it does not assume that economics provides the only rationale for gender equality – a clear ethical case also exists. Neither does it assume that the causes of discrimination either arise solely within the workplace or that discrimination can be resolved through employment-based equal opportunities policies alone. However, the identification of an economic case for equal opportunities often provides a powerful argument for decision makers both within business and government. The aim of the chapter is to clarify the economic concepts, and to illustrate the role that economic arguments play – especially in relation to the labour market – in the debate about equal opportunity issues. It also raises important questions about what is meant by equality and whether equality and difference are compatible.

In earlier years of the debate it was usually assumed that underlying the goal of equality of opportunity there was, first and foremost, some notion of social justice. It was regarded as unjust for some groups to be denied opportunities because of personal characteristics – such as gender, race, disability, religious beliefs, social class background and age – that are irrelevant to the fulfilment of their potential. In response to the evidence of extensive discrimination legislation was introduced making it illegal to discriminate against people on grounds of sex or race in the fields of employment, training and education, and also in the provision of goods and services.

There has also been a recognition that policies for equal opportunities can have some economic impact going beyond the achievement of social or distributive justice that is their main goal, and most recently that there can be some benefit to employers in terms of enhanced economic efficiency as well as some costs. The view of equal opportunities that has risen to some prominence in the last few years in discussion of public policy is neatly summarized by the following quotation from an anonymous writer in the *Employment Gazette* of June 1994: 'More and more employers are coming to see equal opportunities not just in moral terms, but as a way of maximising employees' potential to gain competitive edge.' Implicit in this sentence is acknowledgement that pursuit of equal opportunities may co-incide with the self-interest of employers, but statements of this kind lead to a concern that those measures that would improve equality of opportunity without having any notable advantages for employers are at risk of being neglected.

There is perhaps less emphasis in current policy debate than there once was on the features of the national economic frame-work – and in particular labour market forces and regulations governing the workplace – that have an impact on the opportunities open to women and men, and therefore on the economic outcomes they experience, though there is considerable ongoing economic research on the gender impact of labour market policies (Rubery 1992a, 1992b; Whitehouse 1992; Lindley 1994).

This chapter attempts to unscramble some of these ideas, because, in order to be effective in promoting measures to increase equality of opportunity and in monitoring progress, there is a need to be as clear as possible about the forces at work, about the nature of the goal of equal opportunities, and the extent to which it conflicts with or harmonizes with other goals.

The first part outlines those theories of mainstream economic analysis that seek to explain the position that women tend to reach in the labour market in comparison to men. The second part tries to clarify the concept of equality of opportunity by examining different formulations that have been used in the evaluation of economic policies. The third part outlines the economic instruments available to promote equality of opportunity, and the final part considers the interrelationship between the pursuit of equality of opportunity and other economic objectives.

Explanations of the position of women in the labour market

It is well known that there are two main ways in which the position of women in the labour market differs significantly from that of men: lower participation and lower pay.[1]

Lower participation

Among younger women without children participation in the labour market is very similar to that of men, but falls dramatically when they have their first child. In 1992, 72 per cent of women with no dependent children were in employment compared to 43 per cent of women with a child under 5 (*General Household Survey* 1992). Women's employment rates rise steadily with the age of their youngest child, reaching 76 per cent among those whose youngest child is aged 10 or over, but a large part of their employment is part-time. Recorded unemployment tends to be lower among women, but hidden unemployment, which is not recorded in either claimant counts or surveys asking whether people are seeking work, is high (Metcalf 1992).

Lower pay

Full-time hourly earnings of women are on average lower than those of men. According to the 1993 New Earnings Survey the average hourly earnings of women in full-time employment in manual occupations were 71 per cent of those of men in manual occupations, and among non-manual workers women's full-time hourly earnings were 68 per cent of those of men. The differential has been falling only slowly.[2] Hourly wage rates of part-time workers tend to be lower than those of full-time workers. In 1993, average hourly earnings of women working part-time in manual occupations were 88 per cent of those of women working full-time in manual occupations, and among women working in non-manual occupations, hourly earnings of those in part-time work were 76 per cent of those in full-time work (*New Earnings Survey* 1993). These differentials would be greater if allowance could be made for the significant numbers of part-time employ-ees with low weekly earnings excluded from the *New Earnings Survey* because the sample is drawn from people in the PAYE system.

Most of the differential in wage rates between women and men now comes, not from women being paid less in the same jobs than men, but from:

- occupational segregation – women are disproportionately to be found in certain types of occupation, and in these occupations pay tends to be low;
- vertical segregation – women are disproportionately to be found in lower-grade parts of occupational structures.

The result of these two features of women's employment – lower participation and lower rates of pay – is that their lifetime earnings tend to be much lower than those of men, and lower than those of women without children. Joshi and Davies (1993) show that a woman with two children, who stays out of paid work while her children are under school age and returns initially to part-time employment at gradually increasing hours, typically forgoes £249,000 in gross earnings over her lifetime after the birth of her first child at the age of 25 (at 1991 prices assuming earnings at age 24 of £10,000). This loss is 57 per cent of the post-25 earnings of a childless woman. The earnings loss is attributable in about equal parts to time not in paid employment, time in paid employment but at part-time hours, and reduced rates of pay.

Economists have put forward many theories to explain these features of the differing patterns of employment and earnings among men and women. Some of these explanations emphasize factors on the supply side of the labour market, i.e. personal characteristics such as age, level of education and training, marital status and so on. Other explanations concentrate on the demand side, i.e. the way in which employers have preferences for different kinds of labour. Further explanations focus on the interaction between the two. Some of the theorizing has attempted to incorporate the feedback effects between women's role in the family and their labour market position. The main hypotheses that have been studied are now outlined.

Human capital explanations

Human capital theory assumes that individuals behave rationally in making investment decisions. Education and training are seen as forms of investment in human capital. Human capital can also be increased by work experience. The greater the amount of education or training taken and the greater the work experience, then the greater the stock of an individual's human capital, their productivity and hence their earnings. Women are said to invest less than men in their human capital as the period over which they can recoup returns from the investment is expected to be shorter. At school they tend to opt for subjects that lead to career sectors where women are over-represented. Women in employment now are likely to have left school or full-time education earlier (though girls are now staying on as long as boys and getting as good A-levels). They tend to undergo less in-work training (Clarke 1991). Perhaps most important of all they are more likely to have breaks in employment – mostly for childcare – and therefore do not build up and maintain skills and experience to the same extent as men. As a result of their lower qualifications and longer employment breaks, they are less likely to enter the sort of occupations that have high long-term earnings potential, and less likely to achieve senior positions when they do. They incline towards occupations where investment in human capital is less important, where earnings can commence at an earlier age, and where there is less penalty from work interruptions for child rearing. This under-investment in human capital is partly the result of the expectations of both employers and women themselves that they will have lengthy breaks from paid employment during the years of rearing children, and it may also partly be because women anticipate being discriminated against in pay and promotion.

Human capital explanations view the different treatment of women and men in the workplace as entirely logical. The origins of the inequality largely arise from tastes and preferences which are determined outside of market relations. Thus if equality of outcome in paid work was a social objective then within this perspective attention would have to be paid to the determination of the gender division of labour and gender roles in society more generally.

Reservation wage explanations

The 'reservation wage' is the lowest wage at which a person will be willing to take up paid employment. In a two-parent family the woman's earnings are generally lower than the man's and the expectation is that on having children the woman will give up full-time employment to do most of the child rearing and the man will continue in employment. The woman's wages are then a supplement to the man's, and she is therefore more willing to work for a low wage than if her earnings were to be the main source of financial support for the family, and she is willing to work for a lower wage than a man. (Many other factors affect women's reservation wages, among them: the structure of incentives in the tax and benefit system; the common habit among couples of looking to the woman's earnings as the source of funds for paying for any childcare costs needed for both to have paid employment, which makes childcare costs a form of tax on women's earnings; and women's relative lack of freedom to move residence in search of better employment.) Women work in jobs that pay wages that men who expect at some time to support a family would not accept, and this perpetuates and reinforces any occupational segregation of jobs. If the woman has no partner or if her partner is unemployed – situations that have become increasingly common – the minimum wage she will accept will have to be higher as she will become the sole breadwinner, a proposition that is consistent with the generally lower employment rates of lone mothers and women whose partners are unemployed (Glyn and Miliband 1994).[3]

Overcrowding

Some writers have argued that the tendency for women to offer their labour predominantly in certain sections of the labour market has depressed wages in that sector by maintaining an oversupply of labour relative to demand. Wage differentials between work of equal value to employers in the predominantly female and predominantly male sectors of employment could be eroded by an increase in women offering their labour supply in the male sectors, but the many obstacles in the way of women doing so, for example sexual harassment, even when supported by anti-discrimination legislation, limits the extent to which this happens.[4]

Discrimination

Early versions of economic theories of sex discrimination developed the ideas of Becker (1957), which were originally formulated around the issue of racial discrimination. It was assumed that employers discriminated against groups such as women or ethnic minority groups because they experienced a personal disbenefit from employing them, or because they thought that their other employees or customers for their products or services disliked being associated with them. Employers were therefore willing to forgo some profit by employing men with lower productivity than women. The theory has been criticized for failing fully to explain the continuation of wage differentials: if labour markets worked perfectly non-discriminating employers would reap a profit advantage and drive discriminators out of business. But it can offer a fairly powerful contribution when allowance is made for imperfections in the working of labour markets and for the distribution of prejudice, which may be widespread in those occupations that are predominantly male, and more common there than in the traditionally female occupations.

Later versions of economic theories of discrimination emphasized the role that sex plays as a source of information about people. Employers are disinclined to employ a woman with the same apparent qualifications and suitability for a job as a man because of the expectation that a woman will be more likely to quit early (for child rearing) and to work with lower intensity and commitment (because of family responsibilities) than a man. This has been called statistical discrimination. This practice may be rational economic behaviour by an employer acting in the interest of profit or performance in the absence of full information about individuals, but it is based on prejudice, and will discriminate against any woman who happens to be more 'career-minded' than an equally qualified male candidate, and in such cases the employer will also turn out to have made the wrong choice from a purely financial point of view.

Feedbacks

While each of the theories outlined above tends to emphasize one aspect, most of them give a role to a variety of factors, and the more sophisticated models allow for their interaction in complex ways, and for the direction of causality to go both ways. For instance, many of the theories, as indicated above, give a prominent place to the restrictions placed on women by their traditional role in homemaking and child rearing in explaining their different labour supply behaviour. But they can be extended to show that some features of the working of the labour market act to reinforce the traditional role while others may work to weaken it. For instance, in the human capital model, women end up with lower earnings because of their lower qualifications and experience. A simple extension shows that this earnings differential means that when one parent forgoes paid employment in order to rear children the financial loss to the family will be smaller if it is the woman who does. For example, take-up of schemes giving parents the right to take leave to care for their children is much higher among women than men because the financial loss to the family is then least. However, even where, as in Sweden, the leave can be taken with near to full earnings replacement, take-up is much lower among men – though growing. Thus it would appear that even a generous scheme has limitations in altering the gender specialization of roles, indicating perhaps that although traditional gender roles are reinforced by forms of discrimination within the workplace, their origins may have a deeper social determination. On the other hand, increasing opportunities for women in employment may set in train a series of cumulative mechanisms that in time may lead to a more fundamental change in gender relations.

Other factors

Economic theory tends to neglect forces that it cannot translate into measurable terms, but this does not mean that it does not recognize them as potentially important determinants of economic outcomes, nor deny their role in the feedback mechanism. Some writers have emphasized the part played by power relations in the family and workplace, for example reference has been made to patriarchal relations within work and within the home (Walby 1990) while others have emphasized the behavioural norms arising from years of social conditioning, and the importance of expectations based on these norms. A fully satisfactory theory would have to give both the economic and the social/psychological/historical factors their rightful place, both in cause and effect, but that kind of integration is rarely attempted.

The changing economic environment

Even if all of the hypotheses outlined above have some validity (and they are not generally mutually exclusive), the way that they operate, and the consequences for the economic outcomes for women, change over time. Many major changes have taken place in the recent past. One of the most significant ones is the rise in the real value of earnings (i.e. the value of earnings after allowing for general price inflation), which has been brought about by increasing productivity and economic growth. Women's earnings may still be lower than men's but in real terms they have nevertheless grown, and faster than men's.

Three consequential changes illustrate the impact. First, an increased number of women are now able to earn enough to support a family (albeit at what is for the majority of them a rather low standard of living) independently of a man's earnings, if that is what they have to do or choose to do, and increasing numbers of women are now bringing up children on their own and taking part in paid employment at the same time.[5] Second, few men have increased their share of child rearing work at home, but the earnings of higher-paid women are now enough to cover the cost of childcare, although this frequently relies upon the existence of low-paid women willing to take on these caring roles. However, the general rise in women's real earnings means that it is increasingly in the family's financial interest for mothers to continue in work, and increasing numbers of them are now doing so. Third, there is feedback from the effect of improved earnings potential of women on family relationships – both in the socio-economic sphere (women have gained in power and status), and in personal relationships (two-parent families are less common; fertility rates are lower). (For a fuller exposition of these ideas see Eatwell *et al.* 1989; Rubery 1992a; Humphries and Rubery 1995.)

Equality of opportunity – what is the aim?

In order to appreciate the contribution that can be made to promoting equality of opportunity by legislation and labour market measures it is necessary to be clear about exactly what this much used but rarely defined term is supposed to mean. What exactly is the goal of policies for equal opportunities? How can achievement of the goal be recognized? A scan of the standard works on welfare economics finds long sections on distributive equity, mainly with a fairly narrow focus on the distribution of income, but hardly a mention of equality of opportunity as such, yet this cannot be because the meaning of the term is so obvious that it does not need spelling out. Barr (1993) and Le Grand (1991) offer ideas that can be synthesized to give a conceptualization of equal opportunities that seems to fit well with the common intuitive understanding of the term.

On this basis, the concept of equal opportunities involves two parts: it involves, first, the notion of choice and, second, the

41

notion of chance. Le Grand argues that a set of possibilities for the distribution of jobs, earnings, income, goods in kind, or any other set of economic arrangements (what he calls 'choice sets') will be regarded as equitable if the range of possibilities over which individuals can make their choices is the same for all, regardless of factors such as sex or race.[6] The key question is then: do women and men have the same options open to them? Barr's discussion suggests that equality of opportunity only exists if, having made a choice, the probability of any particular outcome is the same for each individual, regardless of sex or race, etc. The key question is: do men and women have the same chance of success along their chosen path? Equal choice and equal chance are both necessary for equality of opportunity. One on its own is not enough.

It is easier to see how well this two-part definition fits with the intuitive notion of equality of opportunity by examples showing how the economic conditions of women can contravene it. Women do not have the same options open to them in the labour market as men if discrimination means that in certain occupations they would not be welcome, and they will not have the same chance of success in a chosen occupation if discrimination means that they are not paid the same or given the same chances of promotion. A man can, under most current arrangements for combining employment and family life, choose to have children without loss of earnings, but a woman generally does not have this choice: she will lose earnings while out of the labour market, and frequently return to part-time low-paid work; even when she carries on in employment it is harder for her to put in the same working hours and effort as a man while discharging her family responsibilities, so her chances of earnings progression are lower than a man's.

There are two important points to note here. The first is that the preferences of men and women, and consequently the choices they make from among the options open to them, are themselves the outcome of experience, which has been replete with discrimination and role stereotyping, and of expectations shared by all parties in the decision-making process – men, employers and women themselves – of conformity to historic patterns of gender roles in home and workplace. This does not, however, invalidate the concept of equality of opportunity requiring equal choices being open to men and women; but it acknowledges that the choices actually made are dependent on preferences and expectations, which may themselves be the outcome of unequal opportunities, and that full equality of opportunity requires the removal of prejudice and role stereotyping in the formation of preferences and expectations.

The second is that on this definition equality of opportunity does not necessarily lead to equality of outcome, because, on the basis of their preferences, even when the prejudices and practical barriers to women's participation are not in force, men and women may make difference choices.[7] Employment breaks to care for children may be what more women than men choose even if affordable quality childcare and lengthy parental leave is readily available, and even when there is no prior sociocultural assumption that women rather than men will be the main childcarers. Jobs in traditionally female occupations may be still what more women than men will choose even when entry barriers to predominantly male occupations are removed, and conversely fewer men than women might choose predominantly female occupations even when there is equal pay for work of equal value, and even when men do not face prejudice about what is 'man's work'.

However, if the exercise of these gender-differentiated preferences is to take place without sustaining the economic inequality between men and women, then attention must be given to ensuring that equivalence of outcome is obtained. For example, if it becomes apparent that women and men choose different kinds of occupations, then care must be taken to ensure that predominantly male jobs are not awarded higher financial returns simply because it is men that are doing them and vice versa. There may need to be a social re-evaluation of the kinds of jobs preferred by women. Similarly, if women prefer to take more time off to care for young children or the elderly then it should be possible to work shorter hours without incurring long-term penalties in terms of lifetime earnings, employment security or status, as a consequence of their caring role.

Full equality of opportunity will no doubt reduce some of the present gender inequalities in economic outcome, but some residual gender differences may be consistent with full equality of opportunity. This makes the task of monitoring progress towards equal opportunities more complex. If equal participation rates, equal representation in all occupations, and equality in lifetime earnings are not necessarily the endpoint, then how will full achievement be recognized? What degree of equality of outcome can be expected? This paper does not propose an answer, but merely serves a warning to be aware of the question. That said, there is however a presumption embodied in our legislation that in some spheres only equality of outcome can be equitable. One in particular is equal pay for work of equal value, which means that when men and women do work that makes similar demands on them in terms of skill, training, responsibility, effort and so on, they should receive the same pay.

Policies to promote equal opportunities

The discussion of explanations of gender differences in the labour market indicates the complexity of the interaction of the many factors that together determine the economic outcomes for women. In parallel with this complexity there are many and varied ways of introducing change into the processes, and action is needed by a variety of agents: government, employers and individuals themselves. Elimination of sex discrimination is not enough on its own to secure equality of opportunity, which requires many other changes in the position of women in education, training, employment and childcare.

Governments obviously have a key part to play in influencing economic outcomes for women, not just through legislation on discrimination, but also through regulation and legislation covering other aspects of the labour market, which govern the terms on which women can participate in the labour market, and through the social security system, which influences work incentives (for both men and women) and has a significant part in determining women's income independent of men (Lister 1993).

UK legislation makes the important distinction between direct and indirect discrimination. Indirect discrimination occurs when conditions are set – conditions that are not 'justifiable' by the work – that make it more difficult for one group to choose a course of action, or less likely for members of this group to achieve successful outcomes. An example is when an employer requires a technical skill, which is not necessary for the work, and which is more likely to be found in a man. This example (which is taken from the Equal Opportunities Commission's Guide for Employers) is obvious but not very likely. What is much more common in practice, and more subtle, and legal under the terms of the British legislation, is when employers can demonstrate a business case for conditions of employment that are difficult to combine with childcare: examples are a long working week or compulsory overtime, a requirement of availability for travel or overnight stays, or non-standard working hours (of which the House of Commons must be a prominent example). One could also include the lack of assistance with the financial costs of childcare as a factor that indirectly discriminates against parents, in practice usually the mother.

Removal of both direct and indirect discrimination (in the sense broader than the UK legislation) is necessary if all sources of unequal opportunities arising from discrimination are to be eliminated. On its own, the removal of the forms of discrimination illegal under UK law would leave in place many of the conditions that make it harder for women to achieve economic success, and harder for men to take a greater share of child rearing. A particularly helpful amendment would be replacement of 'justifiable' with 'necessary' in the conditions that impose indirect discrimination, as recommended by the Equal Opportunities Commission (1988; see also Clarke in this volume).

An effective approach to mitigating the effects of legal indirect discrimination would be positive discrimination to favour the groups who are currently disadvantaged, but under the UK legislation positive discrimination is not allowed except in limited ways in the field of training and employment to remedy the effects of past discrimination. Thus it is permitted to provide training courses for women only (or predominantly) and to encourage women to apply for jobs where they are under-represented (but not to use sex as a selection criterion).

Indirect positive discrimination is however permitted, and the government itself has used it in more than one instance to favour particular groups. For example, the recently introduced childcare disregard in Family Credit is available to both married and single women (as long as the woman's partner is employed or unavailable for childcare because of disability etc.), yet, because benefit entitlement is assessed on family income, it is known that a higher proportion of those who will be helped by this measure will be lone parents.

The Sex Discrimination Act prohibits discrimination (direct and indirect) against people on the grounds of their marital status, so measures that apply only to lone parents are not allowed. Equal treatment of married and unmarried people can actually work as a form of indirect discrimination against lone parents, who have greater difficulties in the employment field because of lesser access to other family members for informal childcare help, and because the cost of paid childcare has to be met from only one parent's income. For instance, the Training and Enterprise Councils used to be able to give lone parents on training courses a childcare allowance of up to £50 a week, but this was successfully challenged by a married woman as constituting direct discrimination on the ground of marital status, and now, if available at all, the allowance is open to all parents. In its guidance on work and the family the Equal Opportunities Commission warns employers against providing day nursery places solely to lone parents, because this would discriminate against married people. Indirect positive discrimination towards lone parents can be introduced through something like a points system including criteria such as low family income on which they are likely to reach a higher score. The necessity of resorting to such contortions to achieve widely supported social goals suggests an ill specification of the sex discrimination laws.

Employment legislation sets the framework in which men and women work, but many parts of this legislation, apparently unconnected with issues of equal opportunities, are actually rather unhelpful to the promotion of equality of opportunity. Far more women than men work part-time, and this goes with low rates of pay, poor holiday and sickness entitlement, and poor employment protection, especially if earnings are below the threshold for national insurance contributions (so that they do not qualify for national insurance benefits). Following a recent ruling of the House of Lords there is now likely to be a change in UK legislation to give part-time workers the same rights as full-time employees in relation to redundancy and unfair dismissal, but other disadvantages of part-time employment, such as low rates of pay, will remain.

Improvement of employment rights connected with parenthood – whether through statutory schemes or employer schemes – would help both men and women (and children). Longer maternity leave would help more women to return to work after childbirth without so great a loss of pay and prospects. Leave for family reasons would allow parents to take time off work when a child (or elderly relative) or the usual carer is sick, or to attend a meeting with a child's schoolteachers. And, of course, one of the most useful measures that employers can introduce is help with the costs of childcare (Holtermann and Clarke 1992). Joshi and Davies (1993) show that the availability of affordable childcare and the right, as in Sweden, for parents to work 80 per cent of standard hours at full-time hourly rates of pay, could cut the losses attributable to motherhood by more than a half (specifically to about 24 per cent of earnings post motherhood for the mother described above).

Some other changes in terms of employment would help both men and women, but would be especially useful in promoting the involvement of fathers in childcare. Entitlement to paternity leave would allow fathers to be at home at around the time of the birth of a new baby without loss of income at a time when a family is most likely to be feeling economic pressure, and without losing time at home during the annual holiday leave. A scheme for parental leave (which gives a working parent, of either sex, the right to take leave from employment for a period after the end of the mother's maternity leave) would make it much easier for fathers to take an employment break to care for young children, and if, as proposed in the EU draft directive on the subject, the leave were made non-transferable between parents (unlike Sweden, where the right is transferable), take-up by fathers would be encouraged. A higher proportion of British fathers work more than 48 hours a week than any other EU country, and a reduction in the working week of many jobs would allow parents, fathers especially, to spend more time with their children and to take a larger share of domestic tasks. (See Holtermann and Clarke 1992 for estimates of the cost to the state of national schemes for improving parents' employment rights and helping low income parents with childcare costs.)

Some employers have a good record in offering terms of employment that help families, but many do not, and statutory schemes, in line with the proposals of the EU Social Chapter, with much of the cost of allowances paid to parents while on leave funded by the state, would ensure that a minimum standard of provision is available to all employees rather than just those with enlightened employers. Funding arrangements can have an impact on the effectiveness of schemes in promoting equality of opportunity. In particular, if employers have to bear the full cost of the rights of their female employees (as is intended for the recent improvements in maternity rights), then they will have a disincentive to employ women, which would not arise if the cost of these rights were shared by all employers (through national insurance contributions or a payroll tax) regardless of whether they employ women or not.

Economic consequences of policies for equal opportunities

Debate about policies to promote equality of opportunity has to recognize the interrelatedness of economic performance and the goal of equal opportunities. When considering initiatives that could be made, whether by employers or by national government policies, the potential cost incurred by employers has to be addressed. Even when the state covers the cost of allowances to parents on leave there may still be costs to employers. When parents go on leave employers must carry a vacancy or employ a temporary worker who will need induction and training and may be in post for too short a time to reach full productive potential. There is disruption from reorganization of work schedules, and personnel costs of recruitment. If working hours are reduced there will be a need to reorganize working arrangements, and there will be costs associated with taking on extra employees during peaks of activity. But the Employment Department has given exaggerated estimates of some of these employer costs (Holtermann 1995), in particular in its 'compliance cost assessments' of extending maternity rights and the EU proposal for a maximum 48 hour week (Department of Employment 1991, 1992), which are not supported by employer surveys. For instance in the Maternity Rights Survey of 1991 only 13 per cent of employers said that the implementation of maternity rights caused them problems (McRae 1991).

The economic benefits, over and above those arising from improvement in equality of opportunity, must also be counted. The benefits to employers, which have been ignored in government cost assessments, can be substantial, as described in, for instance, Hogg and Harker (1992). When their personal needs are recognized in their terms of employment, employees work with greater commitment and contentment and their productivity is higher and turnover lower. Some analysis of the benefits and costs to employers of providing working parents help with childcare costs has concluded that the benefits to employers, in terms of lower costs of recruitment and training, can outweigh the costs of the help provided by childcare, through greater retention of skilled and experienced female workers and a higher proportion returning after childbirth (Business in the Community 1993).

Government initiatives for the promotion of equality of opportunity also need to be assessed for their impact on the national economy, taking account not just of the costs (of for instance leave payments or help with childcare costs) but also the potential for wider economic benefits. For instance, a reduction in working hours could make a contribution to reducing unemployment, but this has also been ignored in the government's compliance cost assessment of the EU working time directive.[8] Measures to make it easier for women to combine employment with their childcare responsibilities by increasing their access to affordable quality childcare would bring wider economic benefits: it would increase national output; it would ease the skill shortages that afflict the British economy every time it gets going on an expansionary path; and reduce the inflationary pressures that build up all too soon (Holtermann 1992). Implementation of equal pay for work of equal value may, at least initially, require rates of pay that are different from those produced in the labour market (acknowledged to be far from perfect). This can be expected to have knock-on effects in the labour market and beyond, and Rubery (1992a) demonstrates that the wider economic consequences can be beneficial throughout the economy. As an economic measure equal pay for work of equal value is similar in principle to other forms of price control that are intended to promote social or economic aims, such as minimum wages or price regulation of the privatized public utilities.

The potential for employers to make gains on top of the intended improvements in equality of opportunity has recently been given more emphasis in the policy debate, as the quotation from the *Employment Gazette* at the beginning of this article shows. But there is a need to be wary of this development. Any kind of organizational initiative aimed at promoting equality of opportunity can (and should) be subjected to benefit-cost or cost-effectiveness analysis, in order to assess the expected contribution to improving equality of opportunity, and also to assess the other benefits and costs to the employers (the 'efficiency costs and benefits'). Such analysis will reveal that in some cases there will be a net cost in efficiency terms from improving equality of opportunity, while in some cases there will be a net benefit. It is natural that employers will be more inclined to take those steps that have the fortunate outcome of improving their business position. Is it acceptable to give these some kind of priority? The risk is that while the more expensive types of measure may stay on an organization's agenda for social responsibility, they will be repeatedly pushed to the bottom of the list because there is insufficient financial payback to the employer. There is a danger of a shift in attitude towards a position where equality of opportunity is no longer treated as an independent aim, but merely as something that can be pursued if, and only if, it coincides with the employing organization's own self-interest.

It does, however, have to be accepted that there are situations where a gain in equality of opportunity can only be made by incurring some net cost, and there is then a classic trade-off between competing objectives – improvement in one objective (equality of opportunity) can only be gained by some reduction in

50

cost-efficiency – and, subject to complying with legislative constraints, employers will have to decide what balance to choose, according to their own priorities. It is precisely where this trade-off is to be found that there is greatest need for the government, which has a wider set of social objectives than employers, to introduce (and enforce) national minimum standards. The government will itself also have to be mindful of all the benefits and costs arising from its policies for equal opportunities, and will have to take explicit responsibility for choosing a balance, reflecting what it judges to be the preferences of the population, between competing objectives. The spectrum of opinion about the degree to which equality of opportunity should take priority ranges all the way from people who see it as an absolute goal to be pursued regardless of cost, to people who see it as a matter that should only be pursued if there is no cost attached. The present government has shown a tendency to overstate the costs of equal opportunities policies, and to understate their contribution to national economic efficiency, and this biases the estimate of the trade-off between equality of opportunity and economic efficiency against equality of opportunity, even if a fair interpretation of the balance of the public's preferences is made.

Looking at matters the other way round it is just as important, perhaps more so, to evaluate changes in the labour market against criteria that include equality of opportunity. Here, there is little room for optimism. The combination of continuing high levels of unemployment in the UK together with increasing deregulation of the UK labour market has made employment conditions worse for all kinds of employees. Abolition of wages councils, the increase in self-employment, contracting out, short-term working, temporary contracts and so on have increased low pay, insecurity and the risk of unemployment. The risks of adverse economic outcomes have grown for many categories of worker, and for both men and women, both with and without family responsibilities. The adoption of performance-related pay is also thought to be working against the interests of women. These trends in the labour market are in the opposite direction from what is needed to help equality of opportunity (Lindley 1994).

51

Sally Holtermann

Some of the economic foundations for the existence of the unequal treatment of women in the labour market have been examined and although it is also possible to identify an economic case for the pursuit of equal opportunities policies, in terms of gains that would accrue to both organizations and to the wider economy, legislative changes in the UK have tended to move in the opposite direction. Labour market deregulation has been encouraged in the name of reducing labour costs, so that the UK economy can maintain a competitive edge in the international arena. But even if this is an effective strategy for economic growth and employment (and that is highly questionable), there is a distinct danger that these economic goals are being pursued at the expense of further improvements in equality of opportunity for women and men.

Notes

1 The best sources of information on women and men in the labour market are the *General Household Survey* (1992) and the Labour Force Survey. A collection of findings from the Labour Force Survey are presented in *Employment Gazette* (1992) (on women generally) and Bartholomew *et al.* (1992) (on lone parents). The Equal Opportunities Commission (EOC) (1992, 1993) publishes annual summaries of the position of men and women in the labour market and education.
2 The more often quoted statistic from the 1993 *New Earnings Survey* is that among all women in full-time employment hourly earnings are 79 per cent of those of men. But the use of this figure gives a misleadingly favourable view because it overlooks the fact that the wage differentials in both manual and non-manual occupations, when looked at separately as in the text, are greater than the overall differential. The reason for this is that a relatively high proportion of women work in non-manual occupations, where their average hourly earnings are above the average hourly earnings of men in manual occupations. Wage differentials in the UK are virtually the highest in the European Union (EOC 1992).
3 In 1992, 42 per cent of lone mothers with dependent children were in employment compared to 63 per cent of married/cohabiting mothers (*General Household Survey 1992*). Among couples with dependent children, 24 per cent of wives/partners of working men were economically inactive (i.e. neither employed nor seeking work) compared with over half of the wives of unemployed men.

4 There are also high psychological costs associated with pursuing equal opportunities claims and the gains from a successful claim are likely to be greater for women as a whole rather than the individual concerned, which again tends to limit the extent to which such cases are pursued (Bruegel and Perrons 1995).

5 The employment rate for lone mothers with dependent children has been falling (down from 27 per cent in 1981 to 22 per cent in 1990) while the employment rate among married/cohabiting mothers has been rising (up from 47 per cent in 1981 to 60 per cent in 1990) (Bartholomew *et al.* 1992). Although the employment rate among lone mothers has been falling the number of lone mothers in employment has been rising because of the growth in lone parenthood (up from 11 per cent of families with dependent children in 1981 to 19 per cent in 1992 (General Household Survey 1992)). In 1981 there were 395,000 lone mothers in employment compared to 353,000 in 1990 (Bartholomew *et al.* 1992).

6 This is what Le Grand calls 'equitable'. He suggests a slightly different definition for equality of opportunity, which is weaker, and probably too weak to capture most people's idea of equal opportunities. Le Grand and Barr give formal representations of these definitions, but these will not be reproduced here.

7 Any parent, whether man or woman, who takes on the main part of child rearing work by taking breaks from paid employment and then working only part-time, pays a high financial penalty in terms of lost lifetime earnings. There could be said to be discrimination against parents, rather than women as such, but, at present, the costs of children are high and fall mainly on women.

8 For example the working hours of both women and men in Britain are the longest in the EU and have been increasing during the early 1990s. It has been estimated that if these increases had not taken place there would be one million more jobs in the economy (*The Guardian* 1995).

4

THE ROLE OF THE LAW IN EQUAL OPPORTUNITIES

Linda Clarke

The chapter begins by outlining some fundamental issues in relation to the nature of equal opportunities in a liberal society; in particular its focus on individual case law and equal rights meaning the similar treatment of like individuals which immediately poses problems for women given their frequently fundamentally different social roles. This is followed by a detailed analysis of the way in which the Sex Discrimination and Equal Pay Acts have operated in the UK, and then proceeds to a discussion of maternity rights. In each case the limitations of legislation cast within an essentially liberal framework are identified and in each case it has been the European Law, whose origins derive from rather different political traditions, that have brought about more rapid change.

It is now generally accepted that the law has a useful role to play in the development of equal opportunities policies, and in improving rights for women at work. In the UK it is only necessary to look at other kinds of discrimination, such as disability, which have not been the subject of anti-discrimination legislation, to see how reliance on the voluntary development of good practice and fair treatment has failed. Nevertheless, sex discrimination legislation is routinely criticized for having failed to deliver much of what it promised: the average weekly earnings of women still remains at around 71.5 per cent of men's average weekly earnings[1], and women are still generally absent from certain types of occupation, and concentrated in low-paid, low-status, often part-time work. The law is obviously only one element in the development of equal opportunities, but nevertheless it is important to question how the law operates in order to see whether and how legislation and legal practices could be improved.

Sex discrimination law in the UK begins from the classic liberal principle that similarly situated individuals should be treated alike, whereas differently situated individuals should be treated differently. So the Equal Pay Act 1970 originally provided for women to be paid the same as men working for the same employer in only two circumstances: where the woman was engaged on 'like work' with a man, and where the employer had voluntarily carried out a job evaluation scheme which graded the woman's job and the man's job as the same. Similarly, the Sex Discrimination Act 1975 provided that it is unlawful to treat a woman less favourably than a similarly situated man on the grounds of her sex. The problem with this conception of discrimination is that it ignores the fact that discrimination against women is the result of a complex set of interactions, a socially constructed inferiority, on grounds of gender, which the concept of 'equality of opportunity' can only address in a limited and individualistic way. The model of 'sameness', that sex is a suspect classification which simply needs to be ignored in order to achieve equality, fails to address the reality that women's lives are different from men's; it aspires to an assimilationist model that takes the male role as the norm, and aims to encourage and enable women to be just like men. This approach has been criticized by many feminists, who argue that in order to achieve genuine equality it is necessary to break away from the idea of men's lives as the norm and women's lives as 'other', and to recognize that women are different.

This 'sameness/difference' debate is particularly highlighted with respect to paid employment: the public world of work operates on the premise of treating all workers as equally able to meet the demands of the employer. But the reality is that women have two 'jobs' to a much greater extent than men do: in addition to paid employment, women tend to perform many more domestic tasks than men do – cooking, cleaning, shopping, washing. In addition, women are far more likely to be carers – of children, elderly parents, sick or disabled family members. Much of the systemic disadvantage that women suffer in the public world of paid employment results from the fact that working women also have to meet demands in the 'private' sphere of family and home life. Sometimes these demands make it impossible for women to enter into paid employment at all. More frequently, women are condemned to the twilight zone of badly paid part-time employment, with poor prospects of promotion or advancement, and little, if any, job security. It is in this context that sex discrimination legislation must be assessed: if a woman has to pick children up from school in the middle of the afternoon, then the formal right to be treated just like a man would be treated in a job interview is hollow, as she cannot apply for the same job in the first place.

However, the recognition that there are differences between men and women raises further problems: there is a danger that gender roles are simply reinforced, with a continuing identification of women as primarily carers and homemakers, and only marginal workers. The conflict between feminists over whether women should receive equal treatment or special treatment has been highlighted in the USA in the debate over maternity rights (Bacchi 1990a) and has led for a search to find a way out of the polarity of the 'sameness/difference' debate by examining what women need by concentrating on disadvantage rather than difference, outcomes rather than processes (Rhode 1989; Bacchi 1990b). So at some times in a woman's life it may be important to recognize that her needs are different from that of a man – pregnancy and childbirth being an obvious example. At other times, the best way to fight disadvantage may be to campaign for an improvement in workers' rights in general, such as enabling all workers to a certain amount of paid time off for family reasons.

Legal frameworks need to be developed which enable women

to overcome the disadvantages of gender in the workplace, but these legal frameworks cannot be limited to some notion of 'equal opportunities' at work: women's lives are affected by a multiplicity of legal issues, such as access to birth control, education, welfare, child custody and domestic violence, and reform is necessary in all these areas. Ultimately, the public world of the workplace needs to change, to acknowledge that all workers have private lives, involving a multiplicity of other duties and responsibilities. Only when those duties no longer fall primarily on women will there be genuine 'equal opportunity'. It is essential, therefore, that equal opportunities strategists address the question of access to paid employment. The public world of work is fundamentally important in dealing with women's inequality: paid employment is the key to much of the economic and social power in our society, and for women to be denied access to this is to deny women the power to transform their own lives. The systematic discrimination which women face in employment contributes to the lack of power women experience within the private world of home and family: women become and remain dependent upon a male 'breadwinner', or, increasingly, the state. (For a full account of sex discrimination law in the UK see, *inter alia*, Ellis 1988; O'Donovan and Szyszczak 1988; Bourne and Whitmore 1993; and Clarke 1994.)

It is important to understand how the law has addressed these questions, where it has been successful and where it has failed. This chapter will examine the concept of discrimination contained in UK sex discrimination and equal pay law, and the extent to which the law has developed to incorporate notions of difference and disadvantage. Particular attention will be paid to the role of European law in women's rights at work, and recent developments in the field of maternity rights.

The meaning of discrimination

The Equal Pay Act 1970 and the Sex Discrimination Act 1975 are the two key statutes covering sex discrimination at work. The Equal Pay Act 1970 (EqPA) is designed to cover all aspects of sex discrimination in the contract of employment, so that it deals not only with inequality in pay but also other terms and conditions of employment, such as holidays, sick pay and fringe benefits. The Sex Discrimination Act 1975 (SDA) prohibits discrimination at all stages of the employment process, from recruitment, to training and promotion, to dismissal and redundancy. It also contains an important prohibition against subjecting an employee to 'any other detriment' on grounds of sex; this has been used to outlaw a range of unfavourable treatment, including sexual harassment. The SDA also covers sex discrimination in education and the provision of goods and services.

The SDA defines discrimination in two ways: first, 'direct' discrimination, defined by section 1(1)(a):

A person discriminates against a woman . . . if –
(a) on the ground of her sex he treats her less favourably than he treats or would treat a man.

It is also unlawful to discriminate against married people of either sex.[2]

So direct discrimination involves less favourable treatment than a man has received or would receive. It is always necessary to compare the woman's treatment with that of a man, although there is no need to show that a man was in fact treated better: the SDA (unlike the EqPA) allows a comparison to be made with a hypothetical man. However, the comparison must be between individuals who are similarly situated, apart from the difference of sex: section 5(3) requires that:

A comparison of the cases of persons of different sex or marital status must be such that the relevant circumstances in the one case are the same or not materially different, in the other.

This encompasses the principle that like should be treated alike, but also opens the way for the argument that differently situated individuals may be treated differently; at one stage the UK tribunals refused to find that dismissals because of pregnancy were sex discriminatory because men could not get pregnant, and so it was not possible to compare like with like[3]. Tribunals have continued to find it difficult to apply this provision to pregnancy: the approach of the UK courts has been to compare the pregnant woman with the temporarily sick man. The European Court of Justice (ECJ), by contrast, takes the approach that only women can get pregnant, and therefore any unfavourable treatment because of pregnancy is automatically sex discrimination.

It is also essential to show that the less favourable treatment is 'on the ground of sex': it is now clear that this does not mean that the employer was motivated by a desire to discriminate. In James v. Eastleigh Borough Council,[4] a council, for benevolent reasons, allowed women over 60 free access to swimming pools, whereas men had to pay until they reached 65, on the basis of the state pension age. The House of Lords ruled that this was unlawful discrimination: the use of a gender-based criteria (reaching state pension age) was unlawful regardless of the council's motive. The question was whether a man would have been treated differently but for his sex.

The courts have also held that treatment 'on the ground of sex' includes treatment based on stereotypical assumptions about sex. So it was direct discrimination to refuse to employ a woman with young children, where the employer's ground was that women (but not men) with young children were inherently unreliable,[5] or to refuse a woman a two-year secondment to London on the ground that she would not return to Wales at the end of the period because her husband worked in London.[6]

Nevertheless, the concept of direct discrimination is based on the principle that there are differences which justify different treatment. So a woman who was refused a job because she could not work full-time because of her individual childcare responsibilities would not have suffered direct sex discrimination: the comparison would be made with a hypothetical man with similar responsibilities, who would also be refused the job. The SDA recognizes the limits of this approach by outlawing indirect discrimination. The concept of indirect discrimination was developed in the USA as a way of addressing past and institutional discrimination in the context of race, and was incorporated at a late stage into the SDA. Indirect discrimination is based on the premise that certain employment practices which appear neutral between the sexes do in fact have an adverse impact upon women. The key issue then becomes whether or not the employer can justify the practice. The SDA provides that indirect discrimination occurs where a person:

Linda Clarke

applies to [a woman] a requirement or condition which he
applies or would apply equally to a man but
(i) which is such that the proportion of women who can
comply with it is considerably smaller than the proportion of men who can comply with it, and
(ii) which he cannot show to be justifiable irrespective of the
sex of the person to whom it is applied, and
(iii) which is to her detriment because she cannot comply
with it.

Although this concept has the potential to challenge many
discriminatory practices through taking account of differences
between the sexes, the law in the UK has been criticized as being
too technical. A woman has to show that an employment practice
which has an adverse impact on women amounts to a 'requirement or condition'. So a job advertisement which specified that
candidates must be under the age of 28 is potentially unlawful,
but an advertisement stating that preference would be given to
candidates under the age of 28 would not, unless it could be
shown that in practice the age limit operated as a complete bar to
recruitment.[7] Employers can therefore avoid scrutiny of employment practices by keeping their preferences as vague and
discretionary as possible.

It is then necessary to show that any requirement or condition
is such that fewer women than men can comply with it. Here it is
established that the question is whether women can comply in
practice, rather than in theory: so in cases concerning age limits
the courts have recognized that women are in practice excluded
from full-time employment at certain times because of childcare
responsibilities. Nevertheless, the legislation raises problems
which have not been dealt with in a uniform way by the tribunals.
There are divergent views on the appropriateness of using
statistics, with some tribunals requiring detailed analysis of
numbers of women and of men who can comply with relevant
conditions, and others disclaiming the need for detailed statistical analysis.

There has also been a perennial problem in identifying the
correct group for comparison. In Jones v. University of Manchester,[8] the university advertised for a graduate, with relevant

experience, aged between 27 and 35. Miss Jones was 46, and when her application was rejected, she claimed that this was indirect sex discrimination. She argued that the tribunal should compare the proportion of women graduates who had obtained their degree as mature students (over 25), and who could comply with the age requirement, with the proportion of male graduates who had been mature students and could comply with the age requirement. The Court of Appeal ruled unanimously that this was incorrect: the appropriate comparison was not between mature students who could meet the age requirement, but between all men and women graduates, whatever age they obtained their degree, with relevant experience. Miss Jones's case failed because she could not show that the proportion of women graduates with relevant experience who could meet the age requirement was considerably smaller than the proportion of male graduates. Nor have tribunals agreed on the meaning of 'considerably smaller'. If 90 per cent of women can comply with a requirement that they be available for work on Saturday, and 99.5 per cent of men can meet the requirement, is 90 per cent a 'considerably smaller' proportion than 99.5 per cent? Probably not.[9] But what about 85 per cent or 75 per cent? The courts and tribunals have refused to adopt the US approach, that if only 80 per cent of women in the group can meet the condition, compared with 100 per cent of men, then there is a prima-facie case of discrimination.

All of these issues operate as potential traps for the applicant, making indirect discrimination very difficult to establish. Even when it is accepted that an individual woman has suffered a detriment as a result of a discriminatory requirement or condition, the employer still has a defence: the key question becomes whether the employer can justify the discriminatory practice or condition. This incorporates the notion that some 'differences' justify a practice with a discriminatory impact, and that the ending of discrimination, or equality of outcome, is not the goal of anti-discrimination legislation. Rather the discriminatory effect of certain practices is to be balanced against the usefulness of those practices to the employer. The meaning given to 'justifiability' by the courts has varied over time: initially a discriminatory practice has to be shown to be necessary to the needs of the business, rather than simply convenient, but in a series of cases this standard was lowered to one of reasonableness. However, following the decision of the ECJ in Bilka-Kaufhaus GmbH v. Weber von Hartz[10] the courts now require that the measures taken by the employer 'must correspond to a real need on the part of the undertaking, [must] be appropriate with a view to achieving the objectives to be pursued and [must be] necessary to that end'. So the employer has to show not only that there is some business-related objective which is met by the discriminatory requirement, but also that there are not other means, without the discriminatory impact, by which that objective could be met. Although this standard is an important advance, the extent to which tribunals require hard evidence from employers in practice varies considerably.[11]

The concept of indirect discrimination therefore offers considerable potential for dealing with systemic discrimination, but the law in the UK is inherently limited in its ability to fulfil that potential. This is further compounded by the fact that even if a woman succeeds in a claim involving indirect sex discrimination, the tribunal cannot award her any financial compensation unless it can also be shown that the employer intended to discriminate.[12] The essence of the legal system is that it is a stick rather than a carrot, and many employers will only take equal opportunities seriously if the consequences of failing to do so are financial. The SDA originally imposed a very low limit on the amount of compensation that could be awarded to a woman who suffered (direct) sex discrimination: in 1993 this stood at £11,000. However, in Marshall v. Southampton and South-West Area Health Authority (No. 2) [1993] IRLR 445 the ECJ ruled that any financial limit on compensation was contrary to European law, and as a result the government was forced to remove the ceiling.[13] As a result, tribunals have made increasingly large awards, covering not only financial loss, but also injury to feelings: in April 1994 an industrial tribunal awarded £299,851 to a servicewoman who was forced to resign her commission when she became pregnant.[14] The importance of such large awards, and the extension of compensation to indirect discrimination, has enormous potential as a tool for encouraging employers to take the elimination of sex discrimination seriously.

The impact of the European Union

As already noted, membership of the European Union (EU) has had a significant and welcome effect on the development of anti-discrimination law in the UK. Since the UK joined the EEC (as it then was) in 1972, there has been an obligation on the government under international law to comply with Article 119 of the Treaty of Rome: this states that men and women should receive equal pay for equal work. In addition, the EU has passed a number of Directives concerning sex discrimination. These Directives operate as an obligation on the individual member state to introduce domestic legislation which gives effect to the Directive within a certain time. Judges in the UK are then obliged (and have shown themselves increasingly willing) to interpret the legislation in the light of the purpose of the EU Directive. Furthermore, if the government fails to implement the Directive, or does not implement it fully, then a woman may rely on the Directive to claim legal rights against the state itself: this may be against the state as her employer, or by claiming damages against the state for its failure to implement the Directive, thus depriving her of legal rights. Further, the European Commission can bring proceedings in the ECJ against member states over their failure to implement Directives or treaty obligations. (For a detailed account see Prechal and Burrows 1990; Ellis 1991.) In an important recent development, the Equal Opportunities Commission itself took proceedings against the UK government in the UK courts, over the government's failure to provide part-time workers with protection against unfair dismissal or redundancy, on the grounds that this was indirect discrimination against women and contrary to European law.[15] The House of Lords ruled that the requirements in the Employment Protection (Consolidation) Act 1978 that employees had to work 16 hours per week or more for two years, or between 8 and 16 hours for five years, in order to be entitled to a redundancy payment or to bring an action for unfair dismissal, was contrary to Article 119 of the Treaty of Rome. As a result, the government will be required to change the law.

Linda Clarke

Equal pay for work of equal value

The Equal Pay Act 1970, which was not implemented until the end of 1975, originally provided that a woman could claim equal pay with a man doing 'like work', or 'work rated as equivalent'. The Act operates by inserting an 'equality clause' into the woman's contract of employment, so that any contractual term, not merely pay, which is less favourable to the woman is modified so as not to be less favourable. Unlike the SDA the woman must compare herself with a real man working for the same employer. The employer also has a defence to an equal pay claim if it can be shown that there is a genuine material difference between the woman's case and the man's.

Although the EqPA had the effect of raising women's relative pay levels, its impact was inevitably limited. There was no mechanism whereby women could compel an employer to introduce a job evaluation scheme, and the Act was therefore unable to tackle the real problem: the occupational segregation of men's and women's jobs, and the under-valuation of jobs done predominantly by women.

However, the Equal Pay Directive 75/117 states that the principle of equal pay for equal work enshrined in Article 119 of the Treaty of Rome means equal pay for the same work or 'work to which equal value is attributed'. The European Commission successfully brought enforcement proceedings against the UK government before the ECJ and, as a result, the EqPA was amended in 1983, so that from 1 January 1984 a woman could claim equal pay with a man doing work of equal value to hers.

Equal value claims obviously have enormous potential to challenge existing pay structures, and there have been important victories for women. Many trade unions have been successful in using equal value claims in collective bargaining. But the legislation has been heavily criticized for its complexity and slowness, with cases taking up to four years to complete. (For a useful summary of recent cases see EOC 1993.) The Equal Opportunities Commission has pressed the government for amendments to the legislation, with only very limited success, and has now taken the step of referring a complaint to the European Commission, arguing that the UK remains in breach of EU law by failing to effectively ensure or maintain equal pay.

The concept of 'equal value' attempts to incorporate notions of equality and of difference, by recognizing that there are structural obstacles for women within the labour market and pay systems, but that two different jobs, one predominantly female and one dominated by men, can be of equal value in terms of the effort and skill of the employees. Yet the concept has difficulties: measuring how much a job is worth is not as 'scientific' as management consultants would have us believe, and has been beset by the problem of how to eliminate hidden sex discrimination through overvaluing 'male' attributes and undervaluing female ones. It is impossible to eliminate all subjectivity from the process, yet subjectivity inevitably raises the suspicion of sex bias.

Equal pay law is based on the premise that there should be similar treatment for those similarly situated (doing like work or work of equal value) but that different treatment is justifiable for those differently situated. This is translated in law into the concept of 'genuine material difference'. The problem is that the differences which count are themselves rooted in cultural and structural gender disadvantage. So UK law has allowed employers to defend pay differentials on the grounds of market forces, different collective bargaining arrangements and length of service, all factors which tend to favour men. Again, the only ray of hope comes from Europe. Enderby v. Frenchay Health Authority[16] involved speech therapists (predominantly female) in the NHS claiming equal pay with (predominantly male) clinical psychologists and pharmacists. The health authority argued that even if the jobs were of equal value, there was a genuine material difference: that the differences in pay were due to separate collective bargaining arrangements, and in the case of pharmacists to market forces, as there was considerable demand in the private sector for their services. The Court of Appeal decided that the case raised questions as to the correct interpretation of Article 119, and referred certain questions to the ECJ for a preliminary ruling.

The ECJ, in a decision of great significance, held first that where there is a significant pay differential between two jobs of equal value, and one job is done predominantly by men, and one predominantly by women, then this raises a prima-facie case of sex discrimination: the women do not need to prove that this differential is because of sex discrimination, rather the burden shifts to the employer who must show that the pay difference is due to objectively justifiable factors unrelated to sex discrimination.

Second, the ECJ held that separate collective bargaining arrangements for the two groups could not of itself justify the difference. So collective bargaining may explain why the pay is different, but does not justify that difference. Thirdly, the ECJ ruled that market forces can justify pay differentials, but that tribunals should apply the principle of proportionality: in other words, tribunals must determine what proportion of the pay differential is attributable to a shortage of candidates and the need to attract them by higher pay. This decision treats equal pay as a group rather than an individual issue, and again requires that employers must show objectively justifiable economic factors where they pay predominantly female groups less than comparable groups which are male-dominated. It remains to be seen how UK tribunals will interpret this ruling.

Maternity rights

Pregnancy and maternity rights pose particular problems. This is an area of women's lives which is unique: not all women become pregnant, but only women become pregnant. Whether or not pregnant women should be given special treatment has been at the heart of the 'sameness/difference' debate in the USA, but in the UK there has been much less division over the issue. In the UK maternity rights were first introduced as part of a package of individual employment rights by the Labour government in 1975, and were dependent upon a woman having worked for the same employer for two years. Discussion in the UK centred more on how to improve protection, rather than on whether protection should exist in the first place. But the two-year continuous service requirement meant that many women were excluded from statutory maternity rights: in particular, women who became pregnant with less than two years' service were vulnerable to dismissal by employers. The only possible legal redress was an action for sex discrimination, where there is no continuous service requirement. The problem with using the SDA is that a woman has to show that she has been treated less favourably than a man whose circumstances were the same or not materially different. After an initial hiccup (see above and Clarke 1994) the tribunals developed the approach of comparing the pregnant woman with a man with a similarly incapacitating illness, and asking whether the employer would have dismissed the man too.

There are obvious difficulties here: many women were offended by the characterization of pregnancy as comparable with illness, and employers who would dismiss the man about to go off for a hernia operation as well as the pregnant woman were not committing sex discrimination. In some cases, the 'comparative' approach becomes strained, as in Berrisford v. Woodward Schools Ltd[17] where the unmarried pregnant matron of a girls' school was dismissed because of the bad moral example she would set to the pupils.

The approach of the ECJ has been much more straightforward. In a series of cases,[18] the ECJ has ruled that only women become pregnant, and therefore any unfavourable treatment on the grounds of pregnancy was direct sex discrimination. There is no need to search for a male comparator. Webb v. EMO Cargo (UK) Ltd,[19] the latest case to reach the ECJ, illustrates the difference in approach. Mrs Webb was recruited to work alongside a woman who was due to go on maternity leave. The idea was that Mrs Webb would work alongside the first woman, cover for her whilst she was on maternity leave, and then stay on when she returned, as it was envisaged there would be enough work for both women. However, Mrs Webb discovered that she was pregnant also, shortly after beginning work. The industrial tribunal, the Employment Appeal Tribunal, the Court of Appeal and the House of Lords were all agreed that this was not sex discrimination under UK law: a man who was similarly unable to work during the critical period would also have been dismissed. But the House of Lords decided that it was necessary to refer the case to the ECJ, because of uncertainties about the correct interpretation of the Equal Treatment Directive. The ECJ ruled that this dismissal was sex discrimination: where a woman was employed for an indefinite period, her dismissal on the grounds that she would be prevented by pregnancy from performing her job for a purely temporary period could not be justified.

The decision of the ECJ pays considerable attention to the policy issues: the Equal Treatment Directive allows member states to introduce special provisions to protect women in connection with pregnancy or childbirth, and in 1992 the Community passed Directive 92/85, a measure introduced to promote the health and safety of pregnant and breast-feeding workers. As a result of this Directive, the UK government has been obliged to pass legislation which offers considerable improvements to maternity rights in the UK: from October 1994 all women, regardless of length of service, will be protected from dismissal for any reason connected with their pregnancy, and will be guaranteed 14 weeks' maternity leave, on at least statutory sick pay levels. (For a detailed account of the new legislation see Clarke 1994.) As a result, the decision in Webb itself has been overtaken by events.

The 'special treatment' accorded to women under European law has generally been welcomed by women in the UK. But it has also led to fears that such an improvement in maternity rights will eventually harm women's prospects. There is anecdotal evidence that employers will respond by discriminating against women of childbearing age in recruitment, and whilst this may be unlawful, it is also very difficult to prove. It remains to be seen whether this happens in reality. The Webb decision is perhaps most important in its recognition that pregnancy is a temporary condition, lasting only a few months. The major problems that women face as workers begin after the baby is born: it is the lack of adequate and affordable childcare and the inability of the 'public' world of work to recognize that workers also have family responsibilities that are the major obstacles, and ones which last for many years. The way forward must be to concentrate on improving and changing the workplace, and in changing the attitudes and responsibilities of men as fathers. The continued focus on pregnancy as a paradigm of the 'equal treatment/special treatment' debate, and a search for some clear ideological and theoretical response will only continue to obscure the issue of women's needs and responsibilities.

Conclusion

Sex discrimination law in the UK is primarily based on the 'equality of opportunity' model, but has also attempted to take on board, albeit in a limited manner, the notion of 'difference', through indirect discrimination and equal pay for work of equal value. There have been other important developments, such as the recognition of the existence of sexual harassment and reform of inequality in pensions. The prospect of much higher damages being awarded for sex discrimination offers hope in the use of the law as a tool to force employers to take equal opportunities seriously. The lessons of legal strategy over the last two decades demonstrate that it is misguided to search for a clear legal perspective which answers all demands. Sometimes equal treatment is all that women need. At other times, it is necessary to recognize differences in order to ensure that women are in reality treated as equals. Measures involving positive discrimination may be necessary in the short term to enable women to achieve 'starting block' equality, whereas special maternity rights may be needed permanently. It will be necessary to weigh up the advantages and disadvantages, long-term and short-term, in order to see which measures are worth fighting for. But in the end it will be necessary to transform the workplace, to ensure that all workers have real choices about their lives, their jobs and their responsibilities to others.

Notes

1 Figures from the 1993 *New Earnings Survey*, Part A (HMSO).
2 Although UK law does not prohibit discrimination against single people, this is covered by the EC Equal Treatment Directive 75/207, which outlaws discrimination on the basis of marital or family status.
3 Turley v. Alders Department Stores Ltd [1980] IRLR 4.

4 [1990] IRLR 288.

5 Hurley v. Mustoe [1981] IRLR 208.

6 Horsey v. Dyfed County Council [1982] IRLR 395.

7 See Price v. Civil Service Commission (No. 2) [1977] 1 WLR 1417; Perrera v. Civil Service Commission (No. 2) [1983] ICR 428; Jones v. University of Manchester [1993] IRLR 218.

8 [1993] IRLR 218.

9 See Wetstein v. Misprestige Management Services Ltd, unreported, 19 March 1993, where requirement to work on Friday afternoons was held not to be indirect discrimination against Jews. Between 90 and 95 per cent of Jews could comply, as only between 5 and 10 per cent of Jews are strict Sabbath observers, whereas 100 per cent of non-Jews could comply.

10 [1993] IRLR 218.

11 See for example the decision of the Divisional Court in R v. Secretary of State for Employment ex parte Equal Opportunities Commission [1991] IRLR 493, where the court accepted the government's 'evidence' that allowing part-time workers protection against unfair dismissal and redundancy would lead to a decrease in the number of part-time jobs available as 'inherently logical'. This evidence was later described by the House of Lords as consisting of 'an affidavit by an official in the Department of Employment which set out the views of the Department but did not contain anything capable of being regarded as factual evidence demonstrating the correctness of those views'.

12 It is strongly arguable that this is contrary to EU law. In Mulligan v. Eastern Health and Social Services Board (Equal Opportunities Review [EOR] Discrimination Case Law Digest No. 20, Summer 1994) a Belfast industrial tribunal awarded compensation to a woman who suffered indirect discrimination on the basis of the Equal Treatment Directive.

13 Sex Discrimination and Equal Pay (Remedies) Regulations 1993.

14 Note that since this decision the Employment Appeals Tribunal (EAT) has attempted to limit the amount of damages payable to servicewomen dismissed because of pregnancy. In Ministry of Defence v. Cannock [1994] IRLR 509, the EAT held that the correct approach to assessment of damages involves assessing the chances that the woman would have returned to work had she been given a reasonable period of maternity leave. She should not automatically be entitled to compensation for the loss of earnings for the rest of her commission. In particular, the EAT took the view that if a woman was not actively looking for alternative employment six months after the birth, then this could be seen as a failure to mitigate her loss.

15 R v. Secretary of State for Employment ex parte EOC [1994] IRLR 176.
16 [1993] IRLR 591.
17 [1991] IRLR 247.
18 See Dekker v. Stichting Vormingscentrum Voor Jonge Volwassenen (NJV–Centrum) Plus 177/88 [1991] IRLR 27 ECJ; Hertz v. Aldi Marked K/S [1991] IRLR 21 ECJ; Habermann-Beltermann v. Arbeiterwohlfahrt, Bezirksverband Nbd/Opf eV [1994] IRLR 364 ECJ; and Webb v. EMO Cargo (UK) Ltd (*The Times*, 15 July 1994).
19 See *The Times*, 15 July 1994.

5

EMPLOYMENT DEREGULATION AND EQUAL OPPORTUNITIES: THE CASE FOR MONITORING GENDER WORK

Diane Perrons

This chapter considers the changing conditions of employment both nationally, through policies to deregulate the labour market, and within organizations, through the use of more individualized contracts and payment systems, and how these changes make the assessment of equal opportunities policies more difficult. It then proposes a method of monitoring the effectiveness of equal opportunities that would incorporate some of this complexity.

Equal opportunities policies – the framework

Equal opportunity policies exist in a variety of forms. Formal legislation has been in existence in the UK since 1975. It was amended in 1984 in order to allow claims for equal pay for work of equal value to be made in order to comply with European Union (EU) law. Further, from the early 1980s, both public and private sector organizations have increasingly introduced in-house equal opportunities policies. Additionally there is general employment legislation which also has a profound impact on the extent of gender inequality.

The UK government supports equal opportunity legislation and voluntarist initiatives such as those advocated by Opportunity 2000, partly in order to comply with European law but also because it is consistent with a liberal political philosophy. The liberal market model promotes formal equality and it is believed that competition will eliminate systematic discrimination. Where market failure occurs, policies to promote equality in pay between individuals performing the same type of work within a particular firm and which prohibit discrimination on the basis of gender or ethnicity are acceptable (Whitehouse 1992; Clarke, Chapter 4). Thus while equal opportunities legislation, to the extent that it seeks to secure formal legal equality between individual workers, is consistent with this framework, employment regulations or legislative protection that would apply to groups of workers is not and is strongly resisted. Indeed efforts are made to deregulate employment and to restore market discipline.[1]

Company-specific equal opportunities policies were introduced for a variety of reasons: because of a sense of justice and morality, a need to serve and represent the community, to utilize the labour force efficiently, to enhance corporate image and to comply with the law (Jewson et al. 1992; Whitting et al. 1993). In the late 1980s there was also concern about the demographic time-bomb and efforts were made to tap new labour reserves, especially women and ethnic minorities. As a consequence measures associated with being an equal opportunities employer were consistent with commercial self-interest since a business case for greater equality could be defined. However, the labour market forecasts were invalidated by the recession of the early 1990s and some of the enthusiasm for enhancing the role of women in organizations evaporated (Clement 1992). This response indicates that the business case is at least partially associated with cyclical economic change, especially in the case of the private sector, and as a consequence legislation is a necessary, albeit an insufficient, condition for equal opportunities to be realized.

Equal opportunities legislation and in-house equal opportunities policies are generally consistent. The legislation provides a framework for equal opportunities while organizations' policies set out more practical ways of implementing the policy. However, inconsistencies can arise between the equal opportunities policies of organizations and their other objectives and similarly between formal equal opportunities legislation, the more general legislative framework and overall economic policy. Consequently it is important to monitor gender inequality in organizations and in society as a whole in order to evaluate the effectiveness of equal opportunities policies.

So far, despite the policies, the situation for women is far from optimistic. Although some women have moved into professional and managerial occupations they are still vastly over-represented in low-paying jobs with little status or prospect and pay differentials remain wide. Occupational segregation remains immense and on less measurable dimensions of inequality such as employment security, status and control, pension rights, holidays and fringe benefits women have an inferior position (Rubery 1992a).

Moreover, even in those cases where women have obtained managerial positions there is a sense in which they remain on trial, are not fully equal and have to behave in very specific ways in order to be taken seriously (Hearn 1989; Cockburn 1991; Liff and Dale 1994). Further, there are many instances in which having obtained managerial positions the status of those positions has been redefined and frequently downgraded (Coyle 1993; Rubery and Fagan 1994). Thus the quality and type of jobs into which women are entering also need to be considered (Rubery and Fagan 1994). For example, in hotel work and catering nearly 50 per cent of managers are women and the number of management trainees is 75 per cent; however 'as management in this sector is feminized it is becoming a low pay ghetto for women whose earnings as managers are below even average female earnings' (Coyle 1993: 15). Similarly in the civil service 'active measures to increase the recruitment, promotion and retention of women coincided with a decline in the relative pay of middle and higher grade civil servants from 30 to 14 per cent above average pay for men and from 51 to 29 per cent for women (1981–1990)' (Rubery and Fagan 1994: 37). Moreover in banking, again a sector in which women employees dominate numerically but where they have only recently been moving into managerial positions, the management jobs they have assumed 'do not have the authority and control previously associated with management' (Coyle 1993: 15).

Indeed it is interesting to note that those responsible for legislation, such as the Social Affairs Commissioner of the EU, acknowledge that the European legal framework alone 'is insufficient to eliminate the persistent inequality of opportunities for women' (Flynn cited by EOR 1994: 4). Yet at the same time the limitations of in-house strategies are recognized by others and legislation called for. For example, Angela Coyle concluded from her study of local authorities that 'rather than a strategy for women's pay, it is a strategy for low pay that is required' (Coyle 1989: 49) and this perspective is supported by comparative analyses of gender inequality.

In all countries gender inequality in employment exists but there are significant cross-national variations in the extent of inequality (Lane 1993: 275). These cross-national differences appear to be more closely associated with differences in the general legislative framework relating to employment and more widely with the prevailing welfare regime than with equal opportunities policies *per se*. Greater equality is found in those countries which have a more regularized rather than a market-oriented framework (Rubery 1992b; Whitehouse 1992; Blau 1993; Perrons 1995).

In relation to pay, for example, comparative studies of the UK, USA, Italy and Germany indicate that centrally structured systems of pay determination are associated with smaller gender wage differentials (Rubery 1992a; Blau 1993). In the USA, women are relatively well qualified and equal opportunities policies are in many ways stronger than those in Europe with affirmative action programmes and contract compliance being allowed. Thus the comparatively high level of gender inequality in earnings has been attributed to the wide and growing inequality in the distribution of earnings there, especially amongst male workers (Blau 1993), which is in turn attributed to the fragmented structure of wage determination and to the increase in flexible employment practices (Harrison and Bluestone 1990). These inequalities would be reduced with more centralized systems of wage bargaining which would allow agreements made in the larger, more organized firms to be extended to smaller firms in the same industry or sector as occurs, for example, in Germany and this narrowing of overall differentials would also reduce the gender pay gap. Australian evidence also indicates a very strong connection between overall employment regulation and a narrowing of gender inequality in earnings (Hunter and Rimmer 1994). Further, where there is a conscious policy to reduce gender inequalities these can be introduced more speedily in a centralized system (Blau 1993).

Deregulation in the UK

Despite the evidence that more regularized employment frameworks are associated with greater gender equality, since its election in 1979 the Conservative government of the UK has consistently amended legislation in order to deregulate employment in the context of its attempt to create an enterprise economy. 'As a consequence there has been a creeping erosion of the floor of rights on employment protection' (Wedderburn cited by Miller and Steele 1993: 231). Any protective measures that would promote greater equality such as a minimum wage, collective bargaining at the national or occupational levels, the regularization of hours and the harmonization of conditions for full and part-time workers such as those contained in the Social Chapter have been resisted (Rubery 1992a), although European initiatives on equal opportunities such as the Action Programmes and voluntary initiatives by the business sector in Opportunity 2000 have been supported (Fina Sanglas 1991).

More specifically, trade union rights have been weakened, decentralized wage bargaining at the enterprise and individual level has been encouraged so as to reflect both organizations' ability to pay and to enable them to reward individual performances, and wages councils have been abolished.[2] Moreover the nature of many public sector organizations has changed with privatization, subcontracting, compulsory competitive tendering and the decentralization of budget holding. These changes have also contributed to the decentralization and fragmentation of wage negotiation, leading to an increase in wage dispersion, a weakening of the possibility of equal value claims, as these can only be made within a single organization, and to a reduction in the possibility of making progress within the career structure of any organization (Rubery 1992a; Bruegel 1994).

Subcontracting of female-dominated forms of work not only allows equal value claims to be evaded (Rubery 1992a), but may also create the illusion of greater equality. For although equality may exist within the fragmented units, if these are exclusively low-level jobs then inequality will actually be strengthened via the removal of pre-existing career ladders within the more integrated units. Alternatively the appearance of commitment to equal opportunities may be enhanced if some of its operations are subcontracted (Jewson et al. 1992). The decentralization of budget holding will lead to pay being determined at the level of individual organizational units such as a hospital or school, again making equal value claims more difficult. This is very different to the situation in Germany where pay in all sectors tends to move together (Rubery 1992a).

Indeed there is growing evidence that the introduction of deregulation and flexible working practices leads to increasing wage polarization and an expansion in the numbers of working poor, especially women (Michie and Wilkinson 1994). Many public sector organizations had been at the forefront of equal opportunities policies for reasons other than transient commercial opportunism. Their decline and changing nature through privatization and subcontracting is likely to have deleterious effects for gender equality. These changes, together with the new employment practices introduced in the private sector, make the task of effective monitoring of equal opportunities more difficult but more necessary.

Changing employment practices within organizations

Besides the government's desire to weaken trade unions, new managerial theories also emphasize the importance of more individualized systems of pay and contract determination. These developments are associated with the introduction of appraisal systems and performance-related pay. Performance-related pay (PRP) and increasingly individualized performance-related pay became particularly popular towards the end of the 1980s in the context of tight labour markets and the desire to recruit and retain staff. Subsequently, despite the recessionary conditions of the 1990s and research indicating demotivating effects of PRP, its popularity seems to have increased. Indeed PRP based on some form of appraisal is increasingly becoming the only element in pay awards (Bevan and Thompson 1992).

There are a variety of motivations for PRP. Higher salaries could be paid to those staff with high internal and external value without increasing the overall wage bill (Rubery 1992a). It is also seen as a means of restoring or enhancing managerial control, raising worker commitment and motivation while weakening the power of trade unions (Bevan and Thompson 1992; Kessler 1994).[3]

Although more common amongst management, these schemes are becoming more evident in the public and finance sectors where women's share of employment is increasing. In principle these schemes have both positive and negative implications for women. On the one hand, the development of formal appraisal systems can overcome entrenched prejudices and provide opportunities for women to be assessed and rewarded for their individual merits rather than on the basis of stereotyped assumptions of their generally male superiors.[4] On the other hand, they reintroduce discretionary elements into previously formal pay structures which could 'allow gendered stereotyped imagery and evaluation to come into play' (Rubery 1992a: 110), especially since all appraisal schemes seem to contain a subjective element (Bevan and Thompson 1992). Further, given the low external valuation of women's labour and the fact that women are typically constrained geographically (Green 1992), the size of awards necessary to retain women employees is likely to be lower than for male workers.

In the majority of studies of PRP carried out so far gender bias has been found. Promotion potential is often assessed on the basis of qualities considered appropriate to the employee's gender. The qualities sought also vary by the gender of the manager, in both cases leading to a reinforcement of gender stereotypes with male managers looking for characteristics such as intelligence, dynamism, maturity and aggression in male subordinates and dependability, degree of perception, sociability and honesty in female subordinates. These characteristics may in turn influence the kind of jobs for which the appraisees are considered suitable. A tendency was also found for men to be promoted but PRP to be awarded to women. In other words women's talents and skills are valued, but in their existing capacities – an instance perhaps of the glass ceiling (Bevan and Thompson 1992). Thus women receive discretionary awards rather than a permanent improvement in their work situation.

Although PRP should be monitored in order to ensure that it does not constitute a form of indirect discrimination, following the direction of the European Court ruling in the Danfoss case (see p. 184) it seems that in practice few firms are aware of this and little monitoring of PRP awards by gender takes place (Bevan and Thompson 1992). In fact this ruling applies to all pay awards that lack transparency. If the average pay of women workers in a given relatively large pool of workers is lower than that of male workers, then the employer must prove that the system is not discriminatory. Thus, if a merit pay scheme leads to an unequal distribution of payments between women and men, then the employer must be able to show that it is not discriminatory, i.e. there must be objective reasons for the imbalance (Bevan and Thompson 1992).[5] Although PRP awards are often set within boundaries linked with pre-existing pay structures, they nevertheless contribute towards the obfuscation of pay settlements and make equal value claims and indeed an equal opportunities policy difficult to operate if it is the individual rather than the job that is evaluated.

However, another aspect of the human resources management school works in the opposite direction and towards harmonization of the terms and conditions of employment. All staff are taken to be valued employees and as a consequence require similar treatment, leading to a narrowing of divisions between blue- and white-collar workers and between full-time and part-time workers in relation to working conditions and fringe benefits. In the past these benefits have been associated with seniority or long service and consequently disproportionately enjoyed by men and in practice the rate of any harmonization has been slow and in some cases has been associated with a levelling down of conditions (see p. 22). A study in 1989 demonstrated the extent of this inequality, finding that while 73 per cent of male full-time workers were entitled to a pension only 68 per cent of female full-timers and 31 per cent of female part-timers were similarly entitled. In relation to other fringe benefits such as company cars, private health care, etc, only in the case of free or subsidized meals did female full-time workers do better than their male equivalents (Rubery 1992a) and it is highly probable that these took the form of school dinners rather than lean cuisine. This harmonization of basic conditions, however, can take place alongside the continuation of bonus awards, special payments and PRP (Rubery 1992a) in order to allow management to retain some means of distinguishing between employees, and here gender inequalities can be immense (Bruegel 1994).

These organizational changes also mean that monitoring needs to be highly sophisticated in order to ensure that new forms of inequality are not being introduced as old forms are eroded.

Equal opportunities policies and monitoring

Equal opportunities practice is now generally associated with the use of formalized recruitment and selection procedures including the external advertising of all new jobs, measuring equality of access to training programmes, staff development and promotion and the introduction of family-friendly policies in relation to working time, including the possibility of career breaks, job shares and flexible working practices (Coyle 1989). These aspects of equal opportunities policies are introduced to varying degrees in different organizations (Opportunity 2000 1993).

Another necessary dimension of equal opportunities policies is monitoring. While many organizations accept that evaluation is a vital part of the equal opportunities exercise surprisingly few have formal procedures. An Equal Opportunities Commission survey in 1988 found that of 514 local authorities only 26 monitored staff. A higher proportion planned to introduce monitoring but there were few concrete proposals (Coyle 1989). Moreover in Opportunity 2000, where participating organizations commit themselves to 'increasing the quality and quantity of women's participation within their own workforces' and are formally required to monitor their performance, only two-thirds of the members set numerical targets (Opportunity 2000 1993: 4). Similarly, in relation to a study of ethnic monitoring amongst employers who were thought to be among the most advanced, the majority were still in the process of developing their systems (Jewson *et al.* 1992).

At the organizational level attitudes to monitoring vary. In some organizations it has become an integral part of personnel practices and is considered necessary both to systematically evaluate the equal opportunities policy and to evaluate the performance of the equal opportunities officers. It is also seen as part of the growing practice to trace the performance of workers within an organization. Indeed, monitoring by gender and ethnicity has been built into many computerized personnel systems. Computerization has not only 'reduced costs and workloads, increased speed and accuracy, enabled a wider range of issues to be monitored and permitted more sophisticated and more extensive analysis', but has also contributed to the legitimization of monitoring as a routine part of personnel practice (Jewson *et al.* 1992: 17–18). Further, the knowledge that monitoring is taking place has itself contributed to greater numbers of women and ethnic minorities being employed. Equal opportunities officers especially welcome the way in which monitoring provides greater weight to their arguments.

On the other hand some organizations, especially those without computerized systems, are concerned about the costs of monitoring and perhaps also fear that formal monitoring would reveal them to be less than equal opportunities employers, especially in cases where there has been a stable workforce for some time and a low turnover rate. Indeed, where firms operate an internal labour market and recruit at the bottom end of the scale, then vertical segregation would probably continue for some time, even where equal opportunities policies were applied. Further concerns arise over the confusion between targets and quotas and the view that monitoring creates tensions between workers and gives rise to the sense that employees are being promoted on the basis of their gender or ethnicity rather than on their individual merits (Jewson et al. 1992; Maddock 1993).

Sophisticated forms of monitoring that go beyond examining the distribution of employees within and between different occupations and grades may allay some of these concerns. For example, organizations could be in the process of becoming equal opportunities employers provided there are strategies in place to contribute towards this end. Monitoring of all stages of recruitment, from the response to advertisements through to those taking up the appointment and further monitoring a cohort of employees from appointment to departure, examining issues such as the training given, promotions applied for and obtained, PRP awards, levels of responsibility, etc. (Jewson et al. 1992), could determine whether the equal opportunities claim was in fact appropriate.

However, for monitoring to enable equal opportunities policies to be evaluated not only must adequate data be collected and analysed but the objectives of the policy have to be clearly specified. In Chapter 3 Sally Holtermann raises the question of what is meant by equality of opportunity. Within the economics literature reference is made to equality of choice and equality of chance. The former requires that women and men, free from prejudice about gender roles, are equally able to choose from the distribution of jobs available while the latter requires that having made choices the probability of outcome is the same for each individual. This dual conception of equality allows for the possibility that women and men may have different preferences, for example, in relation to taking career breaks or in terms of the nature of work performed leading to differences in occupations and pay levels etc. without there being any inequality or, in other words, that differences in outcome can be consistent with full equality.

However, this conception raises questions of the cost of child rearing, which is considerable and has fallen predominantly on women (see p. 35 and Joshi and Davies 1993), but also of the social evaluation of jobs predominantly carried out by women. The equal value amendment was designed to permit a re-evaluation of women's work but its present effectiveness is undermined by the fragmentation of employment units (Rubery 1992a). Women would probably stand to gain more from a social re-evaluation of their existing activities, rather than entering predominantly male spheres of activity where, in the past, their entry has been associated with downgrading. In any case, many women would perhaps prefer to retain their existing activities, provided they were adequately rewarded, i.e. would prefer to obtain equivalence or equality on the basis of difference (Cockburn 1991).

Thus it is useful to use Cynthia Cockburn's distinction between the short and the long agenda for equal opportunities (Cockburn 1991). For example, in the context of contemporary theories of effective management the objective of equal opportunities policies could be to promote high-flying women to key positions within the existing hierarchical structure of firms in order to capitalize upon the belatedly recognized skills and talents of women. This would be the short agenda, and its effectiveness might be adequately encapsulated in simple measures such as the proportion of women workers occupying different positions in the employment hierarchy. This kind of measure is now contained in many software packages for personnel management.

On the other hand equal opportunities policies could be designed to address equality more fundamentally. Traditional hierarchical employment structures in which women disproportionately reside at the base could be replaced by a flatter structure in which the skill profile of all workers is raised and more appropriately rewarded. This long agenda would require more sophisticated monitoring but would allow a more accurate picture of the state of equal opportunities to be obtained.

Monitoring needs to be carried out within organizations to ensure that there are no practical barriers which work against the overall national framework and to convert 'policy statements into effective procedures' (Liff and Dale 1994: 178), and also at the national level. The national picture reflects the performance of organizations but at the same time strongly influences the terms and conditions in which people are employed. Comparative analysis at this level is therefore necessary in order to determine which kind of economic and political framework is most conducive to gender equality.

While information is now being collected by gender at the national level in the labour force surveys and the new earnings surveys, these sources are far from adequate, particularly in the way that women's occupations are defined. Organizations also complain about the lack of official data at the local or regional level necessary to provide a base against which to compare their own employment profiles (Jewson *et al.* 1992).

Techniques of monitoring

Monitoring needs to take place at the societal and organizational level. Some of the software associated with personnel systems allows for the possibility of gender and ethnic monitoring. However, so far it seems that the form of monitoring incorporated into these systems is fairly limited, only calculating the proportion of different grades occupied by gender or ethnicity. If software to monitor the composition of the workforce is in place, then it would be relatively easy to introduce more sophisticated measures to obtain a fuller picture of the extent of gender inequality.

The technique outlined below is based on the work of Harvey, Blakely and Tepperman and provides a method of incorporating many different dimensions of employment inequality into a single composite index (Harvey *et al.* 1990). The advantage of such a composite index is that it enables an assessment of progress to be made, i.e. whether overall there had been a movement towards or away from more equal opportunities. The technique could be applied at either national or organizational level and it is well suited to analysing changes over time, something that has been requested by employers in order to evaluate their equal opportunities programmes.

At national level the technique has been applied to Canada, the EU (Harvey *et al.* 1990; Perrons 1994) and a similar technique to the USA (Sugarman and Straus 1988) but its usefulness is rather constrained by the lack of detailed gendered data at this level. At the organizational level, however, these constraints do not apply. The only limitation arises from organizations' unwillingness or inability to collect and analyse their data.

To calculate the composite index a number of steps have to be taken. First, the dimensions of inequality to be included in the index have to be chosen. These dimensions or variables have to be expressed as ratios or proportions, e.g. the ratio of female to male earnings or the proportion of a particular grade occupied by full-time female workers. They also have to run in the same direction, i.e. such that as the ratio increases it represents a step towards greater equality. For a satisfactory index there must also be some degree of correlation between the variables.

The variables need to be transformed into natural logarithms in order to prevent extreme values from having disproportionate significance and then standardized to ensure that they contribute equally to the final index (Harvey et al. 1990). If variables are thought to have special significance, they can be weighted accordingly. Standardization ensures that this does not occur simply because of the different units in which the variables have been expressed and is carried out by calculating Z scores,[6] i.e. each variable is recalculated in relation to the mean and standard deviation of the series from which it comes. The Z scores are then converted into index figures in order to measure change over time. These index values for the different variables are then summed for each period and divided by the number of variables to produce the composite index of gender equality (see equation).[7]

$$ IGE \quad = \quad \left(\frac{\sum\limits_{i=1}^{n} Vi}{n} \right) $$

where IGE =   index of gender equality
        Vi =   indexed value for variable i

The actual value of the index is highly dependent on both the variables included and the way in which they are measured. However, provided similar dimensions of inequality and similar ways of measuring them are used then it would be possible to quantify changes in the level of inequality within an organization.

Variables relating to different dimensions of gender inequality can be used. In the case of earnings the effects of bonus, incentive schemes and PRP as well as the hourly or weekly differential could be measured to gain a greater indication of the overall level of inequality. Similarly for participation: in addition to the hours of work, the regularity and security of the contract could be included to see if there were systematic differences between male and female employees. Likewise for employment status: measures which reflect the nature of women's jobs such as the degree of control, the number of subordinates, occupational category, access to training and fringe benefits and so on could in principle be included in the index. The advantage of the composite index over more simple measures such as the proportion of women in different levels of the hierarchy is that it would allow the progress of women as a whole within the organization to be measured, and even if only used for the upper tiers of the hierarchy it could be used to express the feelings of those women managers that somehow they remain unequal. It might also be possible to incorporate some dimensions that would reflect different organizational cultures and resistances to equal opportunities (see Pemberton, Chapter 7).

Whether, and indeed to what extent, employers would be willing to do this is unclear; but given the changes in the structure of employment and the way in which the content of jobs has changed, such monitoring is undoubtedly necessary if the extent of gender inequality in employment is to be measured effectively. Even if only some of the possible dimensions of inequality were included in the index, some idea of how the organization was performing would be obtained and, as with other forms of monitoring, the gathering of information can itself contribute to an increase in awareness of gender inequality.

However, some aspects of gender inequality remain difficult to quantify, such as how women in given positions feel that they are simply tokens or not treated as equals or that they have to follow complex behaviour codes in order to obtain equal treatment (Cockburn 1991; Kanter 1993; Liff and Dale 1994). Indeed the way in which patriarchal power can be exerted in all sorts of insidious ways, which make it very difficult for women to proceed or even want to, must not be overlooked (Cockburn 1993).

Conclusion

Despite the existence of equal opportunities policies at a variety of levels, and despite the limited monitoring that takes place, it is clear that any progress towards the attainment of equal opportunities has been limited. The increase in the deregulation of employment and some aspects of organizational policy are working against equal opportunities and making the operation of the existing legislation more difficult to monitor and to enforce. In this context more sophisticated monitoring of gender inequality is required and a possible technique has been put forward. However, to explain the lack of progress for women it may be necessary to go beyond looking at frameworks for equal opportunities. Employment is only one dimension in which women experience inequality and, until the question of the dominance of male power and masculinity is addressed more generally, it is perhaps not surprising that despite considerable efforts inequality in employment remains.

Notes

1 Indeed Philip Pearson of the London Wages Rights Campaign has argued that 'While Opportunity 2000 is tackling the glass ceiling – the government is taking a sledge hammer to smash the glass floor and the low paid will drop through it' (Pearson cited by Clement 1993).
2 Wages councils had an important role in the narrowing of pay differentials between women and men. In 1970 female–male earnings ratios were the same for wages councils and other industries; by 1991 in wages council industries the female–male earnings ratio was narrower than for all industries, female earnings being 88.1 per cent of male earnings in these industries as opposed to 74.4 per cent in all industries. With their abolition it is likely that the gender gap will increase (Hart 1994).
3 One company studied by Bevan and Thompson reported that 'the

company wishes to have a more flexible approach to encourage a culture of high performance and to stimulate greater employee involvement and commitment to the business. It therefore considers that salaries of individuals should be based on performance only, which reflects their success in meeting personal and company objectives' (Bevan and Thompson 1992: section 3.2).

4 For example, Boots The Chemists have found that 'more rigorous assessment and appraisal techniques began to demonstrate that, as a group, women graduate pharmacists achieved higher ratings against BTC's performance criteria than men'. Moreover, as a result of more objective techniques (in promotion procedures) an increasing proportion of women were obtaining senior management roles; for example, 25 per cent of store managers were women in 1993 as opposed to 18 per cent in 1991, and while 12 per cent of district managers are female compared to only 5 per cent in 1991 50 per cent of the new district managers were women (Opportunity 2000 1993).

5 Thus as Bevan and Thompson argue 'the court established the principle that "the quality of work carried out by a worker may not be used as a criterion for pay increments where its application shows itself to be systematically unfavourable to women"' (Bevan and Thompson 1992: section 1.5).

6 The Z score is equal to (X-Xmean)/St dev X.

7 The values of the Z scores for the base year are set equal to 100 and the values of the other Z scores are transformed accordingly. The transformed value is equal to the sum of 100 and the difference in standard deviation units between the base year and this year. Or 100 + ($Z score_t - Z score_{tb}$) where t = any year and tb = the base year.

TOWARDS THE FAMILY-FRIENDLY EMPLOYER

Lisa Harker

This chapter deals with the long-standing problem of how to reconcile productive and reproductive work. This problem arose with the spatial separation of these activities following the industrial revolution. Consistently domestic work has been seen as the responsibility of women and both organizations and the state have responded to the conflicting demands on women's time according to their own or the economy's need for women's labour rather than on the basis of women's desires for a more balanced existence.

The new features of the 1980s and 1990s are the increase in female labour force participation (including that of mothers with young children), the changing structure of the family (in particular the expansion of single-parent households) and a series of changes in employment practice and the business environment. There has been an expansion of atypical and flexible forms of working and at the same time perceptions that the importance of skills stereotypically associated with women such as communications and caring have become more important. Moreover, these same qualities of concern leading to increased commitment have prompted many organizations to introduce a more caring working environment themselves which recognizes that workers have other responsibilities. As a consequence many organizations have been introducing family-friendly policies. Within this changing context both existing and potential family-friendly policies and forms of legislation are reviewed in this chapter, and the impact of these policies for the individuals, organizations and society more generally are assessed. The context for the introduction of these policies varies between organizations as does the nature of provision. Some of these differences are explored in this chapter.

Changes in family structures

'Family-friendly' is a modern term rather than a modern phenomenon. How women combine their paid work with their family responsibilities has been variously on the minds of employers and governments since the Industrial Revolution. Whilst a higher proportion of women are now in paid employment than at any time since World War II, women's participation in the paid labour force has long been significant, if subject to wide variation over time. Literature suggests that in the pre-industrial period, for example, households often depended on women's wages, frequently earned through agricultural work, textile production, farm work or craft trades (Yeandle 1984). However, it was not until industrialization that the distinction between home and work responsibilities became clear with the emergence of individual wage labour away from the home.

In reality, therefore, the 'male' model of working – a male spouse working full-time away from home with his wife remaining at home to care for children – has never been a persistent one. Nevertheless the dominant ideology of the gender division of paid and unpaid labour has had a considerable impact on policy. Most 'family-friendly' policies have been directed towards enabling women to work as well as take the main responsibility for the day-to-day care of their children. During World War I, workplace crèches were set up by governmental agencies in response to the need for mothers to work to meet labour shortages. Likewise after World War II, when the service sector developed rapidly, part-time and flexitime working practices which fitted around school hours were promoted by employers to encourage more mothers to enter employment (Hallaire 1986).

From the early 1980s women's employment increased rapidly. Between 1981 and 1991 the proportion of mothers with children under the age of 5 who worked increased rapidly from 25 per cent to 43 per cent (General Household Survey 1992). Fears about the falling number of school leavers entering employment and the ageing workforce seemed to provide a real opportunity for women to take a more active role in the workforce. Female employees, particularly mothers returning to the workforce, were seen as an untapped labour source and essential to the maintenance of a skilled workforce at a time when the economy was rapidly becoming more knowledge-based. Labour shortages in the 1950s and 1960s had not had such a significant impact on the number of working women. In the 1980s the combination of the skills shortage with the growing need for two breadwinners to maintain family incomes and the long-term impact of the women's movement all contributed to the increasing numbers of women entering the workforce.

The downturn in economic prosperity stalled the full impact of the so-called 'demographic time-bomb' and consequently threatened to put a brake on the growth of family-friendly employment practices. Nevertheless the reaction to the demographic situation in the 1980s and the persisting skills shortages irreversibly placed concerns about the need for the employers to be more responsive to employees' domestic requirements on the business agenda.

Work–family programmes in the 1990s have begun to move away from the traditional aim of enabling women to combine their work and family lives, towards also encouraging fathers' involvement in the raising of their children. This reflects a wider change in attitudes (Martin and Roberts 1984; Jowell *et al.* 1988, 1990). Evidence of substantial changes in the division of paid and unpaid work between men and women has not emerged, however. Fathers in the UK, for example, continue to work the longest hours in the European Union (EU) (Commission of the European Communities 1993).

In the 1990s the 'male' model of working is not only inaccurate in terms of employment patterns but also in the family structure it implies. The so-called 'traditional' family – where there are two parents and dependent children – makes up less than one-quarter of households and only 28 per cent of such households are comprised of a man who is employed and a woman who is not (*General Household Survey* 1992). The number of dual-earner families has increased at the same time as the rise in unemployment and no-earner households. Furthermore, one family in five is headed by a lone parent (*General Household Survey* 1992). Unless work–family initiatives respond to the nature of families in the 1990s and beyond – rather than focus on the 'traditional' model – they will be ineffective in helping parents combine their work and family lives.

Changes in working patterns

The working model of employment for 48 hours, 48 weeks a year and for 48 years per lifetime no longer exists in reality. Part-time employment is now growing at a faster rate than full-time employment and 'atypical' working patterns are, in fact, not atypical at all. We have seen a revolution in the way work is organized, brought about by a greater proportion of work in the service sector, calls for the reduction in working hours, greater flexibility in operating hours in response to customer needs, improvements in international communications and the increased number of women seeking employment (Hewitt 1993a). The workforce is increasingly being polarized into those who undertake core (permanent, full-time) employment and those employed to take on peripheral (short-term contract and casual) employment, with a declining level of participation in core employment.

Against this backdrop of changes in working patterns, the workforce has remained horizontally and vertically segregated: men and women work in different industries and at different levels in the hierarchy in those industries (Rees 1992). Despite equal pay legislation, even on the most favourable measure – hourly earnings of manual workers – women still earn only 79 per cent of male earnings (EOC 1993). Access of women to training has rightly been identified by some employers as central to achieving a skilled workforce. However, many women returners are still barred from access to training because of the lack of childcare and impoverished information and networks (Rees 1992). Access to training is also restrictive for women employees, particularly those undertaking 'atypical' work.

The question to what extent family-friendly policies fit in with these changing working patterns remains unresolved. Some writers have suggested that the introduction of family-friendly policies has so far been limited, adopted to suit employers as much as families (Simkin and Hillage 1992). As McRae (1989) has pointed out, employers may wish to adopt family-friendly policies because it helps them to accommodate seasonal peaks, operation and customer requirements more effectively, main-taining continuous production without the need for overtime payments. Hewitt (1993b) has argued that the pursuit of 'fair flexibility' – the overlap of policies which benefit employers with those that recognize the needs of employees – is the only solution to this dilemma.

Whose responsibility?

Should responsibility for promoting a satisfactory balance be-tween work and family life rest with governments, employers, trade unions or individuals? The answer, of course, is all of them. But the question of how such responsibility should be shared is more difficult to answer. Peter Moss highlights the centrality of governments' role in promoting family-friendly policies (Hogg and Harker, 1992). In the absence of a policy framework initiated by government, employers' initiatives will only constitute one-off concessions rather than the makings of a family-friendly society (Hogg and Harker 1992). Furthermore, where govern-ments do more to help parents combine their work and family lives, employers are often encouraged to do more. For example, a survey carried out in 1991 in Germany showed that 14 per cent of companies had agreements offering employees a longer period of parental leave (leave taken by either parent after maternity leave);

this was in addition to 18 months' statutory leave, which has since been increased to three years. In countries such as the UK where there is no statutory parental leave provision, employers rarely guarantee such benefits for parents.

Nevertheless employers have significant contributions to make towards changing the workplace culture into one in which parents – with all their familial obligations – are welcome. The Single European Market means greater competition for labour and resources than ever before. Family-friendly policies are emerging throughout Europe as integral to furthering good business practice (Hogg and Harker 1992). In order for companies to have the competitive edge in the new Europe, they will need to ensure that their workforce is fully motivated.

By reinforcing the need for action and representing the needs of less advantaged workers, trade unions have an equally important role to play. In the UK, the number of women in trade unions has not kept pace with the proportion of women in employment (Rees 1992). Indeed, the proportion of employees in trade unions has fallen generally. Family-friendly issues have not been as adequately addressed by unions as they might have been. Facing these issues head-on represents some of the biggest challenges for companies and trade unions as we approach the twenty-first century.

What are the options for employers?

A range of initiatives are open to employers who face the question of how to help parents combine their work and family lives in a way that makes good business sense.

Flexible working arrangements

Flexible working
There are many variations of flexible working practices. Sometimes employees can alter the start and finish times of their working day but they must be present for 'core' hours; 'term-time' working allows employees to work only during the school term, to enable them to take paid leave during the school

holidays; 'annualized' hours provide employees with the flexibility to spread their working hours throughout the year.

Sometimes companies offer a range of flexible working arrangements. At Schering AG, a large chemical and pharmaceutical company in Germany, for example, employees are offered a choice of three different arrangements, working a half day, working one week on and one week off, or working a reduced hour week. This scheme was introduced in 1985 because management saw it as a way of recruiting and retaining skilled employees, particularly those who have family commitments.

Part-time work
Part-time work refers to a working arrangement whereby an employee works less than the full-time hours. The classification normally used for part-time working in the UK is up to 30 hours per week, but part-time working can refer to a working week of any amount of hours up to this limit.

Following a recent Law Lords' ruling (3 March 1994) employers in the UK can no longer offer different redundancy rights to part-time and full-time workers. However, the extent to which the ruling will also cover other working conditions is not yet known (EOC, personal communication, August 1994). Non-statutory occupational benefits, such as pensions, are not covered by legislation and many part-timers do not receive them.

Some employers recognize that part-time employment, accompanied by pro-rata benefits, can enable parents to reconcile their work and family commitments. In the early 1990s Tesco, for example, introduced a scheme establishing rights for part-time workers to career breaks and maternity leave entitlements which were equal to those offered to full-time workers.

Job-sharing
Job-sharing enables two or more people to share a full-time job, dividing the pay, holidays and benefits according to the number of hours that they work. It requires commitment from both colleagues in order to ensure that the work gets done but it has the advantage of providing a mutual support structure.

Teleworking/flexiplace
Flexiplace or teleworking enables employees to work at home. Whilst they may spend some time at the office, the home is identified in their contract as the main place of work. Teleworking normally requires the purchase of equipment in order to undertake work at home, such as a modem and fax.

Oxfordshire County Council introduced a flexiplace scheme in 1990 to enable employees to work at home where possible, as part of a wider package of family-friendly benefits. The scheme has been taken up by men and women alike and enables employees to take a more flexible approach to the working day. As well as being part of the council's equal opportunities policy and drive to help parents combine their work and family lives, environmental considerations were central to the motivation to introduce the scheme.

Teleworking at a location away from the head office but in a 'satellite' office located in the suburbs or closer to the employee's home is increasing in North America and the idea is spreading to Europe. The Telecottages Association was launched in April 1993 in the UK in response to a growing number of satellite office arrangements.

Leave arrangements

Maternity leave
In all countries of the European Union employed women have the statutory right to maternity leave and maternity pay. Some employers, particularly those in the public sector, see statutory rights as minimum standards and offer their employees enhanced maternity pay or extended leave arrangements. Midland Bank offers a maximum of 46 weeks' leave and as a result of this and other family-friendly policies, the maternity return rate has improved with more than 80 per cent of employees returning to work after maternity leave.

Paternity leave
Statutory rights for fathers to take leave after the birth of their child are not available in the UK, unlike in other countries such as

Sweden, France, Spain, Belgium and Denmark. However, some employers, such as Littlewoods for example, offer as much as ten days' paid leave to new fathers.

Parental leave

Parental leave is an arrangement whereby either parent may take paid or unpaid leave following the end of maternity leave. Whilst statutory parental leave may be offered in some European countries, employers may still offer enhanced leave. At Siemens AG, a German electronics company, for example, employees may be allowed to take a maximum of seven years' leave after the birth of their child in certain circumstances such as in the event of the child's illness (Hogg and Harker 1992). In the UK, where there is no statutory parental leave, some employers offer employment breaks for family reasons (see below).

Family leave

Leave to enable employees to take time off to care for a sick child or relative is not a statutory right in the UK, although it is offered by some employers. Employers offer up to fifteen days' paid leave to care for a sick dependant, for example (Labour Research Department 1992).

Employment breaks

Employment breaks allow employees to take time off to look after their children, elderly relatives, travel or study and have a guaranteed job when they return. Employment breaks were first introduced in the banking sector in the early 1980s.

The National Westminster Bank plc, which has developed an employment break scheme since 1981, offers employment breaks of seven years to staff at all grades. Employees may take leave to care for a young child or an elderly, sick or dependent relative or partner. Some employees with particularly good performance records are guaranteed re-entry at the same grade, while others are put on a waiting list and offered jobs at the same level which they were at when they left as they become available.

Childcare

Childcare centres

Helping parents with their childcare responsibilities by setting up a workplace nursery is not the only option open to employers. Employees may prefer to use facilities closer to their home, they may not wish their child to travel to work, and the workplace may not be suitable to meet the standards of a high quality childcare service. However, in some cases, particularly when the local facilities are not adequate to meet the needs of the workforce, a workplace nursery will be the best option. Casterman, a Belgian printing firm, opened a workplace nursery in 1983 to enable their employees, many of whom were shiftworkers, to have access to subsidized childcare services which suited their hours of work. A drop in absenteeism amongst staff has been recorded since the nursery was opened.

Partnership projects

An increasing number of employers are adopting a partnership approach to childcare and the number of workplace childcare places established in partnership now exceeds the number of solely employer-run workplace nurseries (Working for Childcare 1994). In addition to partnerships between the public and private sectors, employers may also work in partnership with private consultancies, voluntary organizations and other employers. Sometimes employers 'buy-in' childcare places in established facilities on behalf of employees.

Childminding schemes

Providing choices in childcare is important for parents. Some companies maintain registers of approved childminders who care for children in their own homes. The service provided by childminders is flexible and can expand according to demand. It is often popular amongst parents who live some way from the workplace or in city centre sites.

In 1990 Elida Gibbs, a manufacturer of health and beauty products, set up a childminding scheme offering all employees places with 'linked' childminders approved by the company. The scheme was set up as a partnership between the company and

Leeds City Council and has been successful in recruiting and registering new childminders as the demand increases.

After-school and holiday care
The time after school and during holidays causes particular problems for working parents trying to juggle their work and family lives. There are a limited but growing number of out-of-school childcare schemes in the UK, some sponsored by employers.

Resource and referral
Childcare information resource and referral services were pioneered in the USA in the 1970s. They provide detailed, localized information and advice about childcare services, normally by means of a computer database. Because they offer up-to-date specialized information, resource and referral services can better match the needs of parents. Employers can establish resource and referral services in-house, or buy-in services to meet the needs of employees, or contribute to a service which also serves the wider community (Hogg *et al.* 1989).

Financial assistance
Financial assistance towards the cost of childcare can be paid to employees through a childcare allowance or voucher. Employers can purchase vouchers from Childcare Vouchers Ltd and distribute them to employees who can use them to pay a childcarer, who is in turn reimbursed by the company. Employers do not have to pay tax or national insurance on the vouchers, although employees are liable for income tax on their cash value.

Eldercare

Despite growing recognition that increasing numbers of employees will be responsible for caring for adult dependants, eldercare has to date received limited attention from employers in the UK. It is clear that before long it will be placed more firmly on the agenda. Initiatives can be aimed at the carers, such as offering flexible working practices, financial assistance, adult daycare services or counselling. Alternatively they may provide direct support for older employees in the transition to retirement, for example.

In 1991 Barclays Bank plc introduced 'responsibility breaks' for all employees with a minimum of two years' service, enabling them to take a complete break or work part-time for up to six months, in order to care for an elderly dependant. After this time employees can return to a job on the same scale as the one they left, take up permanent part-time work or be placed on a reserve list which gives them priority when they wish to return to work (Berry-Lound 1993).

Counselling services

Being a family-friendly employer does not only involve offering practical initiatives for working parents – it also requires recognition of the stresses and strains of parenthood. IKEA, a Swedish owned furnishings and household goods retail company which has a number of outlets in the UK, has a 'check-it-out' service which provides a free general counselling service to employees on any issue. The New Parents Project is part of that service, providing particular support to new parents, especially encouraging fathers to participate in the day-to-day childrearing responsibilities.

Implementing family-friendly policies

There is no one way to become a family-friendly employer; each company has different needs and is made up of a different type of workforce. Nevertheless the outcome will be the same; a family-friendly employer is one that responds to all the needs of all its employees, recognizing that the workforce is comprised of individuals with full lives outside the workplace.

A programme not a policy

In order to respond to the differing needs of employees, a programme of initiatives rather than one or two schemes in isolation will be needed. Eventually, with the successful implementation of a work–family programme, the company culture will become more family-friendly. Successful implementation will be characterized by the integration of work–family programmes into the management at all levels of the company and the linking of the schemes to strategic business planning. Policies should be recognized as being continuous and constantly developing to solve problems as they arise.

The stages to becoming a family-friendly employer

Few of the companies that have been assessed in the USA and Europe have reached the stage of being a family-friendly employer (Galinsky *et al.* 1991; Hogg and Harker 1992), although many companies are making progress towards reaching this goal. It is therefore useful for employers to see how their initial progress will contribute to an overall change in culture. The research of the Families and Work Institute in New York has developed The Family-Friendly Index as a bench tool for US companies (Galinsky *et al.* 1991). It places companies in one of three stages towards becoming a family-friendly employer. The stages may be briefly summarized as follows.

At stage one an individual or group promotes the need for family-friendly policies, stressing the business case and demonstrating possible solutions. However, managers and other staff still see work–family policies as a 'woman's issue' and limited options are considered. Action may only be taken on undertaking a company survey or establishing a focus group, after which one or two *ad hoc* schemes may be implemented.

At stage two the range of policy measures considered is broadened once it is realized that a more comprehensive approach is required. Responsibility for initiating schemes is assigned to an individual or group, often at senior management level. At this stage, the business case for schemes is identified by management and top-level commitment emerges.

By stage three, a fully integrated and coordinated family-friendly programme is established, through support at all levels. Policies are continually developed and company involvement extends to issues and concerns which extend beyond the immediate concerns of employees. Full integration of policies occurs when work–family issues become linked to strategic business planning.

What are the difficulties?

Becoming a family-friendly employer is not easy. It requires resources, commitment and patience. There are many difficulties that will be encountered on the way. Researching the initiative prior to implementation is essential in order to avoid some of the pitfalls. Nevertheless new challenges will be found once the project begins.

Resources

Perhaps the most common concern amongst employers is the cost of funding a work–family programme. A good quality fifty-place workplace nursery may require between £200,000 and £300,000 capital investment (Finch 1993), for example. Flexible working arrangements will require the investment of paid staff time and possibly the purchase of equipment to run new administrative procedures. In addition any new initiative will have to be researched, piloted and promoted by the company, all requiring the investment of resources. However, these costs need to be balanced against the financial returns that accompany an initiative. Once these are considered, the costs are greatly reduced (Business in the Community 1993). Presenting a clear and accurate business plan is an important step in convincing management of the necessity for change.

Support from all levels

Support from all levels of the company is essential if policies are to be implemented successfully. One of the greatest difficulties is changing preconceived ideas. When Levi Strauss & Co. (Europe) introduced its equal opportunities programme in Belgium in 1988, resistance from management was voiced. Personnel staff found that attitudes could be changed by presenting actual examples of success (Hogg and Harker 1992). Real-life case studies of employees who have participated in family-friendly initiatives, publicized in a company's in-house magazine, presented at training sessions or published as a promotional booklet, will bring the benefits of new ideas to the attention of staff at all levels.

The implementation of new initiatives inevitably requires additional work for personnel staff and managers. Planning the introduction of a new scheme over a reasonable period of time will help avoid placing too heavy a burden on these employees. Nevertheless a commitment to increased staff resources or the reorganization of roles will initially be needed even if initiatives become ultimately time-saving.

Support at all levels of the company must be reflected in the planning and management of policies. Flexible working practices and leave policies often require line-managers' time and commitment to make them work. Managers may voice resistance to the introduction of family-friendly policies because they believe that such policies will undermine their control over working hours and not fit with well-established, traditional procedures. Policies need to be integrated into the workplans of all departments rather than treated as a separate agenda where they will be ignored, forgotten or seen as a 'perk'. Nevertheless, an individual 'champion' or group is often needed in order to ensure the successful introduction of policies, to keep up the momentum of projects and to oversee the day-to-day work. A head of equal opportunities or head of human resources may take up this role.

Overcoming resistance
Convincing management about the need for family-friendly policies requires clear presentation of the business case. But resistance can also come from other members of staff who feel that they will not be benefiting from new policies. Some may feel that it is not the company's role to provide support for families – when BMW in Germany first proposed setting up a resource and referral service in the early 1990s some felt that the company should be 'making cars not babies'. Recognizing that all policies may not be positively received by all members of staff and identifying ways in which policies benefit all employees (see Hogg and Harker 1992) is essential when planning or implementing new schemes.

Lisa Harker

Encouraging take-up

Family-friendly policies should aim to support all parents, not only women. In a society which places greater emphasis on women's parenting responsibilities, employers should acknowledge the need to encourage men to take up policies which would enable them to play a fuller role in the care of their children. Support can be provided by offering role models, ensuring that management encourage the take-up of schemes (rather than simply tolerating it) and by providing additional support through workshops or seminars. Employers should be conscious of the eligibility criteria of all their family-friendly policies – they should question whether fathers are encouraged to use the workplace nursery, work term-time hours or receive financial support for childcare, as much as mothers.

However, all parents – men and women – may be reticent about taking up opportunities which new work–family schemes offer. This may be because the scheme is not suitable for their needs or because they fear a possible backlash to their actions, in the form of lack of promotion or redundancy, for example. Those who work other than the full-time norm, for example, can encounter both reduced opportunities and limitations in career progression (Metcalf 1990). Simply implementing a scheme may not be enough. Ensuring that managers are supportive of the initiatives by consulting and discussing policies, offering training opportunities and regularly monitoring schemes is necessary. In anticipating the introduction of new flexible working schemes, managers may be concerned about the impact on their supervisory roles or reticent about the ability of staff to 'get the job done' under the new working conditions. Such concerns should be addressed prior to the introduction of a scheme and ongoing training and support for all staff should be available.

Surveying employees' needs before introducing a scheme can avoid take-up problems. Sometimes a company's perception of what staff require can prove to be different from their real needs. When Ludwig Beck, a German retail department store, surveyed its staff's response to the idea of a workplace kindergarten, they found that the scheme had little support. Staff preferred to use childcare arrangements closer to home but were keen to adopt more flexible working hours. As a result, a company-wide flexible working policy was adopted, enabling employees to draw up individualized contracts with their employer to work between 60 and 163 hours a month (Hogg and Harker 1992).

The key to the success of any work–family policies is planning and monitoring initiatives. Listening to employees, either in a formal (through a trade union or other workplace representation) or informal but open way, will ensure that the needs of all employees are recognized and balanced with the needs of the company.

The impact of family-friendly policies

If you don't do it, you don't know what you are missing.
(Pierre Vanassche, Head of Personnel, Casterman S.A.,
Belgium)

The impact of family-friendly policies on women

Family-friendly policies enable mothers to combine paid work and family life without loss of status and income. Joshi and Davies (1993) have estimated that the average loss of earnings experienced due to disruption to working patterns and absence of childcare by a woman who has two children amounts to £249,000 over a lifetime (see Holtermann, p. 35). Assistance with childcare and flexible working practices with pro-rata benefits would enable mothers to return to work, if they wish, whilst their children are still young without significant detriment to their career. Family-friendly policies are therefore an important contribution to equal opportunity programmes to allow women to overcome the barriers they face to reach the higher levels of the workforce.

The impact of family-friendly policies on families

Successful work–family policies challenge the assumption behind the male model of working and the sharing of domestic responsibilities. If implemented effectively, they promote fair division of family responsibilities, encouraging fathers to play an equal role in the upbringing of their children. Family-friendly policies, by counteracting direct and indirect discrimination in the treatment of workers with children, particularly women, also facilitate the increase in household earnings of families with children and thereby improve their opportunities.

The impact of family-friendly policies on the workplace

Family-friendly policies benefit all employees, not just those who are experiencing difficulties reconciling their work and home commitments. Working for a company which recognizes and responds to the needs of its employees is rewarding and motivating. Crucial to the success of equal opportunities pro-grammes, family-friendly policies contribute towards equal rep-resentation of men and women at the workplace. Men and women who do not have family commitments will respond to the recognition that support will be there if or when they require it. In one of the few existing studies of the effect of introducing a work–family programme, the Families and Work Institute's survey of Johnson & Johnson staff found that more than half of the employees not using the company's flexible working time and leave policies said that the policies were nevertheless 'very important' to their decision to stay with the company (Families and Work Institute 1993).

The Johnson & Johnson survey also found that a higher percentage of workers 'strongly agreed' that their supervisor was supportive over work–family matters than before the company's work–family programme was implemented. These employees were also found to be less stressed, more loyal to the company, more satisfied with their jobs and more likely to feel that they were successful in balancing their work and family life.

The impact of family-friendly policies on employers

Family-friendly policies mean better business for employers. Whilst the initial outlay of a scheme may seem expensive, once the costs of losing qualified staff – costed in terms of the resources required to recruit and retrain another employee – are balanced against the initial set-up costs, the difference is more marginal. The business case for introducing family-friendly policies also extends to less quantifiable benefits to companies: the benefits of improved staff relations, loyalty to the company, enhanced publicity and reductions in staff turnover and absenteeism, for example. Even in periods of high unemployment, employers have been found to introduce family-friendly policies in order to retain staff with specialist skills (Rajan and van Eupen 1989).

Being seen to be a company which is concerned about the needs of working parents can also have a considerable impact on the company's customer base. Companies are already extremely sensitive to the importance of maintaining a good public image and acknowledge the link between public relations and maintaining a customer base. Family-friendly policies are beneficial in publicity terms too.

The impact of family-friendly policies on society

Since the war, women's position in the labour force has been undermined by a strong, underlying ideological opposition to the employment of women with young children. The view that such behaviour is harmful to children and irresponsible of mothers persisted and was fuelled by government statements and fashionable child development books.

More recently greater acceptance of mothers who go out to work when their children are young has emerged, although work–family issues remain largely perceived as women's issues. It is important that policies which help parents combine their work and family life aim to be 'family-friendly' and not only 'women-friendly'. Only through the ultimate 'mainstreaming' of work–family issues – when they apply to men and women equally – will society truly value the contribution of family-friendly policies in the workplace.

Acknowledgement

The author would like to thank Sally Holtermann and Marion Kozak for their helpful comments on an earlier draft of this chapter.

7

ORGANIZATIONAL CULTURE AND EQUALITIES WORK

Carole Pemberton

Ten years ago, twelve women left a postgraduate programme in women and education, determined to translate into action the ideas which had stimulated their thoughts and engaged their emotions. A belief that others would come to recognize the value of women in work, and that discrimination had to be challenged, led several to seek equalities posts. The years that followed could be summarized as a journey from evangelism to disillusionment. Egos were bruised, confidence sapped, and career progress halted. Eventually they all abandoned their roles to escape back into mainstream organizational jobs.

As one of those women, I have had cause to reflect on why able, committed individuals were able to achieve so little at such a high personal cost. From the vantage point of the management centre where I now work, I have concluded that the reasons lay in our inability to understand and interrogate the organizational cultures of which we were part. Had we done so, we may have decided not to join or at least recognized the need for different strategies to achieve our ends.

This chapter offers a framework for understanding organizational culture in order to identify the processes operating at the organizational level which may enhance or obstruct the implementation of equal opportunities. By recognizing that approaches to equality are part of the organizational culture of 'how things are done here' (Ouchi and Johnson 1978), I hope to help both those with a commitment to making gender work and individual women seeking to develop their careers to recognize the specific challenges they face within their own organizations.

The concept of organizational culture

The concept of culture as an anthropological field of enquiry is widely recognized. The methodologies of researchers spending extended periods of time living with a small group, visibly different to their own culture, have been well developed in the twentieth century. The researcher acts as observer and interpreter of their habits of daily living, rituals and relationships. The application of the same methodologies to organizations was not, however, suggested until Pettigrew (1979) argued that, in order to understand organizations, the focus should be shifted from what they do to the less rational, more expressive social qualities that give tasks their meaning. To understand an organization, he argued, it is necessary to understand the context in which it operates, the content of its cultural knowledge, and the social processes which are in operation. For organizations, like tribes, have belief systems about the rightness of certain social arrangements which motivate their actions.

Once Pettigrew had shown the way, the concept of organizational culture became increasingly popular as a means of understanding how organizations deal with issues of control and commitment. Studies of organizational or corporate culture multiplied, particularly in the context of comparative management. However, although widely appropriated, the concept of culture is neither simple nor uniform. Broadly, it has been used in three ways. First, as a societal or external variable that affects how particular organizations operate in different national or social contexts. Second, as an internal phenomenon that organizations try to create and re-create in order to enhance their performance and, finally, as something which derives from the basic assumptions and beliefs held by the members of the organization, a root metaphor (Smircich 1983).

Comparative management

The most influential of the comparative studies was a study by Hofstede (1980) of 116,000 IBM employees operating worldwide. He proposed four cultural dimensions along which countries might differ and which could be critical for the success or failure of any organization, even one such as IBM which prided itself on the strength of its own culture. These dimensions are the degree of power and social distance that is accepted between a subordinate and their boss; the emphasis placed on individualistic or group working; the extent to which rules and regulations are used to control uncertainty; and masculinity or femininity of values attached to work (Hofstede 1980). Together the dimensions can be used to separate out countries, and to produce a cultural matrix which could indicate both openness to equal opportunity and the ways it might be achieved.

In Hofstede's economic categories the UK and Netherlands occupy the same grouping, but in cultural terms there are significant differences. The Netherlands has a very low masculinity index, while the UK's is significantly above the mean for the forty countries in the study. The UK has a higher focus on individualism than the Netherlands, and a lower need for regulations to avoid uncertainty. The consequences can be seen in approaches to equality. A study of European values reported that the Dutch have a stronger belief in equal rights for men and women in work than do the British (European Values Group 1991). The Dutch regulate their commitment through an Equal Opportunities Policy Coordination Department within the Ministry for Social Affairs, while the UK has opted for an Equal Opportunities Commission with restricted powers. The Netherlands has long offered parental leave and contractual protection for part-time workers. In the UK such regulation was resisted, until imposed by the European Union. The UK profile suggests that moves towards equality will focus on empowering individuals rather than groups, and that rules and procedures will not be seen as absolutes in guiding behaviour. Such differences are made visible in outcomes. In the Netherlands, legislation and social benefits have led to a higher percentage of part-time working women than in any other European country (EOC 1994), but a significantly lower percentage of women managers than in the UK (International Labour Office 1992). Although those who look at the greater progress made in Scandinavian countries find support in Hofstede's work, his conclusions are challenged by those who view organizational culture as an internally created variable, and therefore one capable of manipulation through direct intervention (Hofstede 1980).

Corporate culture

The next strand in applying the concept of culture to organizations treated culture as a tool, something that organizations could introduce and develop to enhance performance. This could include informal practices such as giving gifts to departmental secretaries, the annual golf match and after-work pub sessions, as well as the creation of company champions and the commissioning of a corporate logo. These are all ways of developing rituals and culture designed to integrate and unify the workforce (Deal and Kennedy 1988).

Peters and Waterman (1982) extended this approach by arguing that companies with strong cultures were high performers. The subsequent failure of many of these companies led Peters to focus instead on speed of response to changing business conditions, and a willingness to embrace chaos as the cultural phenomena which may work as good indicators of performance (Peters 1993). Nevertheless, the message that organizations should actively intervene to create the culture that businesses need, has been widely accepted in UK public and private sector organizations. Organizations have accordingly issued mission statements, changed corporate logos and invested heavily in corporate communications. If little has subsequently changed, it is because changing the packaging of culture is significantly easier than moving the corporate mind.

An offshoot of the view of culture as a management tool is the structure-culture model which sees culture as shaped by the form of the organization. From this perspective Harrison and Handy have identified four clear cultural orientations which may be matched against organizational shape (Harrison 1972; Handy 1985).

1 A power culture: here advancement depends on the patronage of a few powerful organizational members. Policies are shaped by individual will rather than consensus or negotiation and subordinates are tightly controlled.
2 A role culture: here there is concern for order, rationality, and procedural equity which is made visible by the development of formal recruitment, selection, training and reward procedures. This model is more likely to be found in large organizations where competition is limited.
3 A task culture: where the superordinate goal is to get the job done well, thus anything that gets in the way of achieving the goal will be removed. This would seem to offer a more open climate for equality because concern for capability will override considerations of gender, race, age or disability.
4 A person culture: this refers to *ad hoc* and short-lived cooperative arrangements between members to meet specific needs. Issues of organizational equality are unlikely to be considered because members will see themselves as personal agents responsible primarily for and to themselves.

Equalities initiatives and the designation of equal opportunities posts have been more evident in large public sector and private sector organizations where role cultures are more common. There were committed attempts to change organizational beliefs by directly intervening in the ways in which people behaved and thought. Equalities departments were created, resources were dedicated to new development schemes, awareness training was offered or mandated, and recruitment practices changed to create a workforce which more closely matched the local population. However, small organizations in specialist areas such as IT, advertising, media and consultancy, where the task culture is more prevalent, have modelled new ways of working and appointed women to senior positions.

While role cultures have the structural conditions for intervention, they also harbour the conditions for failure. Harrison (1972) criticizes them for their lack of flexibility, their inability to respond quickly, and their protection of the security of the status quo. Indeed, although the systemization of recruitment practices within the public sector has been shown to assist women's advancement (Powell and Butterfield 1994), organizations have discovered that changing culture is not as easy or speedy as management writing assumed. 'We do all the right things, and yet nothing is right', was the *cri de coeur* of at least one equal opportunities manager.[1] Evidence accumulated that attempts to change attitudes in the workplace frequently met with overt and covert resistance, regardless of what official policy may have prescribed.

Culture as root metaphor

An explanation for that resistance lies in the third model of organizational culture, that of a root metaphor deeply embedded in the organization's history. Here culture is seen as what an organization is, rather than something it has. The organization is a subjective experience, and therefore the purpose of studying an organization is to discover the shared cognitions and beliefs: to understand the rules that collective minds have generated and which guide action (Smircich 1983).

The most influential of such writers is Schein (1985) who argues that the term culture 'should be reserved for the deeper level of basic assumptions and beliefs that are shared by members of an organization, that operate unconsciously, and that define in a basic "taken for granted" fashion an organization's view of itself and its environment' (Schein 1985: 6). From this perspective culture develops over time in response to the need to solve internal and external problems and, having proved its value, it is passed on to new organizational members as the correct way to perceive, think and feel.

The power of Schein's approach is that within the context of management and organizational change it identifies three operational levels of culture: artefacts, values and assumptions and in the latter part of this chapter I indicate how it might be adapted to

Table 1 Organizational values and equal opportunities

Value	Business artefact	Equal opportunities artefact
Differentials are important as motivators of individual effort	Gradations in company perks	Women appointed on lower entry point salaries than male colleagues
Loyalty is important	Award ceremonies for long service	No career break scheme since breaks in service imply disloyalty
Giving time is a performance measure	Commitment is measured by the number of hours given each week	Resistance to flexible working practices
Importance of understanding and reflecting customers	Senior managers talk of the business advantages of a wider recruitment base	Active recruitment of diversity
It is important to create an environment of equality for all employees	Progress is reported in the Annual report and is an ongoing agenda item at Board meetings	Policies are monitored. Managers are held accountable for progress in their department

help prospective employees assess future employers. Artefacts are easy to get hold of; they include job titles, policies, dress, rules, language and how space is allocated – they are a first-level guide to how seriously committed an organization might be to equal opportunities. Values may be a little harder to access, but they are generally explicit enough to be discussed and must be engaged with if change around equal opportunities is to be pursued. Assumptions, however, are often the hardest to grasp and to deal with, partly because they have become habitual but partly because they deal with almost metaphysical issues such as human nature. Table 1 identifies values which may be operating within an organization and their visible manifestation in organizational and

Table 2 The equal opportunities implications of organizational assumptions

Assumptions	Equal opportunities implications
What is real	We know what is going on, we don't need figures
	vs
	Data are important to establish reality
What is truth?	No senior manager could be responsible for sexual harassment
	vs
	All allegations must be investigated regardless of rank
Human nature means . . .	Women are more comfortable in support roles
	vs
	Women have diverse capabilities, we need to maximize them
Human relationships mean	You can't expect an older man to be managed by a younger woman
	vs
	We have to find ways of facilitating male–female working
Women are . . .	Unlikely to be able to go on an overseas assignment
	vs
	Overseas assignments should be made more manageable so that women don't exclude themselves

equal opportunities terms and Table 2 shows how these assumptions shape how equality is interpreted within an organization.

By separating out levels at which cultural paradigms are passed on, Schein (1985) highlights the naivety of approaches which focus on changing artefacts without recognizing the values and assumptions embedded in those that already exist. For those working with gender, Schein's work is cautionary. It points to the need to unearth values and assumptions in order to recognize where problems may arise in implementing change, and of evaluating where the strengths of a culture lie before looking to change it. His work supports Helen Brown's argument in Chapter 8, that organizations which are serious about equal opportunities need to devise ways of linking the leverage between new policies (artefacts) and changes in people (values) to initiatives which have the capacity to address processes and cultural dimensions of organizations.

Recognizing that organizations are simultaneously operating systems of value and meaning alongside socio-structural systems (Allaire and Firsirotu 1984) which may or may not be in harmony, helps understanding the difficulties of being a change agent. As Judi Marshall and Adrian McLean counsel:

> In seeking to introduce change into any organization, it is wise, therefore to identify and pay attention to those factors which underpin the present way of operating. Being clear about what is happening before concentrating on what should happen gives any change solid foundations. Understanding fully the characteristics of the current culture is a starting point for change.
>
> (Marshall and McLean 1988)

The culture of equalities work

Equalities work has struggled to establish its place in organizations for over twenty years. As a consequence it has often created its own subculture. This culture may reflect that of the organization or directly challenge it. For those working in equalities departments the creation of a subculture may be absolutely necessary to sustain motivation, self-confidence and group identity. Ideally the department creates its own artefacts, beliefs and assumptions which then interact with the values and assumptions that the organization holds concerning equality.

Thomas (1990), writing of the US experience, has suggested that equalities initiatives in the 1970s and 1980s were driven at a societal level by values of social justice. However, arguments based on these values generally fail to exert any influence at the micro level of the organization. As a result, US legislation included measures of contract compliance which meant the loss of government contracts for those organizations who failed to reach targets on the recruitment of women. However imperfect its application, this at least ensured that organizations had to address issues of social justice even though they would be interpreted and acted upon differently by organizations according to their prevailing cultural norms.

For Cox (1991) legislation interacts with the organization's culture to produce six dimensions along which the nature of the equality environment can be measured:

1 Acculturation: the extent to which minorities are expected to assimilate into the prevailing culture, or are encouraged to bring in their difference.
2 Structural integration: the extent to which equality measures are structurally integrated through supporting policies and procedures.
3 Informal integration: the extent to which minority groups are included or excluded from informal contacts.
4 Cultural bias: the extent to which there is prejudice against particular minorities.
5 Organizational identification: the extent to which minority group members feel they belong and are committed.
6 Inter-group conflict: the extent to which there are power struggles between minority groups competing for attention and resources.

The profile that emerges from rating organizations on these dimensions can then be plotted on a continuum between the monolithism of a white male majority culture and the pluralism of a multicultural diversity: a pluralism based on the active management of diversity, rather than the containment or denial of difference.

Cox's use of words such as multiculturalism and diversity are in themselves markers of a shift in the culture of equalities work (Cox 1991). The talk is now not of social justice, but of encouraging and utilizing difference as a business weapon. For Thomas, 'managing diversity does not mean controlling or containing diversity, it means enabling every member of your workforce to perform to his or her potential. It means getting from employees first everything we have a right to expect, and second – if we do it well, everything they have to give' (Thomas 1990: 17). Gaining equality should not depend on the will of those holding power to dispense justice. Instead, it should gain its own momentum through a focus on performance improvement.

Supporters of managing diversity as an instrument of change point to evidence of reduced turnover and absenteeism where diversity is encouraged. The link with corporate culture is transparent. By creating a strong culture of diversity organizations can gain a competitive advantage hence the business case for equal opportunities, emphasized in Opportunity 2000.[2]

Equalities as a culture change issue

Making the conceptual link between equality and business has further strengthened the argument that equalities work is an aspect of cultural change. In preparing the rationale for the Opportunity 2000 campaign, Hammond and Holton (1991) looked at companies worldwide who had successfully implemented culture change programmes. They concluded that the factors which had been successful in effecting change for business goals should also apply when attempting to change the balance of the workforce. These factors were commitment from the top, behaviour change, ownership, and investment of resources. For those wanting to work with gender, these factors provide a set of criteria with which to assess the likelihood of equal opportunities policies being effected in any organization.

Conducting an equalities audit

Once equalities work is recognized as part of an organizational culture, then a new agenda emerges for those charged with being organizational catalysts, either as consultant or employee. The individual now becomes an auditor of the equalities culture. Cultural auditing, previously seen as a consultancy tool (Sidney 1994), is potentially a technique that could be used for screening organizations. By combining an analysis of the existing organizational culture with an analysis of the likelihood of organizational change a comprehensive equalities audit would be obtained. The section below outlines possible components of such an audit.

The first task would be to collect information on the culture of the organization in terms of the artefacts, beliefs and values and assumptions shared by the members of the organization.

1a Artefacts
These could include:

(i)   Publicity: are equality issues referred to in public documents such as mission statements, annual reports, recruitment and promotion literature and in personnel policy?
(ii) Existing gender balance: what is the gender balance of the workforce overall by level and function, e.g. what percentage of the senior management team and of the company board are women and what is the gender composition of different salary grades?
(iii) Family-friendly policies: does the organization permit flexible working or provide help towards childcare?
(iv) Goals and responsibilities: what goals has the organization set for changing the balance of the workforce and where does responsibility lie for effecting progress towards these goals?

Answers to these questions, many of which will be available in published sources, give a first indicator of company culture, but by themselves they can delude. It is the beliefs driving the use of those artefacts which are a better guide to the culture in action.

1b Beliefs and values
Interpreting official policy can be helped by discovering how far decision makers in the organization believe the following statements.

(i)   Increasing the number of women in the organization will increase creativity and improve the quality of decision making.
(ii) It is important to encourage women to move up the organization, and this means active support.

(iii) The introduction of more varied working arrangements including emergency leave enables a better balance to be obtained between work and personal commitments and does not imply a reduced ability to contribute.

(iv) Men are preferred employees because they do not make the demands on the organization that women do.

Unearthing the answers to such questions is much easier as an insider than as a prospective employee. For a candidate, requesting an informal discussion before placing an application offers a more honest arena for raising such questions than the interview itself. For an equalities postholder, or an external consultant brought in to advise on equality, it is through such questions that the shape and texture of commitment emerge.

1c Assumptions
Given the hidden depth of assumptions, discovering them is more likely to involve interpretation of actions than receiving direct answers to questions. Acting as organizational anthropologist will require devising a framework against which actions can be set. That framework might include the following.

(i) What does that decision or action assume about the career aspirations of women in this organization?

(ii) What does that policy assume about who has responsibility for equality within the organization?

(iii) What does the speed with which new practices are introduced assume about the tolerance of employees to changes in the workforce make-up?

(iv) What does the visibility given to and speed of implementation of equalities policies assume about their relationship to business success?

Having investigated the existing culture of the organization the likelihood of a proposed change being successful can be gauged by determining the extent of real commitment to equality issues in terms of the resources and personnel devoted to their attainment. Answers to the following questions would be required.

2a Commitment from the top
(i) Who are the champions of equality within the organization?

(ii)   What statements and actions have senior management made in support of the change?

(iii)   Where is the equalities department placed on the organizational chart, how powerful is it perceived to be and does it have direct access to the board?

2b Defining behaviour change

(i)   How does the organization say it wants to be different as a result of your intervention?

(ii)   How will the organization measure any change, e.g. in job applications, recruitment procedures and in work being done differently?

(iii)   Will rewards be given for achieving change, e.g. to managers using more 'feminine' managerial skills, for acting as performance coaches, and for preparing women staff to take on greater responsibilities?

2c Ownership

(i)   Do managers own equal opportunities as a business issue?

(ii)   Do line managers feel that equal opportunity is a managerial responsibility or only a concern of personnel?

(iii)   Do employees feel they have any responsibility for creating an environment of equality?

(iv)   How wide is the network of support that a person with an equalities responsibility can call on?

(v)   Who believes they will gain, and who thinks they will lose as a result of the change?

2d Resources

(i)   How much time have senior managers given to informing themselves on equalities issues, and signalling their involvement?

(ii)   How much time has been spent in educating managers and developing appropriate skills?

(iii)   How large a budget does equalities work have compared to other change initiatives?

(iv)   What resources of staff, space and equipment are available for equalities work?

(v) Have resources been targeted mainly at women already judged most able, or used to increase the skills of women below managerial grades?

(vi) How much has been invested in organizational communications, so that people understand what is happening and why?

By using a methodology or scheme which locates equalities work as a culture change issue, individuals will acquire both evidence of the organization's will to change and a language framed by organizational development from which to argue their case.

Conclusion

The purpose of this chapter has been to establish the strong relationship between equalities work and organizational culture. Through using models derived from management research, I have argued that within each of them lie explanations of why the implementation of equality is challenging, and at times overwhelming. Through developing personal checklists to explore both the nature of the existing equalities culture and the likelihood of being able to bring about change, I have suggested that a more realistic assessment of the outcome of equal opportunities policies can be obtained. Individuals will also be able to assess their personal values against those of the organization.

I am not proposing that making gender work is a no-win career choice. Rather, that taking time to understand the organizational culture and the culture of equality will better equip individuals to escape the feelings of personal blame, incompetence and dented self-esteem that marked many of those who entered the gender employment arena unprepared. It is an equally valid tactic for women looking to identify those organizations which are most likely to encourage their career potential. Collecting the data may lead individuals to look elsewhere for their career satisfaction, or it may increase confidence that it is possible to work with the culture, once opportunities and constraints are identified. The audit also provides a starting point for those seeking to investigate the extent to which different organizations have a serious commitment to equality.

Notes

1 There is one serious limitation to the structure-culture model. It assumes that culture follows structure. If the organization has to change its structure, as a result of competitive tendering, deregulation, global competition or recession, then the logic suggests that culture will change in response. This is not supported by evidence. Throughout the UK, role structures are rapidly turning themselves into task structures. Management talk is of team working, flattened hierarchies, project teams and reward for performance, yet the values which prevail are those of the past and do not change so fast. When knowledge, values, motives and expectations have served employees well and enabled them to survive in the organization they are not easily discarded. It is, as Gillian Stamp argues in Chapter 13, not surprising that resistance by the dominant group becomes all the more determined.

2 Opportunity 2000 is the initiative launched by Business in the Community – although it has full government support it is financed by industry.

Part 2

MANAGING EQUAL OPPORTUNITIES: PRACTICAL ISSUES

Jenny Shaw

While some of our contributors have concentrated on describing the changing economic and legislative frameworks and employment policies within which equal opportunities initiatives unfold, others bring experience of particular sectors, public, private and voluntary, to bear on the linked questions of if, when and how gender is defined as a problem at work and by whom? Consciousness-raising is only a first step, and not always a straightforward one, especially if gender is put into a 'problem' framework rather than a 'rights' one. However, in this section we start from the practical position that equal opportunities are there to be managed, that readers are interested in what interventions seem to work well and how to avoid the most common pitfalls. We also start from the assumption that recognizing and respecting difference is at the heart of all equal opportunities work: that is, understanding the differences which occur between and within firms, industries and sectors (public, private and voluntary), as well as between individuals; knowing when differences should be ignored and when they should be taken into account. This is the basic craft skill to be developed. The person moving from one organization to another, from the culture of trade unions to that of voluntary organizations or a local authority needs to be aware that what may be taken for granted in one setting might need very careful preparation in another. Are letters, for example, routinely scrutinized by superiors or do people at all levels have the authority to write on their own behalf? It is easy to make mistakes, particularly in the early days, and in a sensitive area like equal opportunities this is a risk that cannot be taken.

Although equal opportunities posts are often positioned at the margins of the organization, their brief is an all-encompassing one requiring both pan-optic vision and depth of focus. It is, of course, an exercise in the art of the possible and demands a sense of what in-house initiatives are possible as well as what external initiatives such as Opportunity 2000 might be of strategic use. As we suggested in our introduction, gender work is a developing field and, like all new subjects, is eclectic in its origins and style. Though a culture of equal opportunities is emerging and, probably sooner rather than later, will lead to a more uniform mode of doing and writing about gender work, at present there is a healthy variety of styles and practices. This is reflected in the way that our contributors have approached the task we set them, of thinking about the practicalities of gender work and of mining their own experience to inform the next stage. Some aim to draw out lessons to be learned, to warn of unviable strategies and spell out minimum targets, others aim to reaffirm the value of gender work in the face of what may sometimes seem like slow progress or setbacks, whilst still others aim primarily to encourage introspection and reflection about the nature of the work and its consequences.

Most, like Helen Brown, acknowledge the long-term and difficult nature of the attempt to coordinate changes which arise at different levels but nevertheless offer interim goals which will effect some leverage on change. In her case she recommends the need to develop an operational definition of success in equal opportunities so that it can become the focus of a shared vision. The value of this can easily be seen in the context of the rest of her chapter which compares three domains from the public and voluntary sectors – the NHS, housing associations and higher education – to illustrate differences in progress made towards implementing equal opportunities or in creating a culture in which such initiatives might thrive. Many of the contributors converge, for example, on the need to establish targets and monitoring procedures, but there are differences, too, in orientation towards change strategies.

Margaret Hodge, whose chapter is an exercise in reflective learning in local government, private consultancy and professional politics, agrees with the need for targets, monitoring and training so that women will move up the hierarchy, but finally plumps for a national framework of rights, minimum wages and rights for part-time workers which would benefit men too. Together with Rita Donaghy, whose chapter describes UNISON's path-breaking decision to build the principles of proportionality and fair representation into its constitution, Margaret Hodge's chapter shows how the theory of role modelling can be more relevant to organizations than to individuals. As Rita Donaghy argues, trade unions can do more than wait to fight individual cases of discrimination, landmarks though they often are, and must accept their role of redefining the bargaining agendas of industrial relations and as exemplars of good practice. Trade unions, political parties and local authorities can be 'organizational role models' as well as seedbeds for experimentation.

However, it would be wrong to see all good equal opportunities initiatives as emanating from this sector. Whilst local authorities, with their tradition of public service, may seem the 'natural sponsors' of equal opportunities, it is Business in the Community, a private sector organization, that is the actual sponsor of Opportunity 2000. Moreover, there are many variations between and within local authorities. A department with a tradition of largely employing men, say, an estates department, will not have the same collective experience to draw upon to make sense of a recently imposed equal opportunities policy as, say, an infant school where the employment of women was not exceptional. Yet both can belong, formally, to the same organization and be bound by the same policies and mission statements. Reflecting on how East Sussex moved from a 'paper' to a real policy Paul Burnett indicates that it was directly traceable to the appointment of a small number of senior personnel and thus he makes a theoretical point about the level at which change is possible, although he also stresses refinement and the nitty-gritty tightening up of procedures – an emphasis which is traceable to Opportunity 2000 and makes his chapter more than just a study of a local authority and more one of the application of Opportunity 2000 methods.

Ruth Valentine's chapter takes a different approach; it is more personal and invites the reader to look long and hard at what they do and feel. Though it deals specifically with voluntary organizations and their staffs, the attention it gives to unconscious desires and drives, to the ambivalence which characterizes so much of our behaviour, to our tendency to collude, deny, control obliquely and to displacement activity generally, can apply to any and every gender worker. Like any work, gender work offers individuals opportunities to work out personal anxieties and dilemmas. As Ruth Valentine points out, many qualified, able women traditionally gave their time and energy to voluntary work because they were blocked from finding other outlets for their talents. Whilst, on the one hand, this produced low cost, sustainable, flexible organizations which appeared quite woman-friendly, it also produced a certain complacency about equal opportunities. A self-righteous maternalism made many staff overly controlling and defensive, and their organizations resistant to change.

Gillian Stamp too explores what can be done at the level of the individual with the technique known as Career Path Appreciation. Dealing with the social, company and individual costs of undervaluing and underusing employees, either because of straightforward prejudice or a more complex failure to recognize their potential, her chapter returns in a practical way to some of the themes set out in Sally Holtermann's chapter on the costs and benefits of providing, or failing to provide, equal opportunities. Career Path Appreciation is not only a way of overcoming 'wastage' of resources, it is a face-saving way of puncturing managers' assumptions and helping them perceive the capability of people.

A common theme in all the Part 2 chapters is the danger of

complacency, its role in resisting change and the unintended or counterproductive consequences of much equal opportunities work. In some organizations or departments the values and language of equal opportunities have become widely accepted, and attempting to do further work in an organization already publicly committed to social justice may be seen as unacceptable criticism or as divisive, whilst formalizing equal opportunities through, for example, women's units which were seen as 'remote' reduced participation of women at many levels. There is also the danger, again mentioned in the introduction, that the more gender work is professionalized, the more likely it is to create a career structure up which men will proceed – the 'glass escalator' effect. This pattern is well established in what were once called the semi-professions, school-teaching, social work and librarianship, but it is likely to affect gender work too as the recent and controversial appointment of a man with a history of making misogynist remarks to a position of responsibility for equal opportunities in the European Commission perhaps demonstrates.

Just as in public contexts gender work has to compete with other similarly pressing claims, so many of our contributors have to contain and resolve within themselves the desire to contribute to various causes. All write from the experience of being steeped in the conflicts that inevitably accompany gender work and the pressure to prioritize, both personally and politically. Choices have to be made about where and how to attempt gender work, from the bottom or the top, through paid work, voluntary activities or politics and, if the last route is chosen, through local, national or European politics? The following chapters suggest some of the opportunities and difficulties entailed in the different routes and, with the benefit of hindsight, indicate the more promising strategies. There are, inevitably, gaps. We do not, for example, consider the media and how this may advance or obstruct equal opportunities. Nor does private sector experience feature as much as we would have liked, largely because the culture of the private sector does not encourage its employees to write self-reflection of the kind collected here on a semi-charitable basis. However, mitigating the gaps, we trust, is the practical focus of our contributors who lay themselves on the line and make recommendations of what should be done.

8

WOMEN IN THE PUBLIC AND VOLUNTARY SECTORS: CASE STUDIES IN ORGANIZATIONAL CHANGE

Helen Brown

The process of successful equal opportunities implementation is best seen as an exercise in cultural change in organizations. Using a simple model of organizational change this chapter will examine aspects of effective equal opportunities implementation in the public and voluntary sectors, focusing particularly on the NHS where considerable headway has been made in the past few years, on the housing association movement where there is recent evidence of a determination to change, and on higher education where, for perhaps the first time, there is an acceptance that 'natural' progress towards equality is unlikely to lead to any real difference. The focus is on equal opportunities for women where most progress has been made, but there are also clear links to other forms of discrimination. In the NHS work is now under way to develop ways of addressing race discrimination, while in higher education discrimination in terms of gender, race and disability is being addressed at the same time.

In each of these sectors the role of a central body in developing guidelines and examples of good practice is important in creating both an acknowledgement that there is a real problem to be dealt with and a general climate of urgency. The Women's Unit of the NHS, the National Federation of Housing Associations (NFHA), and the Committee of Vice-Chancellors and Principals (CVCP) have each created clear guidelines and, in the case of the NHS, a strong programme of positive action, properly resourced, has been introduced. These central drives often signal a degree of readiness – a sense that the time is right to change – but of themselves cannot create fundamental organizational change. For that to happen we need to first understand in more detail the dynamics which position women in certain ways, both in different sectors and in individual organizations, and second to develop ways of influencing those dynamics. This chapter outlines briefly the position of women in each of the sectors considered, but the concern here is less with the (none the less essential) diagnosis of barriers to women's advancement than with proposing a framework which should shed light on the range of efforts needed to bring down those barriers.

Fundamental organizational change in the sense that it truly reaches all parts of an organization can be conceptualized as being made up of a number of linked changes in different dimensions of an organization. At its simplest this can be described as changes in:

- policy – the formal aspects of an organization, its rules, regulations and structures;
- people – the mix of individuals in the workforce, their skills, attributes, behaviours and training;
- processes – the 'way things are done here', the informal and cultural aspects of an organization.

The management of change, in relation to any new issue, involves the identification of these different sets of changes and their coordination. Part of the management problem is to ensure that major sets of changes do not get overlooked. However, many equal-opportunities-inspired attempts to bring about change focus narrowly on the first dimension, changes in policy, particularly in the early stages of a new initiative. In parts of the public sector, such as the civil service, the existence of central bodies makes it relatively simple to disseminate codes of practice, or to encourage a given level of performance against targets. Similar, although somewhat less forceful, encouragement is provided in local government through the work of the Local Government Management Board (LGMB) and the local authorities associations. Within individual public sector organizations this process of creating formal codes of practice and equal opportunities procedures continues, a good example being the BBC where a considerable amount of work has been done in relation to gender and race. These framework documents are useful, probably essential, but without further work rarely result in fundamental change. In fact one of the commonest concerns and complaints about the reality of equal opportunities policies is that they may look wonderful on paper but that in practice they fail to 'live'. In some instances, inspired particularly by the work of Opportunity 2000, public sector organizations have taken a further step to strengthen formal equal opportunities requirements by establishing targets and timescales to achieve certain proportions of women in various grades or professions. These can be used to demonstrate some sense of public accountability through the publication of annual monitoring reports. While these are to be welcomed, without additional efforts the reality is too often a report of limited progress and, after a number of years, a sense of 'getting stuck'. If the good practice guidelines are in place, along with the supporting research, how is it that little changes?

One fundamental reason for this failure is that attention to the formal aspects of an organization, or to an entire sector of the public services, affects only the most superficial aspects. It does little, of itself, to address the complex and diverse ways in which organizations are able to persist in successfully discriminating against women. Another is that some of the formal mechanisms which regulate behaviour of and within organizations are not available to be used as a means of emphasizing or enforcing equal opportunities policies. An important example here is the current restriction on including terms and conditions in the specifications for compulsory competitive tendering (CCT). This limitation is now being challenged by the Equal Opportunities Commission. Increased use of subcontracting arrangements may also mean that traditional forms of career progression are no longer available (see Perrons, Chapter 5).

The second dimension of organizational change is the people who make up an organization. Many public sector organizations are developing positive action programmes for women which are intended to increase their skills so that they are at least formally qualified to move up the organization. Measures are also taken to ensure that there are women who meet the relevant job and person specifications on shortlists. These initiatives have the effect of bringing the 'women problem' into sharper focus; the dangers are that unless the case is well-argued (for example, in terms of diversity, business strengths, and service delivery which meets the needs of all sectors of the population) it can too easily be perceived as special pleading and a distraction from effective discharge of the tasks in hand. At times when demands for efficiency and resource constraint appear paramount it can be too easy to identify positive action programmes as a low priority which can be put on the backburner until such time as external pressures and demands reduce which, in practice, can mean never. At the same time as core personnel, who may be well supported by their organization, shrink and are replaced by an increasing periphery of contract workers, the proportion of those who are not protected grows. There is enough evidence to suggest that women are particularly affected by the reduced support and protection afforded to part-time and contract workers for this to be a cause for concern. There is a danger, too, that positive action programmes which can make a real difference to women, such as those which seek to bridge the gap between administrative and professional jobs and managerial ones, can be perceived as in some way 'remedial' and of lower status than other forms of management development. Experience strongly suggests that this is rarely the case; nevertheless the perceptions of those who seek, whether overtly or covertly, to maintain the status quo are enormously important, and have major implications for the effectiveness (or otherwise) of equal opportunities policy initiatives.

To achieve fundamental and persisting change organizations which are serious about equal opportunities need to devise ways of linking the leverage provided by changes in policies and in people to initiatives which are capable of addressing organizational processes and the cultural dimensions of organizations. This area is the hardest to affect but is nevertheless essential. It involves developing an in-depth understanding of how an organization or sector operates, the forces for and against change, and the leadership requirements for making change both desirable and acceptable. None of this is easy, but progress can be made where there is a full knowledge of what is involved and a shared vision of what 'success' will look like. Arguably, we need to devise wide-ranging and challenging definitions of success which have the capacity to inspire and enthuse others, whilst being willing to work doggedly at the detail as opportunities arise. At a recent conference I proposed the following (far from perfect) definition of 'success' which was an attempt to capture the complexity of fundamental change and also to convey its transformational nature.

Success is where women form 50 per cent of the workforce at all levels; where we lose the distinction between men's work and women's work; where women are fully integrated into the labour force and in the process have actually transformed the nature of the organizations that they work for and the services those organizations provide. Most importantly, success is where women feel comfortable in the work that they are doing and do not have to prove themselves over and above the demands of the job (Brown 1993).

Whilst I accept the enormity of the task that achieving this vision represents, I am convinced that keeping the big picture in view is helpful in maintaining momentum and motivation while working to understand and overcome the various barriers facing women, and at the same time recognizing how even small gains represent progress towards larger goals. The remainder of this chapter examines how three areas in the public and voluntary sectors are moving towards a situation which contains at least some of the elements encompassed by this definition of success through understanding and utilizing the levers for change which are specific to that sector.

The National Health Service

Throughout the 1980s the NHS was subjected to an almost endless stream of research reports documenting the discrimination against women in the health service. Successive studies consistently identified barriers facing women at work, highlighting outmoded attitudes about the 'proper' role of women, evidence of both direct and indirect discrimination, the absence of effective childcare provision and inflexible patterns of work (see, for example, Davies and Rosser 1986; Bevan *et al.* 1989; Davies 1990; Department of Health 1991). In 1989 women occupied only 17 per cent of general management posts and only 3 per cent of general surgeons were women (Brown and Goss 1993), in a sector where around 75 per cent of all employees are female. In 1988 the National Steering Group on Equal Opportunities recommended urgent action. Its report concluded by pointing out how the organization and management of the health service at that time was based on male norms:

> It could be assumed that the NHS would offer conditions of employment commensurate with its dependence on female talent for delivery of care to patients. Such an assumption would unfortunately prove incorrect, as shown by comparisons of their financial rewards, job and career prospects and working lifestyles with those of men working in the NHS . . .
> The NHS expects the majority of its workforce to conform to the working patterns of the minority.
> (Department of Health 1988).

Following the publication of this report good-practice guidelines were produced together with training materials, and regional health authorities were required to produce equal opportunities policies.

However, in spite of the recognition that change was essential, by 1990 it was increasingly clear that little real action had resulted from the actions taken in the wake of the Steering Group's report. A critical report by the Equal Opportunities Commission (1991) concluded that, while the majority of health authorities had equal opportunities policies on paper, they were not being implemented effectively. Potentially unlawful discrimination was still occurring in recruitment and selection, and most health authorities were not providing sufficiently flexible arrangements for working and training. It was clear that emphasis on formal aspects of change had resulted in little change on the ground, except in the most enlightened authorities, and there was little enthusiasm for yet another 'new initiative' on women.

Recognizing that the traditional means of effecting change had been tried and found wanting, the NHS Management Executive commissioned the Office for Public Management to devise some alternative means of bringing about change. In our conclusions (Goss and Brown 1991) we argued that there was little need for further research to document discrimination, except in a few specific areas; what was needed were ways of harnessing and celebrating the good practice which did exist in many health service organizations, together with clear leadership and direction from the centre. In the process of exploring just what was happening to women in the NHS at that time two things became clear. First, considerable progress had been made in many parts of the health service, but it was often progress 'by stealth', unacknowledged and with a sense of sometimes 'breaking the rules'. Many creative managers had introduced flexible 'women-friendly' working arrangements or childcare provision but had stopped short of developing a policy on flexible working which met women's needs. In other words, changes had been made to some process aspects of the organization but no link was made to the policy aspects. Consequently, changes were often made on a case-by-case basis and remained largely invisible to others. This failure also signalled a reluctance to integrate equal opportunities into broader organizational strategies. Closer examination of the range of equal opportunities practices which lay behind the formal policy statements showed, somewhat ironically, that more was happening in the health service than in, for example, some private sector organizations who communicated their intentions and achievements more effectively. In our research we found many examples including working from home, childcare support, split or short shifts (for nurses) which minimized their need to arrange childcare, and job sharing, all of which worked well for women who had access to them, but good practice was not easily shared or spread.

A second and related concern was the fragmentation of linked areas of policy within the Department of Health and the considerable difficulty this caused in assembling an accurate picture of just what was happening. It appeared as though equal opportunities was at the same time everyone's and no one's business. All three reports mentioned here called for the establishment of some kind of high-profile unit at the centre to monitor, support and publicize progress on equal opportunities for women.

The establishment of the NHS Women's Unit has met many of the criticisms of the previous situation; there is now a clear focus, earmarked funding, energetic promotion of good practice, and a substantial positive action programme. The new approach recognizes that it is no longer either feasible or acceptable to presume that things will get better in due course. Instead equal opportunities in the NHS is positioned as part of the core business of individual health service organizations. The health service as a whole has become a member of Opportunity 2000 and established goals and timescales for change in eight key areas.[1] Importantly, the then Secretary of State used her rarely exercised 'reserve powers' to require individual health service organizations to comply with these goals, rather than leaving change to individual discretion. Some of the effects have been dramatic:

- 37 per cent of vacant chief executive posts from April 1992 to March 1994 went to women;
- 50 per cent of trainee accountants are women;
- four NHS Regions have already exceeded the targets for women consultants;
- the target for women members of authorities and trusts has been exceeded; 41 per cent of 'fourth wave' trust chairs and non-executive directors are women.

The successful achievement of targets cannot, of course, in itself be taken as evidence that fundamental change is occurring. However, coupled with substantial investment in training and development (£3 million over two years), in childcare support (in over 50 per cent of health authorities and trusts) and job share registers (particularly in the London area), the signs are encouraging. It remains to be seen whether ways in which the new freedoms for NHS trusts to establish their own pay and conditions of service are exercised will operate for or against the interests of women employees.

This overview of approaches to change within the NHS should not, of course, be taken to imply that there is little more to be done. To do so would be to deny much of the day-to-day experience of women (and men) within the service. Nevertheless the substantial shift in strategy, with an emphasis on raising the profile of women, providing clear leadership and support for local initiatives and for individual women, linking equal opportunities to mainstream organizational agendas, together with rigorous monitoring provides a template for effective change which could well be adopted elsewhere.

Housing associations

In 1992 the National Federation of Housing Associations (NFHA) surveyed its membership and discovered, or perhaps confirmed, the typical pyramid distribution of women employees. Overall 63 per cent of employees in housing associations are women. In the most junior grades 79 per cent are women; at director level the figure is 24 per cent. However, particular concern was generated by the realization that women made up only 15 per cent of recent appointments to director-level posts, apparently reversing a trend that had increased the employment of women in top managerial jobs from 21 per cent in 1985 to 34 per cent in 1990 (NFHA 1992). The housing association movement is not a single organization in the same way as the NHS, and there are no simple ways to direct the pace and direction of change within what is a loose association of a large number of independent organizations who vary considerably in size. In this sector change is most likely to come through influence and alliance building and by persuading managers in individual associations that change has value for them and for the services which they provide for tenants.

In response to the survey report a conference was organized later in 1992 by NFHA, the Housing Corporation and the Office for Public Management (OPM 1992). The intention was to draw on the experience of senior women managers working in the sector to develop an agenda for change which could then be debated more widely at local and national level. Four key messages emerged:

1 The business case – failure to develop the potential of women staff represents an enormous waste of resources in, for example, the costs of recruitment when turnover is high.
2 Management responsibility – housing associations and the Housing Corporation have an important role to play in demonstrating that performance in equal opportunities is as important as performance in other areas of management responsibility.
3 Expert support – the NFHA offers an important source of leadership, support, guidance and advice, and these resources can and should be mobilized to promote and enable change.
4 Exchange of learning – there is a need to maximize the exchange of learning between organizations and from elsewhere to provide ideas for those leading change within their own associations.

These four messages recognize the reality of the housing association movement. There are few 'central' funds available, individual managers may feel isolated in their efforts unless they are equipped with arguments for change and practical tools and support, but nevertheless the 'central' bodies can play a major role in creating a climate for change. Locally committee members can be encouraged and supported to provide appropriate policy direction within the voluntary housing sector. Voluntary management committee and board members are particularly important as a locus for change since they carry responsibility for senior appointments as well as much policy making. However, in comparison with similar public positions, such as councillors or health authority members, they often receive less training for their work.

The partnership for change, suggested by this conference, was formalized into a tripartite working party consisting of representatives from housing associations, NFHA, and the Housing Corporation. Its brief was to document good practice both inside and outside the housing association movement and to provide a practical guide for managers. The practical aspects are emphasized in the report (OPM 1994) of the working party by listing 'possible problems' and 'ways forward' against each aspect of equal opportunities implementation so that, ideally, potentially isolated managers can draw on the experience of others in how to bring about change as well as what to change. This emphasis was introduced following the realization that, while many associations have good formal policies covering, for example, recruitment and selection, they are less well equipped to address the informal and cultural issues which were identified as the single most important factor in helping (or preventing) women develop their full potential as managers. A particular problem, common in many organizations, is the 'long hours' culture, which results in staff value or commitment being judged by the number of hours spent in the workplace, rather than by the quality or quantity of work performed, and effectively discriminates against people (usually women) whose caring responsibilities prevent them working long hours. When housing associations can appreciate that working long hours, to take just one example of where cultural and attitudinal change is needed, is in practice counterproductive to both individual and organization, they can begin to make changes which bring positive benefits beyond a narrow equal opportunities agenda.

Higher education

The higher education sector provides an interesting example of sustained systemic resistance to women's advancement, possibly representing a harder nut to crack than either the NHS or the housing association movement, essentially because the levers for change are obscure and deeply embedded in the culture. Changing people is slow since few enter from outside, and managerial initiatives which go beyond paper policies can often be resisted. There are differences between the 'old' and 'new' universities but these are largely those of degree rather than of kind. Referring only to the old universities the influential Hansard Society Commission report (1990) commented, 'it is wholly unacceptable that the centres of modern academic teaching and excellence in Britain should remain bastions of male power and privilege'. Recognition that there is a problem which needs attention on a sector-wide basis has arrived slowly. In 1991 the Committee of Vice-Chancellors and Principals (CVCP) issued guidance notes which captured standard good practice in equal opportunities. This was followed by the establishment of a Commission on University Career Opportunity (CUCO) which reported in 1994. The main task of the Commission was to survey equal opportunities policies and practices in higher education. It found that 93 per cent of institutions have now formally adopted an equal opportunities policy, but that so far only 37 per cent have put in place action plans (CUCO 1994). This may mean that the gap between the best and worst institutional practice will widen.

Since the Hansard report appeared an increasing number of universities (currently 28) have signed up for Opportunity 2000 and committed themselves to a positive action programme. Nevertheless, to date the progress of women working in higher education remains slow, with only limited gains over the last decade. There are some interesting contrasts to be drawn between the progress of women undergraduates and women academic staff. Between 1965 and 1988 the proportion of women undergraduates increased from 28 per cent to 44 per cent; between 1980 and 1989 the proportion of women professors in old universities remained constant at 3 per cent, well short of the proportion of women in the age cohort who might now be expected to occupy senior positions, and strongly suggesting that academe does not offer an attractive employment option to women.[2] While similar vertical segregation exists in other spheres of employment, within a sector where promotion, ostensibly, depends on individual merit and excellence these figures are perhaps particularly hard to justify. To understand how discrimination against women works, and therefore consider how it can be rectified, we need to delve deep into the culture.

One of the first universities to join Opportunity 2000, Sheffield Hallam, has produced a detailed code of practice. Crucially in the preface the vice-chancellor states that, 'providing equality of opportunity is concerned with the elimination of discrimination by removing unfair structures, biased policies, prejudicial practices and oppressive behaviour', recognizing that deeply embedded features of organizational culture are likely to be major contributors to discrimination, and therefore need to be addressed if real change is to occur.

There are a range of cultural and organizational barriers facing women in higher education, all of which need to be addressed if progress is to be made beyond policies on paper. Research into the realities of recruitment practices (Collinson *et al.* 1990) shows that women are more often judged informally and subjectively on the basis of their perceived 'suitability' for a post or for promotion. Judgements are made in terms of assumptions about commitment, ability to fit in, or about the assumed relevance of experience which may have little bearing on the job in question. Job-related criteria such as age are likely to be based on the career norms of the majority (i.e. men), neglecting the fact that women are often older at the same stage in their career. In universities this form of discrimination was encapsulated in the 'New Blood' scheme, designed to encourage younger people into universities, which had an upper age limit of 35. This was successfully challenged and an industrial tribunal ruled that the scheme constituted unlawful sex discrimination because fewer women than men could comply with its terms. However, the scheme for 'New Academic Appointments' which replaced it, while having no formal age limit, still enshrined the notion that academics are 'normally' at a certain stage in their careers at a certain age.

These notions of 'suitability' and 'normal' career paths pose difficulties for women at all stages of their academic careers. Even as undergraduates women learn to believe that they are less able than men and attribute their achievements to 'luck' rather than capability. This self-perception is reinforced by a number of factors: women gain fewer firsts than men except at the Open University, tutorials can often demand a confrontational style which women are uncomfortable with, and they are less likely to have women lecturers or tutors to provide role models. The reflections of women staff and students paint a picture of a highly politicized world where success depends on the ability to play the game by male rules. There is also evidence that the expectations of male and female staff are different. Women are more often expected to play a major role in student support, in part because of inadequate performance in this role by men and in part because it is what many students prefer (Brown forthcoming).

Success in higher education depends heavily on good networks and in turn success allows access to networks. O'Leary and Mitchell (1990) found that women who characterized themselves as well connected produced more research than those who considered themselves poorly connected. Interestingly, 75 per cent of poorly connected women in their study described their interests as outside the mainstream of their subject, suggesting that it is not only the volume of work that is an issue, but the definition of what constitutes 'proper' academic work. In this world men reach their peak of research productivity between 45 and 49 while women follow some five years later, between 50 and 54. There is evidence (Brown forthcoming) of processes of cumulative advantage or disadvantage which reinforce early career positions. The myth of collegiality can obscure the many small instances of discriminant behaviour which lead to the clearly marginalized position of women in higher education. The danger for higher education at the present time is that narrow adherence to formal equal opportunities practices may make it appear that 'justice has been done' (Jewson and Mason 1986) while failing to address the informal processes of discrimination which continue to thrive. The focus on individual achievement, within a culture of liberalism and collegiality, can end up effectively obscuring or denying evidence of systematic group disadvantage (Brown forthcoming). The best managers in higher education understand this, and understand why change is necessary to revitalize the sector, but I suspect there will still be an uphill struggle.

Conclusion

The impact of equal-opportunities-led change through the 1980s was in many respects disappointing (see, for example, Coyle 1989; Figes 1994). Too often the strategies adopted assumed that it was only necessary to ensure equal opportunities for individuals, and failed to recognize the need to build new organizational cultures, new attitudes and new values. Where change did occur it was frequently at the cost of assimilating women into the dominant culture, so that they were led to behave as surrogate men – working long hours and adopting a macho management style. Nevertheless many parts of the public and voluntary sectors have now learnt from the failures of the previous decade and are attempting, as the case studies have illustrated, to introduce more effective approaches to change. Some of the key learning points from the 1980s experience are as follows.

1 Fundamental change takes time and requires sustained commitment from managers, staff and members. An overall vision of success needs to encompass both structural and cultural change.

2 The need to develop a pluralistic approach which tackles organizational change at different levels (rather than, for example, relying on training alone). Interventions on a number of fronts help to generate a 'critical mass' of women which in turn speeds the change process, and helps to institutionalize the change and resist backlash.[3]

3 The need for equality issues to be understood as intrinsic to business planning processes and central to the management task. In the past equal opportunities units and other activities were often 'bolted on', and given only temporary legitimacy until the economic or political context changed.

4 The need to monitor the outcomes of policies and initiatives, to learn what works and in what circumstances, and to avoid cumbersome bureaucratic procedures which become ends in themselves – thus losing sight of the vision.

5 To recognize that those in existing positions of power and influence will, in all probability, resist change through both overt and covert means. Successful change strategies will anticipate this resistance and devise tactics to counter it.

The task of challenging discrimination and building organizations which acknowledge, value and utilize the different experience of women is still considerable. We are now in a better position to understand and implement equal opportunities strategies which are likely to lead to much-needed change in organizations, but the difficult and continuing task (Marshall

1992) is to assert women's diversity while standing firm against restrictive policies in the name of women's interests.

Notes

1 Women in the NHS – the goals:
   1 Increase the number of women in general management posts from 18 per cent in 1991 to 30 per cent in 1994.
   2 Increase the number of qualified women accountants to 35 per cent by 1994.
   3 Increase the number of women consultants from 15.5 per cent in 1991 to 20 per cent by 1994, necessitating an annual increase of 10 per cent. Accelerate the rate of increase in the number of women consultants in surgical specialties from the current 9.7 per cent per annum to 15 per cent per annum.
   4 Increase the representation of women as members of authorities or trusts from 29 per cent in 1991 to 35 per cent in 1994.
   5 Introduce a programme allowing women aspiring to management positions to go through a development centre with a view to establishing their own personal development needs.
   6 Introduce incentives on recruitment and retention to ensure the number of qualified nurses and midwives leaving the profession does not rise.
   7 Ensure that following maternity leave or a career break all women, including those returning to nursing part-time or as a job share, are able to return to a grade commensurate with their leaving grade and to work of a similar status.
   8 Monitor the time taken for nurses to reach management positions to ensure that men and women have equal access to these positions.
2 There has been some improvement in the 1990s. In 1993/4 319 out of 5844 professors in the old universities were women, i.e. 5.5 per cent (Association of University Teachers 1993–4).
3 It is possible that the gains women have made recently may lead to another period of backlash. However there are suggestions (Wilkinson 1994) that the world-views of young women and men are converging, offering the future possibility of more fundamental change.

9

WORKING WITHIN LOCAL GOVERNMENT: LESSONS LEARNED

Margaret Hodge MP

<hr>

In the mid-1970s when I was first involved in local government, women were emerging as important players in community politics. It was women with young children who set up under-5s' playgroups to meet their own needs. They moved from running their own groups on a voluntary basis to demanding action from their local councils. They lobbied for support and funding to expand under-5s' facilities and to bring in professional and paid support. During the same period, radical Labour authorities developed new forms of tenant participation in council housing. Working-class women turned from running the social events on their estates to promoting and defending the interests of their fellow tenants in relation to both the government and the council. Women had started to participate in politics at the local level in a real way.

At that time, I chaired the Housing Committee in the London Borough of Islington and more and more women came forward as chairs of their tenants' associations. Our campaign against the government's IMF-imposed cuts on our housing improvement and development programmes was led by a woman from the tenants' movement and the majority of the tenants' leaders were women. Yet, when gender emerged at the top of the political agenda for radical Labour councils in the 1980s, many working-class women stopped being active on the local political scene. It seemed that far from moving forward on some aspects of gender equality, we moved back and women retreated from partici-pation in the political process. They could not relate to the agenda and priorities set by us, left-wing politicians. Sadly for me, much of the 1980s felt like a time when women's equality suffered a severe battering. We saw progress achieved in earlier years reversed as we alienated many women from our cause. It would, however, be wrong to write off all the work on gender during this period. Things were achieved; many of the initiatives on which we embarked and which were pilloried and ridiculed at that time have become accepted orthodoxy today. For instance, our early monitoring of the workforce by race and gender was considered absurd then. Today even Opportunity 2000, supported by a Conservative prime minister and many establishment enter-prises, supports monitoring. It has become generally accepted that monitoring is an essential prerequisite for an equal oppor-tunities policy. When we, in Islington, set up our first workplace nursery in 1983, we were viciously attacked for wasting the ratepayers' money on irrelevancies. Less than ten years later a high street bank sought our advice on how to establish a workplace nursery. Similarly, changes we promoted to the use of language which reflected institutional sexism and racism were ridiculed, but today sensitivity to sexist and racist language is widely understood.

Radical change will always excite controversy and those seeking change at the local level are bound to attract critical comment, especially in the popular press. In particular, local government has always been considered good knocking copy and good for a dig; so, when local government politicians attempt radical change, they are more vulnerable than most to cheap and contemptuous attacks. At the same time, it is not enough to simply blame the tabloid press for working to bring our policies into disrepute. True, we did embark on some important and good policies, but too often they were lost in other gestures and structures which alienated those very people whose interest we sought to promote.

When Ken Livingstone became Leader of the Greater London Council in 1981 and new councillors secured leading positions in various London and metropolitan authorities in 1982, we thought that we could use the power of the local state to both challenge Thatcherism and promote a new politics in which gender was to have a key part. By building a rainbow coalition of all those groups who were oppressed in society we could defeat the Thatcherite Conservatives and secure socialism! The oppression experienced by different groups – such as women, people from the black and ethnic minorities, the disabled and lesbians and gay men – united them and gave them an identity of shared interest. We thought that by simply bringing them together we could build a majority of people who were 'on our team', supporting us and voting for us.

But this notion of a rainbow coalition was deeply flawed and many of those whom we included in the coalition did not identify with each other or with us. We found that you cannot construct a majority by forcing together different minorities. In the real world those groups believe that their interests and disadvantages differ. Young Afro-Caribbean men in the inner city do not easily find a community of interest with white women meeting a glass ceiling in a local government bureaucracy, or with gay men harassed in a Soho pub. Also, by focusing on a range of so-called oppressed minorities, we alienated many, particularly among the aspiring working class, who did not define themselves as being part of a minority group and who felt that Labour ignored them. They believed that the Labour Party was not concerned with their problems and their interests and this contributed to a poor electoral performance for Labour, especially in London. By trying to construct a majority from a rainbow coalition of minorities we lost the support of many of those who saw themselves as part of the majority.

At the same time the deck was stacked against us. We had a prime minister who was determined to stamp out all centres of opposition to her authority. She wanted to undermine local authorities in the same way that she had weakened the trade unions. In the case of the Greater London Council, she first weakened it by removing some of its powers, and then abolished it altogether along with other metropolitan authorities in order to remove its influence and opposition. Furthermore, we had a popular press which prospered by the continued promotion of sexism, with the Page 3 nudes seen as a strong selling point. Our equality policies were a challenge to their marketing strategy which therefore had to be undermined. So the GLC funding of one or two voluntary organizations was used to ridicule all the equality policies.

In Islington we were treated in a similar way. Take one example: we funded a number of tenants' associations and women's groups to run self-defence classes so that women were less frightened to go out alone. One of the women's groups to whom we gave a grant of £500 to purchase gym mats for the self-defence class was a group of lesbian women. Never mind that other groups received similar grants; never mind that £500 represented a minute sum in relation to our overall revenue budget of nearly £200 million. The grant hit the headlines and we were labelled as loony left and hugely wasteful. The grant overshadowed the rest of our programme promoting equality and became a lasting symbol of loony Leftism in London for the best part of a decade. The press distorted the issue, but we should have known better and handled things differently.

I do not think that we began to understand the intensity and depth of the prejudice in our local communities. Perhaps this was the most important lesson to learn from our 1980s' experience and which should inform our policies in the future. When I moved from local government, first into the private sector as a consultant with Price Waterhouse and then into the House of Commons, I realized how far advanced we were in local government on gender equality in comparison to both the other sectors. Things I took for granted in local government have not yet touched the cultures of other organizations. This both demonstrates the importance of what we did achieve and our failure to recognize the extent of the institutionalized disadvantage we had to challenge.

We thought if we simply passed resolutions in the town hall or in smoke-filled meeting rooms outlawing inequality, it would happen. But you do not change the world by passing resolutions or enacting legislation, particularly when the prejudice is so strongly felt and so firmly entrenched. You have to start from where people are and move forward from there. Innovators need to demonstrate leadership, but they must also take people with them if they are to achieve lasting change.

Most women experience the daily pressures of living on low incomes in a society which is now more divided than at any time during the last hundred years. More and more women are becoming lone parents in a society which increasingly blames and condemns them; and a majority are managing the conflicting pressures of holding down a job while still fulfilling their traditional role, both in the home and in caring for children or sick relatives; whilst virtually all have to cope with a growing fear of crime which keeps them at home at night. Yet in the 1980s we focused more on policies and issues which, though important, were marginal to most women's daily concerns. Women might have felt able to start addressing issues such as sexuality and rape sentencing if they felt we were also addressing their immediate needs. But many women felt that Labour councils were ignoring or marginalizing those needs and they felt alienated from a perceived emphasis on what they thought were peripheral issues.

If we are to recover the support of those women who were beginning to participate in politics in the 1970s and who became disillusioned in the 1980s we must prioritize those issues which reflect women's immediate concerns. So a concern with developing a range of appropriate, high quality childcare and early years educational services is vital; appropriate after-school care to help women at work is important. Better lighting schemes, good security in council homes and more community policing to respond to women's fear of crime should be a priority. Support for Sunday trading which has now begun is also relevant so that women who work can shop more easily. If we start by focusing on these policies, which are by no means exhaustive we will at least start from where women are and with things that matter to them.

The 1980s also saw the emergence of women's committees and

women's units in town halls up and down the country. The contribution to change was, in my view, limited, though the lessons learned from this are invaluable. The establishment of women's units seemed to offer women an institutional answer to their daily needs, but it did not make sense to most women. They could not understand how more bureaucrats sitting in the town hall would make any difference to their lives. In fact, many women felt that the money spent on the units and the committees could have been better spent expanding under-5s' services. This alienation from the women's committees and units was partly an inevitable consequence of the structure, but it was also partly the result of the way we chose to operate the mechanisms. Separate units and committees allowed the bureaucracy and the politicians to marginalize issues relating to gender equality. Too often a personnel, housing or social services committee used the existence of a separate committee to sideline equality matters by refusing to deal directly with the issues and simply referred them on to the women's committee. At the same time, many of the committees and units marginalized themselves by focusing on the wrong issues – those which were not of relevance to most women.

The challenge for the future is to find a more effective means for achieving change. We need to reflect on what did work and what did achieve lasting change. My own experience has led me to the view that we were most effective where we had people (mostly women) committed to pursuing equality in key decision-making positions in both the bureaucracy and the political structures. The Thatcher era taught us that simply having women in key positions is not enough, but having women committed to gender equality in key positions is important.

For instance, in Islington we introduced a radical maternity package for our workforce which was enjoyed by all those who worked for us, regardless of their length of service. Many of the men, both members and officers, argued that we would open the floodgates to pregnant women if we abandoned the two-year eligibility rule before women became entitled to the maternity package. With a woman leader and a woman personnel chair we were able to resist the argument, insisting that the eligibility criteria would not be the deciding factor in determining where women work or when they reproduced! Time proved us right; Islington Council did not have more women on maternity leave than other similar employers. Our women staff on the other hand enjoyed a better and more appropriate package of maternity benefits. This package would not have been adopted without the commitment of two people at the heart of the political machine. So having people in key positions within the mainline bureaucratic or political structures is one effective way of achieving change. They are more likely to reflect a gender perspective in what they do.

If we want to change the composition of our structures, we need to monitor for gender. Also setting targets is important. Our legislative framework prohibits open positive action, but monitoring and target setting are vital forms of effective action. Local authorities were partially successful with their equal opportunities recruitment practices. More women and people from the black and ethnic minorities were employed in council jobs, although rarely in management roles.

Furthermore the recruitment policies engendered conflict and resentment as white men believed they were being discriminated against. As an extreme example of this, the Commission for Racial Equality took on and won a case against Hackney Council on behalf of local white men, when Hackney tried to recruit people from the black and ethnic minorities to work as gardeners for the Council. Hackney wanted to ensure an equal representation of races among their gardeners who were all white at that time. Local white men felt they were being discriminated against by this policy. The courts backed the white men. This case demonstrated both the constrained statutory framework within which we had to operate and the resentment the equal opportunities policies caused in local communities.

A few committed women in key positions is not enough. A critical mass is necessary for sustained change. Again our experience in Islington bore this out. When we had women in influential positions we were able to promote and defend gender initiatives; when these women left men were waiting in the wings ready to take back the reins of power and they soon started to dismantle some of the programmes. For instance, under-5s' facilities, previously protected from financial constraints, were cut; women in senior management positions became more isolated and left. Lasting changes depend on there being enough women to defend the changes; reaching this critical mass is a vital task for the future. Vigilant monitoring and appropriate recruitment and promotion policies will help, but a commitment to change across an organization is also imperative. We have to create a 'pro-woman' culture among both men and women so that all support the changes we wish to promote.

The late 1980s and early 1990s saw a shift in local government policies and activities on gender equality. This came about for a number of reasons. First, political lessons were learned from the failures of some of the early experiments. In particular, politicians were influenced and chastened by the 1987 General Election results with a disappointing performance by Labour, especially in London. To the extent that the equality policies were seen to contribute to that poor performance, they became the victim of Labour's electoral defeat. Furthermore the campaigning against rate-capping and the government-imposed cuts on local authority budgets also ended in failure. Labour councils thought they were leading a populist campaign to defend jobs and local services but soon realized that few people, apart from the activists and those who worked for local authorities, were prepared to do anything to defend them.

Our priorities changed as we tried to rebuild Labour's fortunes and restore confidence in the worth of local public services. This involved a switch of focus; we needed to make sure that the bins were emptied efficiently and promptly, that the streets were kept clean and that the telephone was answered politely. Getting the basic services right was vital if we wanted to restore confidence and defend our services against further cuts. At the same time, building support for the Labour Party also meant focusing on the basic services. The rainbow alliance of support had never materialized and traditional Labour voters were alienated by the language, the resolutions and the gestures. We had to regain the confidence of our traditional base which meant concentrating our efforts on improving universal local services.

By 1994 we started to see that the switch paid dividends with a dramatic improvement in Labour's electoral fortunes, partly due to a changed perception of Labour local councils; the loony left image no longer rang true. The switch also meant that equality policies and programmes moved down the political agenda. Some of the more controversial and radical initiatives were curtailed; no more grants to lesbian groups for gym mats, no more funding of Babies Against the Bomb. However, the pendulum swung too far in many places. Many Labour politicians, anxious to court popularity, were willing to drop everything on equality. Yet, for as long as discrimination and disadvantage remain so firmly embedded in our society, equality must remain a central issue for politicians. Some of our methods may have been less than perfect in the early 1980s, but the objective was right and remains important.

Two other factors changed the approach by local authorities in the late 1980s, both as a response to government action. First, local government was faced with severe budget cuts as the government attempted to rein back public spending. Ironically, the government's failure to control their own expenditure meant that they were even tougher on local authority spending. Councils were therefore forced to abandon many of their radical initiatives in the struggle to maintain properly funded statutory programmes. Women's units and women's committees were an easy target for cuts; training programmes, essential to support positive action promotion policies, also lost out. The non-statutory youth clubs, afternoon school clubs and under-5s' groups were closed as councils tried to protect the statutory school budgets. Maternity packages also became a victim as authorities were forced, year after year, to reduce spending. Second, the introduction of compulsory competitive tendering (CCT) had a significant impact on gender policies. The first services which were subject to CCT were predominantly those which provided part-time jobs for women, like school cleaning and catering. Councils were forced to cut costs to compete effectively to retain the work in-house. This was because private sector competitors operated in an increasingly casualized and non-unionized environment where it was easy to pay low wages and where it was common practice to limit rights to holiday, sick pay and overtime. CCT often meant a loss of earnings and a worsening of conditions for the low-paid women council workers. Paid overtime had to go; maternity packages which exceeded the statutory minimum were written off as uncompetitive; entitlement to paid time off work to care for children who were ill was struck out of employment contracts. For services where a high proportion of total costs are staff costs, cost cutting to achieve a competitive edge inevitably meant cutting wages and conditions. At the same time, an environment has been created in which any new initiative introduced for the benefit of women is more likely to be rejected because the price tag will be deemed to be wasteful at a time of financial constraint. At present the prevailing view is that investment in women is not a good investment for society as a whole; so long as this persists we may be winning the moral argument, but we have not succeeded in making a good social and economic case for our cause. Attempts by local authorities to introduce improvements in pay and working conditions and which reflect a concern for equality have been undermined by government-imposed cuts and CCT, which demonstrates the limits of the power of local authorities. Only a national framework of rights, with a national minimum wage and national conditions covering matters such as the rights of part-time workers, maternity rights and rights to time off will stand the test of time and last. These rights will, of course, also benefit men.

In the environment of the 1990s with a Conservative government still in power and a 'new realism' being shown by Labour councils, the question of whether progress on gender issues may still be achieved becomes acute. Yet, equality must remain a policy priority. For as long as disadvantage and discrimination on the grounds of gender exists, politicians, officers and others who are committed to equality and fairness must work towards the eradication of that disadvantage. All local authorities, not just Labour ones, can build on the experience and achievements of the 1980s. This involves working sensitively with a bottom-up as well as a top-down approach – from the community upwards as well as from the town hall downwards. Policies need to be developed with the consent of those in whose name they are being formulated, which for women means building from their concerns rather than from the preoccupations of an elite. The political and financial climate may act as a constraint but it need not halt progress.

You only have to observe how the equal opportunities recruitment policies piloted by local authorities in the 1980s now provide models for establishment businesses in the 1990s to see that some progress is possible, even in this environment. Furthermore, as power transfers from national government to the European state, the political and constitutional framework will change, as we have already seen with the impact of European equal pay legislation. Local authorities' recruitment policies were clearly successful in altering the composition of the workforce. The emphasis now needs to shift to providing training so that women can develop the appropriate skills to move up an organization to senior positions. The legislative framework does not inhibit organizations from specifically targeting their training resources on particular groups; the opportunity therefore exists to take action which will help the promotion of women and those from black and ethnic minorities.

The early equality programmes in local government concentrated on changing the nature of the workforce. Little was done to look at access to services from a gender or race equality perspective. Yet there is much evidence of disadvantage in the delivery of local services. For instance, elderly women are less likely to be allocated a home care service than elderly men, because social workers assume that women are better at managing in the home. Meals-on-wheels are not prepared taking into account varying religious, ethnic and cultural preferences. We need a range of new policies and approaches to tackle inequality in the delivery of council services. We can only make our services universally good if we recognize the diversity of the community – its different needs and preferences. Few authorities have started to monitor who gets what, or tried to set up a database which would enable access to services to be analysed. Yet this is a key task. Only when we have identified disadvantage and diversity can we start to take the appropriate steps to counter the inequality.

Local authorities still have a role in developing new initiatives and new modes of action. Many pieces of national legislation have developed from policies introduced by local councils. This is true for all the political parties: CCT, for example, developed as a national policy after a few councils introduced competitive tendering voluntarily; the Citizen's Charter emerged from attempts by local authorities to address quality issues; comprehensive education originally evolved from policies introduced at the local level by a few councils. The diversity of local authorities remains one of the key strengths of local democracy. This diversity enables initiative to flourish and that initiative is essential if we are to tackle the many complex issues which confront us in society today. If policies work well in one locality they can provide a model of good practice and other local authorities or government itself can build on that positive experience. This is of particular importance in the field of equality where we do not know which policies will be effective.

I have described some of the initiatives sponsored by local authorities to promote gender equality since the early 1980s. A vital prerequisite for any progress is the presence and strength of a political will determined to pursue equality and support the necessary changes. Equality should be a core value for politicians on the left. Sadly, all too often the commitment to equality within the Labour Party is superficial. The Labour Party is still a very male-dominated institution where many of the men are far from ready to share power with women. This can be seen in the hostility to working with a minimum quota of four women in the Shadow Cabinet. It is obvious in the hostility to having all-women shortlists for 50 per cent of the 'safe' parliamentary seats which will become vacant in the run-up to the next General Election and it can be seen in the hostility towards changing the working hours for Parliament so that women with caring responsibilities can put themselves forward as candidates more easily.

The situation is not very different in local government. It took two years of persistent argument for a few of us to persuade colleagues in our Labour Group that we should start our evening meetings at 7.30 p.m. instead of 7.00 p.m. so that mothers with young children could find life a little easier. There are still very few women leaders in local government and the percentage of women councillors on my Labour Group was marginally lower when I gave up being a councillor than when I first became a councillor more than twenty years earlier! Women still feel they have to be more than perfect to succeed in politics.

The culture of politics remains inimical to women. Politics

appears to thrive on aggression and confrontation. At present it still operates in a fiercely competitive and individualistic way. To succeed, you do not just have to wipe the floor clean with the opposition, but you are expected to do down your own colleagues. Much of today's alienation from politics is the result of the confrontational nature of the process. Women, in particular, feel more comfortable in a cooperative environment and tend to walk away from conflict. So if women are to take part in and believe in politics, the culture and nature of the process must change. At the same time, one of the ways of making it change is to have more women MPs. The project is to try and break the vicious circle so that with more women MPs, working together, we can make a real difference to the way in which we conduct our democracy.

This reflection on the past decade of gender politics and policies in local government demonstrates that we enjoyed some successes but were also responsible for some failures. Some initiatives which were dismissed as outrageous and absurd ten years ago are commonplace today. Others alienated those whose interest they purported to promote. If radical policies which challenge traditional orthodoxy are to succeed they need to be rooted in the immediate concerns of people. In that way they will engender support and we can move society forward; leadership with the people rather than for the people is what is required. Local government must continue to work to develop gender policies. In fact its contribution is vital. Local authorities can and should innovate and experiment. They enjoy greater freedom in this regard than the central state. If things work – or fail – in one locality, other institutions can learn from that experience. If the central state gets things wrong, it is much more costly and difficult to put it right. Innovation and experiment is especially important in difficult areas of public policy, like gender policy, so local government's contribution is important.

Whether politicians of both the main political parties are really willing to revitalize local democracy to enable local authorities to fulfil their potential is, of course, another question. But even within the present constrained framework, there is room for local authorities to try some new and radical measures which could further the cause of gender equality.

10

IMPLEMENTING EQUAL OPPORTUNITIES IN A LOCAL AUTHORITY: A CASE STUDY

Paul Burnett

Like many other public sector organizations, East Sussex County Council has had a policy on equal opportunities for many years. In the decade following the adoption of its first equal opportunities policy in 1982 a number of practical initiatives developed to support the achievement of the objectives of the policy. These included the introduction of more flexible working arrangements; the establishment of workplace nurseries; improved access to county council buildings; active membership of the Sussex Local Employers' forum on disability; a range of joint ventures with local ethnic minority representative groups; equal opportunities action programmes and a wide range of training and development programmes. Nevertheless, little had been done to assess and evaluate the real and positive impact of the policy and the initiatives which had sprung from it.

In 1992 a decision was taken to review the county council's existing policies and their application. The aim of the review was to establish the facts about the impact of the policies on the county council's workforce; to look at changing trends in legislation and the approach taken by other progressive employers; to recommend, if appropriate, changes in the existing policies and the introduction of new policies; and to recommend a range of practical and positive measures which the county council could take to ensure that the revised policies could be implemented effectively. This chapter is presented in the form of a case study to illustrate, for others working in the field, the criticial influences which led to the review, the findings of that review, the lessons to be learned and the fundamental elements of the new approach which has since been adopted in East Sussex. Whilst the review encompassed a range of equal opportunities issues, the focus here is on gender.

Why, then, did the review take place? The commitment, attitudes and expectations of employers and employees are critical for the effective formulation and implementation of any policy. In the years preceding the review perceptions across the organization suggested that whilst there were specific individuals and groups who actively sought to promote equal opportunities, they did so in a vacuum and without the levels of support and resources necessary to maximize progress and achievement. This will not be an unfamiliar scenario for the reader. Any meaningful review or creation of robust policies and their comprehensive implementation will always depend on strong, committed leadership.

Lessons learned from Stage 1 of the policy and its review

The principal lesson learned from the review was the influence of a few key individuals in first establishing the equal opportunities policy and later in its review and change. The appointment of a number of senior managers in key positions created an environment within which real and positive action could be taken. These appointments brought to the county experience of organizations which were leaders in the field of equal opportunities and provided an influx of ideas, a raised awareness and, most importantly, knowledge and experience of how to get things done. Even more significant was the influence such individuals and their explicit commitment to equal opportunities had on staff across the organization. This increased the motivation of those who had previously sought to promote equal opportunities and led to changes in the behaviour of others. Whilst some of these changes in staff attitudes may not necessarily reflect fundamental changes in belief, and may not always have been for the right reasons, the net result was that equal opportunities began to rise in the list of policy and operational priorities in parts of the organization where previously there had been limited or no action at all.

However, key individuals were not the only source of changes in the attitudes of staff, and employees were not only influenced by key individuals. In the years since the introduction of the first equal opportunities policy there had been significant developments, not least those stemming from EU legislation and directives. The Opportunity 2000 initiative had acted as a catalyst to many large and small employers in the private, public and voluntary sectors, leading many to take a hard look at their existing policies and procedures. As a consequence employee and public expectations had risen. Nevertheless research on local authorities had shown that while 82 per cent of local authorities had equal opportunities policies, and many had introduced positive measures and initiatives in support of these policies, progress in terms of increasing the representation of women, the disabled and other minority groups, particularly at senior levels, remained relatively limited (Coyle 1989).

In the light of these developments the county council decided that the review was necessary to ensure that its equal opportunities policies and practices not only met current needs but could withstand future demands. At the heart of this decision lay the view that in the competitive and complex public sector working environment of the 1990s there was a need to make the best possible use of the organization's existing and potential workforce. As the county personnel officer pointed out in outlining the background to the review, the council should avoid unlawful and unfair discrimination in any of its practices or procedures but, beyond this, it also needs to be taking practical and positive steps to provide opportunities to attract, develop and retain good quality staff drawn from all sectors of the East Sussex community and, where appropriate, beyond.

The review was carried out by an inter-departmental working group on equal opportunities with representatives from all departments to establish the current position in all parts of the organization. It aimed to bring together examples of proven good practice and implement it across the organization. This second stage of the equal opportunities policy was designed to grow out of the best practices in the different parts of the organization rather than from a formula designed and imposed from the centre, which would be divorced from the body of the organization.

The first stage of the review was an evaluation of the effectiveness of the 1982 policies and focused on data on the composition of the organization's workforce and emerging trends. Immediately the review group became aware of the paucity of such information. The existing policies had had no formal monitoring or evaluation built into them and information was either patchy or unreliable. It was, therefore, difficult to identify trends or measure either the effectiveness of the policy or the initiatives which had sprung from it.

However, a number of important facts about the composition of the workforce and the changes in gender composition since that first equal opportunities policy were established:

- women accounted for nearly 75 per cent of the council's total workforce (part-time and full-time);
- the number of women employed by the county council in the previous six years, as a proportion of the total workforce, rose from 68.5 per cent to 72.3 per cent;
- the gender balance in the total workforces of individual departments varied considerably – in social services women accounted for around 80 per cent of the workforce, in education the figure was 75 per cent, but in other departments the figure was as low as 40 per cent;

- around 63 per cent of women employed were part-time workers whereas only 24 per cent of men were part-time. In the previous six years, however, the proportion of men working part-time had increased from 16 per cent to 24 per cent.

The variation in the gender balances of departments is not surprising in the light of traditional stereotypes. Departments such as highways and property, where engineering and construction are still largely regarded as 'masculine', have a smaller proportion of women than education, social services and libraries, where the work is not traditionally regarded as the preserve of males or females. However, had existing policies been influential, there should have been a higher correlation between the proportion of women in each department and the proportion of women in management grades in that department. This was not the case. Overall, little more than a third of management posts were occupied by women. The review concluded that whilst men formed 28 per cent of the total workforce, they occupied 64 per cent of management grades, whilst women, on the other hand, formed 72 per cent of the workforce, but occupied only 36 per cent of its management grades. The conclusion was that men were four or five times more likely to reach management grades than women. In addition, statistical analysis of gender representation across management grades showed that the gender ratio worsened in the higher levels of the hierarchy and culminated in a position where men were about twelve times more likely to attain middle and senior management posts than women. Whilst there were differences between individual departments the proportion of men in management posts was significantly higher than their proportion in the total workforce in all departments.

Further internal research into the proportions of the workforce from ethnic minorities or those with disabilities was similarly disappointing. However, the apparent lack of progress cannot be explained simply by the fact that existing policies were not working. Any change in the composition of a workforce as large as the county council's is bound to take time, particularly when wastage rates are low. Moreover, in relation to gender issues alone, there are other factors which organizational policies may not be able to shift. These include factors such as women's motivation to pursue a career or take on managerial responsibility, their self-confidence and self-image and the difficulties of operating effectively in a management environment and culture which remains predominantly masculine. All of these may have contributed to the overall stasis.

Nevertheless, the review team concluded that the county council's equal opportunities policies have had a relatively marginal effect in increasing the prospects of women progressing up the grade hierarchy when compared to their male colleagues. The main impact of the policies seems to have been in deterring overt discrimination but the policies had not been as successful as had been hoped in changing basic attitudes. The challenge became to find a way of achieving results which would match the laudable words. In terms of sex discrimination this meant creating a policy framework able to challenge basic attitudes and achieve positive results. To do this it was necessary to gain a better understanding of what the workforce, both men and women, wanted, how they viewed the opportunities open to them, and what they saw as the barriers to their progression.

The outcome of the review was to recommend that the three existing county council policies on equal opportunities, disability and HIV/AIDS, should be revised to bring them up to date with current needs. It also recommended the introduction of two new policies to help prevent sex and race discrimination and a harassment policy. The policies were to be seen as a family of documents – a general policy statement stating clearly where the organization stood on the overall issue underpinned by the other more specific policies.

Whilst the type of general statement which had featured in the original policies was retained, the new policy established a clear and explicit set of strategic objectives within which the operation of the county council's business would be managed. These objectives incorporated the five fundamentals of the new approach: responsibility; action; targets and standards; monitoring and evaluation; and training and support.

Responsibility

The review had established that good practice was evident across the county council but that it had often been operating in a vacuum. Comprehensive and effective policy implementation and action required clear identification of responsibility. As the new 'Equal Opportunity in Employment Policy' pointed out:

> Case law has shown that the management of an organisation can be held as vicariously liable for acts of unlawful discrimination carried out by those whom they manage, even if management had no knowledge of the action at the time. It is essential for management to be able to demonstrate not only that a policy to prevent unlawful discrimination exists, but also that they have taken steps to ensure that their employees understand and comply with the policy.

To this end the policy explicitly outlined the responsibilities of chief officers, managers and employees in implementing the family of policies which had been formulated. It made clear that the responsibility for implementing the policy lay with all chief officers and established that they were required to ensure that managers and staff in their departments observed the policy, received appropriate information, guidance and training, and adopted the right approach. In addition they needed to ensure that equal opportunities were an integral part of all management, supervisory and induction training.

Individual managers now have to ensure that policy is implemented in those parts of the organization for which they are responsible in accordance with departmental guidelines and in the context of the strategic objectives. In some departments this is supplemented by the inclusion of specific tasks and targets for individual managers within the performance management scheme which is operated across the organization. Consequently, some managers might identify specific equal opportunities targets relevant to their particular area of work, the achievement of which would determine whether performance pay rewards would be forthcoming at the end of each financial year. Individual employees, for their part, are expected to understand and adhere to the principle of equal opportunity in employment. The policy explicitly points out that the achievement of equality of opportunity and the avoidance of unfair and unlawful discrimination are matters of personal and individual responsibility. Finally, the new approach established that failure to comply with the policy and its supplements could result in disciplinary action.

Thus the roles and responsibilities of all working within the organization were redefined to ensure more effective implementation of the aims and objectives. To support this departments were advised to nominate an identified equal opportunities coordinator. In addition a regular review of the policy and its effectiveness was to be instituted through annual reports to the county council by the county personnel officer.

Action, targets and standards

Identifiable responsibility without clear action planning and target setting would not have been an advance and could weaken the potential of the policy. Consequently, a feature of each of the new policies has been to list the required management action or the specific measures which managers need to take. These action plans and targets provide the corporate framework within which all departments must now work and to which they will be accountable in the annual report to the county council. Thus all departments must now have in place measures which:

1 ensure that no applicant for a post or any employee will receive less favourable treatment on the grounds of gender, marital status or sexual orientation;
2 monitor recruitment, selection and promotion procedures and investigate any evidence of adverse impact against women or men to ensure that all applicants are receiving equal treatment and that appointments are made solely on the candidate's ability to do the job;
3 provide facilities, terms and conditions in a flexible way so as to encourage women to secure employment and to return to employment with the county council without detriment when they make career breaks;
4 join Opportunity 2000 and seek to meet the commitment to

developing the careers of women which membership demands, including increasing the percentage of women in
management (the target set by the county council was to
increase the percentage of women in middle and senior
management positions from the existing 38 per cent to 54 per
cent by the year 2000);
5 ensure that all employees, regardless of their gender, receive
the same opportunity to develop their skills and potential and
have full access to training, development and promotion
opportunities available according to their abilities;
6 provide specific training to encourage women to develop their
careers in supervisory and management posts and to help
senior women managers operate effectively in what can be a
relatively isolated environment;
7 make awareness training in this area an integral part of all
management and induction training.

Monitoring and evaluation

Monitoring and evaluation of the policy is an integral part of the
new policies and is a responsibility of all departments. Whereas
no provision for such activities featured in the previous policies,
arrangements are now in place to ensure that the effects of the
new policies are monitored, that information from departments
is collected and evaluated and a report submitted annually to the
appropriate county council committee.

This monitoring process focuses not only on the groups who
apply for jobs with the county council, but also to their representation in long and short lists and to the relative rates of
appointment across the groups. A critical element in this area has
been the introduction of a monitoring questionnaire which is sent
to all applicants for posts. The information has proved invaluable
in establishing where discrimination occurs in the recruitment
process and in eliminating a number of myths which have
developed in recruitment lore. For example, it is now possible to
identify whether the relatively low number of women managers
is due to fewer women applying, or to the fact that discrimination
is occurring within the selection process.

Training and support initiatives

The publication of a policy does not, in itself, constitute action. Equal opportunities are only achieved when people throughout the organization possess the necessary commitment, awareness, skills and competencies to carry out their individual roles and responsibilities in ways consistent with the policy aims and objectives. This was recognized at an early stage of the review and particular attention was subsequently given to providing the relevant training and support in order that the policy objectives be achieved.

The starting point for the training and support programme was an attitude survey of men and women across the county council to find out what they wanted, how they saw opportunities already open to them, and what they regarded as the main barriers to their career progression within the organization. Out of this grew the first awareness-raising programme which took all managers, across the organization, through the new policy, the roles and responsibilities of individual managers, the key aims and objectives and the actions required to achieve them. From this point individual departments were then able to pursue courses relevant to their particular fields.

Subsequent corporate training programmes have focused on particular targets within the policy. For example, training initiatives have been launched such as the 'Springboard' programmes to encourage women to enter supervisory and management posts, and a women's management support network to help senior women managers overcome the difficulties of working in an often isolated environment has been developed.

It is too early to judge whether or not the tangible results sought by the new equal opportunities policies will be achieved. Laudable words have been spoken and published before and, as cynics point out, minimal progress achieved. However, the policy framework now in place is more robust than that established in 1982. It has moved beyond laudable words to focus on intended action and outcomes, it explicitly identifies responsibility and accountability, sets targets and establishes processes for ongoing review, monitoring and evaluation. Above all, the organization is committed to supporting and empowering individuals to achieve their potential and to break down barriers. At the very least, when the next review is undertaken, possibly after another decade, there will be much more information with which progress may be evaluated and success judged. At this stage we are confident that the outcomes will be more positive.

11

EQUAL OPPORTUNITIES AND THE VOLUNTARY SECTOR

Ruth Valentine

The voluntary sector's understanding of equal opportunities

Here is a paper called 'Equal opportunities and the voluntary sector'. I find it in a journal, or given at a conference, or in one of the still fairly rare books about voluntary organizations. I am (as I am) a consultant who works with the sector; or (as I've been) a manager, a staff member, a committee member, a volunteer, one of the many people involved in more or less formal ways in this culture. What am I expecting?

First, I know that it's not likely to be saying: we think the voluntary sector needs equal opportunities policies. There are still voluntary organizations, notably some of the large and long-established ones, that don't have such policies, but they're in the minority. Even they are likely to respond with 'We're already doing it' rather than 'We don't believe in it'. It's a brave man or woman working in the voluntary sector who says openly

170

'We don't believe in it' these days. So far so much progress. There has been progress.

Second, it won't be just about the position of women. It will talk about 'disadvantaged' or, more assertively, 'oppressed' groups: minority ethnic groups, people with disabilities, lesbians and gay men, working-class people, people with HIV or AIDS. The list isn't comprehensive, and most of us have stopped thinking it can be: we will go on discovering to our shame that there are other groups that we have excluded from employment and services, that there are more unconscious prejudices to work on.

This second point should have a profound impact on the stance of the paper. I hope the writer will accept that we cannot use our status as victims of someone else's oppression to claim immunity from being ourselves oppressors. This applies to all of us, but perhaps especially to the white middle-class women who have traditionally staffed and managed voluntary organizations. I don't just mean the often dedicated and resourceful women who have been derided as the 'twin-set and pearls brigade' (prejudice comes in many forms), but people like me, feminist, left-wing and university-educated. We have had for twenty years or more a great deal of power in the voluntary sector, and our egalitarian principles haven't always been matched by our day-to-day practice.

Women and the voluntary sector

Perhaps this is the moment to look at the history and culture of this odd voluntary sector. A definition may be useful. Voluntary organizations are helping and campaigning agencies which have been set up not by local or national government, but by concerned individuals. They may or may not (since this is a common misunderstanding) work through volunteers. Shelter and Amnesty are voluntary organizations; so is your local Citizens Advice Bureau, or disability group, or Asian women's refuge.

Many voluntary organizations were, and continue to be, started by women; and even where men have provided the impetus, it is rare that women have not been closely involved in the actual working. Voluntary organizations are set up in response to a need which has been observed not to be met by existing providers, statutory or voluntary. This means that they are likely to start small: trusts may be found to provide some funding, then perhaps local authorities; years later there may be a network across geographical areas. The huge government-funded 'welfare bureaucracies' that are the most influential part of the voluntary sector still started like this. This shared history is a key factor in the present-day culture of voluntary organizations. At best, it shows in a flexibility of approach, a readiness to rethink services in order to meet the needs of users: the kind of openness that equal opportunity thinking demands. It can also be seen in a mistrust of hierarchy and bureaucracy; a frank ridiculing of overt power-seeking; an assumption that everyone involved has some-thing to contribute to the thinking of the organization. These values seem to me to come largely from the thinking and the preferred working styles of women. They are explicitly cited by many, women and men, as reasons for making their careers in this sector.

The downside

It would be reassuring to claim that the voluntary sector is characterized only by these positive values. Alas, they have, like all belief systems, their shadow side. Flexibility too often has become an inability to set reasonable boundaries on what the agency can do for its users: 'I swear', said one observer, of the founder of a new agency, 'if a client came in and said she wanted to learn to knit, X would assign a caseworker to teach her.' Responsiveness and commitment too often end up as a collusive exploitation, with both staff and management taking excessive overtime and extreme stress as a norm.

Another besetting sin of the traditional voluntary sector is maternalism: the unconscious assumption that the agency knows best what will be good for its users. There has been a culture change over the last twenty years that has brought in the vocabulary of consultation and choice; but it has not always been matched in practice. Maternalism shows the class and gender origins of the sector: middle-class philanthropy, and a kind of oblique controllingness, recognizable in women who have had inadequate outlets for their abilities – mother knows best. Many black, or working-class, or disabled users and colleagues have found us as guilty of maternalism as our foremothers, however much we consciously reject their values.

Similarly, women's traditional desire for relatedness at work can turn sour. What starts as constructive mutual support may end up oppressive, punishing those who can't or won't merge with the dominant group. The desire to merge, to deny conflicts and differences, seems very powerful in many voluntary organizations, particularly those run by and for women. The feminine environment is seen as contrasting with the masculinity of the outside world: it should therefore be perfect, warm and accepting – the organization as mother. There is a primitive rage resulting from the disappointment of this fantasy that has racked many an otherwise capable organization, and bewildered all those affected.

The masculinization of the voluntary sector

There has been a reaction against all this: necessary, but not always helpful in its impact. Of course, voluntary organizations are not the only ones to experience a passage from creative chaos to bureaucracy. There is a pattern common to all types of organization: the founder-led, inspired agency outgrows its strength, needs to bring in order and system, and risks being paralysed by too much order. In the voluntary sector, this transition has in many ways been a gendered one: a move from stereotypical feminine to masculine values, and more literally from female to male management. As organizations have grown, they have become assertive, and recognized the need for non-exploitative pay structures; and as pay has improved, more men have been drawn to work in a traditionally female field. The result in the 1990s is that many voluntary organizations have a staffing pattern with women constituting 50 per cent or more of staff below senior management level, but very much in the minority in management teams. Chief executives these days are more likely to be male than female. A concomitant of the necessary 'professionalizing' of work in this sector has therefore been a loss of opportunity for women. This in some cases is exacerbated by a double standard in recruitment practice: staff are recruited according to good equal opportunity practice, but senior managers, whose recruitment is the responsibility of honorary officers, may go through a much more traditional, and discriminatory, process.

Issues for women

All this means that a woman entering the voluntary sector is faced with a specific set of issues and a specific culture. In many ways the environment is more obviously welcoming; she is very unlikely to be the only woman (though she may be the only woman in senior management); she is unlikely to have to fight to defend the concept of women's oppression. These are no mean achievements.

Nevertheless, she will not find the battle definitively won. Precisely, she may have to deal with the assumption that it is. The sophisticated understanding of equal opportunity as affecting everyone oppressed by an unequal society can offer a kind of opt-out in relation to women: aren't other groups' needs more pressing? This is of course an old trap for many women, as well as for men who don't want to look at their own behaviour. The task of equal opportunity may be felt to be overwhelming, and one response is the creation of an unspoken 'hierarchy of oppression', a competition for the role of most-oppressed. There is enough truth behind this philosophy to make it compelling: after all, there are more white women as managers than black men, or more gay men than women or men with disabilities. The notion of a hierarchy, however, reflects something crucial in our puritan culture, an idea which itself is inimical to the practice of equal opportunity: that only one set of needs can be considered, that only absolute neediness and powerlessness deserve our attention. In this philosophy, only those right at the bottom of the hierarchy can get their needs met. This is a mean and punitive spirit, and it has to be replaced with one which is both more generous and more honest. This is one of the key tasks for women and men in the voluntary sector who want to make the rhetoric of equality into something nearer a reality.

For women, this has two implications. The first is the need to identify, and speak about, the ways in which women in this sector are still oppressed. These include the 1980s culture of macho management, enthusiastically embraced by some as the antidote to woolliness; the favouring, in status and pay, of 'male' activities – financial management, PR, contact with politicians and high-ranking officials – over 'female' work with service users; and the range of ordinary oppressive behaviour that has not been eradicated – sexual harassment, bullying, the appropriation of women's ideas. Too often women complain to each other about these things rather than developing strategies for countering them. At work as well as domestically, we can get into the pattern of accepting behaviour which diminishes and depresses us as inevitable or immovable. Understandable though this may be, its results can look remarkably like collusion.

Women and power

The second task is for women to acknowledge the degree of power they do have, and tackle their own oppressive behaviour. We have too often used the hierarchy of oppression model, not only to deny our own needs (something we tend to see rather ambivalently, as if it didn't itself result in our martyrish oppression of others), but to reassure ourselves that we are after all powerless and therefore innocent. Precisely because women, and particularly white women, are the traditional workforce of voluntary agencies, we have considerable power. We know the ropes; we understand the culture, what's done and what isn't; and like girls in the playground we can make life very uncomfortable for those who don't conform. Furthermore, as managers we have power in the real world, power to recruit or turn down staff, to encourage or discipline subordinates, to make or break careers. If our own need to be victims overwhelms us, we will make these decisions badly, ruled by unconscious rage and prejudice. Many women in management in the voluntary sector are honourably occupied in finding a style of management that is congruent with their values, that enables them to be honest about the extent of their power and to use it responsibly.

This task is frequently made harder by the responses of both female and male staff to women in authority. The problem is of course not confined to the voluntary sector, but its manifestations here are shaped by the particular culture. In a culture where dissent is accepted, it is in some ways easier for a member of staff who sees every woman manager as the witch-mother to express that feeling directly. Women making difficult decisions – about redundancies, say – may be told that they are 'like Margaret Thatcher'. Women in management have to find ways to handle this kind of criticism. They need to understand it as about something other than themselves, to fight the temptation to experience themselves as powerless victims, and to use their power responsibly to set boundaries for the appropriate expression of dissent.

Equal opportunities and service provision

There is also the question of the core work of the organization, its face-to-face service to users. The high profile application of equal opportunity principles has been in recruitment and employment practices; but although these are vital, not least to the quality of service provided, they are not the whole story. Again, the issues are sometimes blurred because women are the traditional users of helping services, for themselves and on behalf of their families. Many agencies have worked hard at re-examining their services to ensure equal access for all groups in their community. The defensive statement 'we treat everyone the same' can still be heard, but there are also organizations that have women-only sessions because they have realized that for some women sitting in a mixed waiting-room is an unacceptable or a threatening experience; or that work in partnership with refugee community organizations, or tenants' associations, or disability groups, to see how their original, culturally-determined services can be applied and adapted to meet other needs. There is in general far more work to be done on these issues of service delivery, on appraising day-to-day work practices as well as major structures and priorities.

Working in the voluntary sector

The opportunities for women to make use of their understanding of gender issues in this sector do therefore exist, but they are not straightforward. There are very few posts for which this knowledge will be a sufficient qualification. Experience of work in the substantive field – housing, or advice work, for instance – is likely to be required for any designated women's post. It is also true that these posts tend to be targeted at the needs of particular groups of women – refugee women, or women with disabilities, or women in bed and breakfast, for instance – so that the applicant will need to combine a feminist awareness with an understanding of some very specific needs.

For the woman who wants to work in the helping professions, however, the opportunities to make use of her feminist standpoint are there. Jobs in the voluntary sector are as hard to come by as any others, and in a culture that values experience above qualifications, there is no easy way in on the strength of academic study. Nevertheless, there is an exciting role for women to contribute to the re-feminization of the voluntary sector.

12

TRADE UNIONS AND EQUAL OPPORTUNITIES

Rita Donaghy

The traditional role of trade unions was perceived as mainly to defend their members' interests in the labour market. Any analysis of their role started from a description of who their members were, on the one hand, and what was happening to labour markets on the other. When the members were predominantly male, many union policies and strategies were distinctly un-woman-friendly, and not always inadvertently. In the 1930s, the National Association of Schoolmasters energetically promoted a bar, such that women teachers lost their jobs on marriage. Other strategies to raise wages, such as the claim that men had to earn more than women because they, men, had families to keep, were double-edged. The living standards of some wives may well have been raised as a result, but for many women who either were not married or who themselves had families to keep, their position was much worsened as they had to survive on lower wages for the same work.

For substantial periods of history, and in certain occupations, women workers represented a challenge and a threat to existing male workers who were 'the members', and many unions actively developed strategies which kept women out of the labour force, while other unions were simply passively resistant to the idea of equal opportunities. However, in the last two decades, unions have made great strides towards formulating policies in this area. They have been in the vanguard of establishing workplace nurseries, maternity leave rights and childcare allowances. On their own, and in partnership with the Equal Opportunities Commission, they have fought a series of landmark equal pay and discrimination cases. This shift in perspective, however, was not automatic and is the culmination of a learning process both within and without the trade union movement.

As the composition of the labour force and the political environment changed, unions began to rethink their role in relation to gender and equal opportunities. Traditional male-dominated sectors of employment declined and service-oriented sectors, which employed more women, grew. Family patterns and household composition altered too. It was not just that more women worked, more parents, especially lone parents, worked (see Holtermann, p. 53). Divorce rates rose and the idea of a traditional breadwinning male earner with a dependent wife became increasingly outmoded. Union membership fluctuated, but when it grew, the biggest gains came from women. In the political arena, there was a marked break in consensual or corporate politics expressed by a sharp shift to the right and an unbroken sequence of Conservative administrations from 1979 to date. A growth in income differentials and polarization between both individuals and households has marked the last two decades in which the political mould has been irrevocably broken. Individualism has been energetically promoted and the death knell of collectivism sounded more than once. As Eric Hobsbawm (1981) proclaimed at the start of the period, the 'forward march of labour' had halted and the formation of new alliances with different interest groups became an urgent priority for trade unions as well as left politics in general.

In this context it was no longer possible to see unions as narrowly negotiating employees' interests with employers, although it is arguable whether trade unions ever saw themselves exclusively in this narrow role. Political intervention had recast the ground rules with at least ten pieces of legislation in the last fifteen years and made it much harder for unions to defend their members' interests. This forced unions into a more complicated relationship with the general public as well as with their members and with employers, one that was increasingly dependent on media coverage. The net effect of these changes was to establish that unions were not simply creatures of the labour market who could only operate within its terms, they were not just reactive, but major players in the formation of public opinion who could accelerate social change by being exemplary as well as by fighting cases of injustice. Undoubtedly weakened by privatizations and the contraction of firms and organizations, each producing higher unemployment and a reduction or fragmentation of the workforce over twenty years, unions were forced into a rethink. Recruiting and retention became harder as workplaces splintered and employment became more intermittent. As more people moved in and out of work, identifications between those in and out of work became more complex.

For many years a view prevailed that conflicts of interest between equal opportunities and trade union practices were inevitable. For example, positive action policies such as career breaks for childcare were expected to clash with a last-in-first-out policy and it was tacitly accepted that unions could back only some aspects of equal opportunities. It is my view that there is no area where a trade union should not bargain legitimately on equal opportunities and there is no excuse for partial support. In the context of rapid political and labour market restructuring, equal opportunities, which has been creeping up the union agenda, has to be continuously reviewed in the light of changing circumstances. For although the principle of equal opportunities is now widely endorsed within the trade union movement, finding ways to implement it is still a problem.

Equal pay legislation and subsequent strategies

The failure to bridge the gender gap more than marginally between men and women, despite legislation, remains a challenge for trade unions and demands strategic innovation. Women still receive only 79 per cent of the hourly rate paid to full-time working men and, in the ten years since the equal value amendment to the Equal Pay Act (see Holtermann, p. 52 and Clarke, Chapter 4), there have been only twenty-two successful claims made by women. Compared with the rest of Europe, Britain fares particularly badly with, for example, non-manual women workers who earn only 53 per cent of the male rate in banking and finance and only 61 per cent of the male rate in retailing. These are the lowest rates in Europe.

There are, of course, no single solutions and many of the instruments of change are far from perfect, but they are what we have to work with at present. Legislation is absolutely essential and, whatever its weaknesses, it is important to use both British and European law. Similarly, though the Equal Opportunities Commission has been systematically underfunded, it has played an important role and could play an even greater one if it was properly resourced; especially if it took on the task of monitoring an equal opportunities code of practice which had the same status as employment rights. Of course, unions could do more still if they had the ability to take collective as well as individual cases to court, as they can in the USA. But at present they cannot and, without stronger legislation and a more sympathetic political climate, progress is bound to be slow and piecemeal as it is obliged to proceed largely by championing individual cases which test the legislation.

Within industry there is some scope for systematic and coordinated campaigns. For example, the electricity industry, which was deeply divided by gender with a predominantly female clerical staff and a predominantly higher paid male blue-collar staff, was the object of a mixed campaign of legal action and negotiation. By selecting a series of strong cases in each electricity company UNISON either negotiated improvements which would have a general application or took the cases through industrial tribunals. When the first claims were submitted the pay difference between the top of the manual grades and the top of the clerical grades was £709 p.a. and after four years' service the difference was £2,663. UNISON's four-year campaign of combined legal action and bargaining compared jobs as telephonists, wordprocessor operators, accounts clerks and sales with those of store keepers and meter readers and reached agreements with eleven out of the nineteen privatized companies who admitted that they had underpaid 11,500 clerical staff, most of whom were women. Ultimately, about 20,000 women are expected to benefit, but already £70,000 back pay has been secured. Some companies settled out of court and began to negotiate new grading structures, whilst others negotiated new deals without litigation.

For many women it is their status as part-time workers that is the crux of their economic disadvantage and discrimination. Four out of five part-time workers are women and the number of part-time workers has risen by a third since 1979. Yet there is no legislation on compulsory breaks or holidays for the 28 per cent of the workforce who are part-time workers, and little sign of a commitment to remedy this. Indeed, it was in order to preserve this situation that Britain energetically negotiated an opt-out to the Maastricht Treaty. Yet, despite a climate which still does not favour part-time workers and exploits the expressed preference by many women for part-time work, some progress in establishing rights for part-time workers has been made. In 1990 UNISON took up and won the case of two part-time women domestic cleaners made redundant from their jobs at Woodilees Hospital in Glasgow after four years of work. One had worked seven hours a week and the other fourteen. As they had worked less than twenty hours a week they found that they were not entitled to redundancy pay. The case made by UNISON on their behalf was that this threshold discriminated against part-timers and, because most part-timers were women, it amounted to sex discrimination. After a four-year-long trail through the Industrial Tribunal to the Employment Appeals Tribunal and, finally, to the Court of Session (Scottish Court of Appeal) the two women were awarded their redundancy pay plus 15 per cent interest. This was a landmark ruling preventing future discrimination against part-time workers and has been followed more recently with a House of Lords ruling which grants part-timers the same rights as full-timers in regard to unfair dismissal and rights to redundancy pay if they have worked more than eight hours a week.

New developments: personal contracts and performance-related pay

Performance-related pay schemes have become extremely popular amongst employers and are generally a key part of personal contracts which, in turn, are justified on the grounds that they link pay to effort and performance. In reality, the links are not so clear. Trade unions are becoming increasingly worried that whilst some people may in the initial stages of the scheme earn more, often in excess of national agreements, this increase is not sustained or sustainable. Some schemes only allow a fixed proportion of employees to qualify for the higher bands of pay, regardless of their performance, many schemes are non-pensionable and very few cover part-time or temporary workers. Similarly, very few personal contracts contain provision for maternity, paternity or parental leave, for job-sharing or part-time working and they rarely, if ever, cover career breaks or childcare provision. Although an employer has a legal obligation to pay employees equally for work of equal value and not to introduce differentiation which would lead to different rates of pay between men and women, the privacy which surrounds individual contracts nullifies much of the legislation, though it also makes such schemes highly vulnerable to claims that they are discriminatory. It is hard for individuals to know the details of other people's personal contracts and the scope for restoring and even increasing income differences between the sexes is hugely increased by this development.

In any job evaluation it is impossible to specify all aspects, and in the case of process or people-work, where a majority of women are located, it is especially difficult to quantify caring, listening and facilitating into targets. However, most discriminatory for women, black and older workers and other 'diverse' sections of the workforce are schemes which link pay to the subjective judgements of higher managers. For not only do senior men tend to promote those who mirror their own characteristics, there is growing evidence that success by female and male workers is explained differently, with male success being attributed to ability while female success is explained as luck or an easier task.

Support for the view that performance-related pay may have a discriminatory impact comes from a 1989 European Court of Justice case widely known as the 'Danfoss' case. This held that a pay structure linked to quality of work and the employees' sense of initiative could constitute direct discrimination against women. If the employer could not clearly show what criteria were used to assess employees' performance then the burden of demonstrating that their practices were not discriminatory lay with them. This case is part of a series revealing a sea change of attitudes. In 1988 the Department of Health was obliged to review the NHS general managers scheme following a complaint by the Equal Opportunities Commission because it excluded part-time workers. And in 1990 the Court of Appeal ruled in the case of Briggs v. North Eastern Education Board that expecting a teacher to work after hours was discriminatory because it amounted to a requirement which fewer women than men could fulfil.

Though legislation is clearly a major and necessary way of levering employers towards negotiations it is not sufficient. In 1987 almost a million manual workers in local government were covered by a major restructuring, which included a job evaluation scheme which gave due weight to skills, responsibility, mental effort and initiative as well as to physical effort and working conditions which had previously dominated job evaluation schemes. But getting the 'correct' grade does not, in itself, solve the problem of low and unequal pay for women. Most job evaluation schemes are inherently discriminatory: even if they permit a degree of tinkering, they formalize differences, many of which turn out to be trivial, for most job definitions cover only a fraction of the skills which employees bring to their work. But the limitations of all such schemes is that they ignore most women's inability to work overtime or on shifts, to participate in bonus schemes or to travel extensively because of their other commitments. Thus, as long as unions negotiate such schemes with employers without taking these other factors into account, they will help maintain discriminatory structures. More worryingly, as labour market conditions change, a new range of practices are becoming common which need to be studied carefully for their equal opportunity implications.

The welcome given by the government to the spread of personal contracts because they are seen as a way of ensuring 'the aspirations of individual employees to deal directly with their employer, rather than through the medium of trade union representation or collective bargaining' is alarming, first because it marks a further stage in attempts to undermine unions and collective organization, and second because it opens the door ever more widely to individual discretion which is the vector through which most discrimination is effected. The personal contract assumes that employer and employee meet on equal terms, though this is far from the case. Although an employer cannot legally and unilaterally decide to change a contract, for example by excluding the right to belong to a union (if this is done it amounts to a breach of contract which gives grounds to the opposing party), in effect this practice is growing and has not been successfully challenged. On the other hand, however, so far as the push towards personal contracts is driven by a desire to reduce union power it does not seem to be successful.

The long-term effects and costs of personal contracts in, say, litigation costs remains to be seen, as does the effect of performance-related pay on morale as well as output. At present unions supply advice to members on the implications of personal contracts which includes the formal recognition that an employer's withdrawal from collective bargaining does not immediately alter an individual's terms and conditions of employment or diminish their individual rights. Any terms within a collective agreement which are capable of being incorporated within an individual's employment contract are presumed to have been so incorporated. The existence of a contract implies agreement on its terms and that these cannot be changed. Unions always advise members to take care over any contract which seeks to bind the employee to any future and unilateral changes by the employer. Wide clauses which include phrases such as 'you shall perform such duties as the company may from time to time require, either orally or in writing, provided that in changing your duties at any time the company shall not act unreasonably' give the employer almost total control and restrict the basis of a challenge wholly to interpretations of what is 'unreasonable'.

Rita Donaghy

Playing a leading role and setting the bargaining agenda or following majority values?

Unions are not confined to using existing legislation to fight cases of discrimination. Their role is also to set bargaining agendas and to lead in rethinking the nature of work and its place in the modern world. They can and should articulate a progressive view of social relations. Taking their equal opportunities brief seriously is a tremendous aid to this task, for women's collective experience in thinking about and managing the dual and often competing demands for domestic labour and caring responsibilities is a rich source of information which is becoming increasingly relevant for the majority of workers. While many of the issues dealt with under the heading of equal opportunities may have started out as women's problems, especially as they related to job insecurity and part-time work, they are fast becoming everyone's problems. In these circumstances unions have a huge responsibility to be forward thinking. They can and must raise consciousness, articulate issues and demonstrate good practice.

However, not all trade unions are equally well placed to do this. Differences of size and membership, as well as the contexts in which they work, are critical. But public sector unions may have a particular responsibility, a legacy perhaps of the public service ethic or rationale which once underpinned the whole sector and led many to seek work within it and its unions. The public sector has generally, but not exclusively, led the private sector in equal opportunities and, in principle at least, the ethic of public service is more compatible with equal opportunities than with that of profit maximization. Some of this has changed in recent years with the introduction of internal markets, and simple dichotomies have lost their earlier clarity, but as public and private sector distinctions blur, the chance of transferring or exchanging collective wisdom and experience grows.

Nevertheless, trade unions have not always given equal opportunities as high a priority as they might have, or followed through a commitment to ensure that women can achieve, and remain in, leadership positions. Claims that are important in equal opportunity terms have sometimes started high on the agenda but, in the face of hostile employers' insistence that they be costed as part of limited packages, they have often been transformed into a choice between a basic pay rise or progress on equal opportunities. Such packages are always sent out to the membership for consultation, and in the course of this process equal opportunity measures are known to get lost, for unions generally reflect rather than lead society's priorities.

To take another example, internal union mergers have often affected women's leadership positions, both on the elected and the full-time officer side. Without institutionalized support women find it virtually impossible to achieve the continuous and often long service required to gain important leadership positions. Union mergers often lead to staff reductions which, as in any organization, inhibit career and promotion prospects for those remaining. This slows down the process of implementing positive policies to promote women. Yet mergers, as with any structural change, also offer an opportunity for reorganization along more progressive lines, as the case of UNISON may demonstrate for, at its inception, it adopted a policy of proportionality.

Exemplary action: proportionality within UNISON

By the end of the 1980s equal rights had become relatively fashionable, but practice still lagged behind rhetoric. A succession of male general secretaries had espoused the cause of equal opportunities at the annual TUC conference, but a suspicion remained that the new-found interest in women was based almost wholly on the opportunity that they offered to boost flagging membership. The merger of the public sector unions COHSE, NALGO and NUPE, and their reorganization into one new union UNISON, represented a unique chance to do something radical about equal opportunities.

The new union was set to have over a million members, three-quarters of whom would be women, and from the very start of discussions about merger there was a clear sense that this was the moment to depart from practices which had traditionally obstructed women within unions and led to their less than full participation. However, the gender composition of the soon-to-be-merged unions was not the same. COHSE had 80 per cent women members, 44 per cent on its National Executive, 52 per cent stewards and 32 per cent branch secretaries. NALGO had 51 per cent women members, 41 per cent on its National Executive, 44 per cent stewards and 27 per cent branch secretaries. NUPE had 74 per cent women members, 46 per cent on its National Executive, 42 per cent stewards and 27 per cent branch secretaries. The strategies chosen to establish a different gender composition in the new union were the two linked policies of 'proportionality' for women and 'fair representation'. If they succeeded, the experiment was expected to have implications throughout and beyond the trade union movement. If it failed, it would add, sadly but importantly, to our knowledge of the difficulties of turning policy into practice.

Accordingly, when UNISON established its rule book it not only incorporated a general anti-discrimination policy which stated that 'The Union shall seek to ensure that discriminatory acts are not committed against any person by the Union, or by its organs, members or officers, on the grounds such as race, gender, sexuality, disability, age, creed or social class', but included in its aims and objectives the principles of proportionality and fair representation. Proportionality was defined as 'The representation of women and men in fair proportion to the relevant number of female and male members comprising the electorate', whilst 'Fair representation' was taken to mean that a 'broad balance should be aimed at between different groups within the electorate, that is, between manual and non-manual, full time and part time workers and those with different skills and in different occupations within the union as a whole'. The specific commitment was 'To promote fair representation in all the Union's structures for women, members of all grades, black members, members with disabilities and lesbians and gay men.'

The first merger report to the three national conferences had stated:

In developing the structure of the New Union, it is necessary to understand the way in which current trade union organisation often discourages women's participation, for example, through restrictions on standing for elected posts, the time and venue of meetings and the conduct and language of union business. It is necessary to take account of the demands and patterns of women's paid work and their unpaid work and responsibilities at home. Male trade unionists need to re-examine their attitudes and behaviour towards women in the workplace, in the union and in the home.

This statement was a recognition of the role women had already played in modernizing the three unions and in shifting their policy agenda towards a commitment to equal pay, minimum wages, part-time workers' rights, childcare and equal opportunities more generally.

Women had broadened the horizons of the unions by making them take on issues of sexual harassment, abortion and health care rights and become more responsive to the communities of which they were part. But, though organizational and policy changes had been achieved to meet some of the demands made by women, the structures and agendas had remained governed by male assumptions and traditional outlooks. In the light of this perception, the formation of a new union allowed a real root and branch change and various options for effecting change were examined, including proportionality, quotas, reserved seats, informal arrangements and self-organization. Without all or some combination of these, the principles of equal opportunities and fair representation would not be achieved.

Whilst undergoing this major reconstruction UNISON did not only try to make itself more woman-friendly via proportionality, it aimed also to attend to the claims of three other historically disadvantaged groups, that is, of black people who form a large section of public sector employees, of lesbians and gay men, and of those who are disabled. The strategies considered to be potentially effective in promoting and including members of these groups included self-organization, separate national conferences and positive action policies; and all were to be allowed at branch, regional and national level. Self-organization was justified as enabling these groups to determine their priorities, elect representatives at different levels, provide access to resources, training, publicity, build confidence and raise participation generally. Perhaps most important of all was the express provision for disciplinary action if acts of racism or sexism arose.

Branches and regions were given a deadline of the year 2000 to achieve proportionality. Targets covering the composition of all UNISON committees, conferences, meetings and delegations were to be agreed, with a timetable and mechanisms, including guidelines, training and education programmes for their achievement laid down. If earlier results were possible, they too were to be agreed; and all were urged to avoid rigidity and excessive red tape. The goals of proportionality for women, fair representation overall and support for women's self-organization were to be simultaneously pursued, monitored and reviewed. It was a revolutionary programme. However, just as discrimination does not disappear once there is a rule forbidding it, nobody expected proportionality to be achieved overnight, and throughout the period the other side of raised hopes was disappointment that change did not happen fast enough.

In the four years of consultation exercises leading up to the merger, there was a strong, though contradictory, sense of *déjà vu* alongside a palpable fear of breaking the mould. We were used to the structures that we knew and we recognized that to make the new union truly woman-friendly would mean changing the internal distribution of power and influence within the union. The four hitherto excluded groups wanted a share in decision-making powers, they wanted to influence policy and, in turn, they wanted to effect change in the external environments of work, public policy, education and wider social attitudes. But they knew that power is never given away, it is fought for and redistributed only with a struggle, even if there is a fair degree of good intention. It was clear that implementing the policy of proportionality meant close scrutiny of UNISON's existing employment policies and a programme of positive action on recruitment, retention, promotion, training and arrangements for part-time working and job-sharing. Although it is far too early to say that proportionality is firmly in place in UNISON, the mechanisms have been put in place at national and regional levels. As branch mergers take place, proportionality is being addressed at local level, admittedly with varying degrees of enthusiasm. Although the principle is still questioned by some, my belief is that its philosophy was so fully embodied in the formation of UNISON that only the most foolhardy would forecast its future demise.

In some respects the three constituent unions had already pioneered change, although such change was uneven. As an administrator within an 'old' university for over twenty-six years, and chair of NALGO's committee responsible for negotiating for all white-collar non-teaching staff for sixteen years, I had witnessed the variable and erratic progress that had been made in equal opportunities, even within the same union. Although in 1973 I was still referred to as 'Chairman', in many ways our committee was ahead of the rest of the union and the union movement generally. The proportion of women on the national committee reflected the fact that 95 per cent of the membership were women, priority had been given in wage negotiations to boosting the pay of the lowest grades, part-time workers had been admitted to occupational pension schemes, and the maternity leave scheme negotiated in the early 1980s was still better than many negotiated later and included rights for those who had undergone the nightmare of a stillbirth. However, a parallel national committee representing white-collar staff in the former polytechnics was, by contrast, almost entirely male-dominated: partly because in that sector of higher education NALGO represented all the clerical and administrative grades, whereas in the 'old' universities NALGO represented only the lowest-paid half. The lessons to be drawn from this comparison are, first, that a female-dominated committee gives priority to equal opportunities and, second, that unions can all too easily take over and reproduce the structural inequalities of the organizations which they are attempting to reform.

Nevertheless, for those women and men who had spent the 1970s and 1980s arguing against reserved seats for women, parallel structures and other so-called privileges, these developments appeared as an ultimate defeat. Certain women who had succeeded under their own steam feared that the strategies proposed would undermine their achievements. Against this view though, it can be argued that the bargaining agenda has to be changed and women have to be in a position to change it.

Women are still overwhelmingly lower paid, less secure in their jobs and less likely to enjoy pension rights or access to overtime work or bonus rates. They still suffer disproportionately from the effects of privatization, from job losses and cuts in pay and conditions, and from the abolition of the wages councils. Unless structures are created which ensure the full participation of women at all levels in the trade unions, the bargaining agenda will not, in practice, change. This is a matter of survival for trade unions as well as for equal opportunities.

Conclusion

It is important to recognize both the scope and the limitations of trade unions in promoting equal opportunities. The bargaining agenda is getting ever broader and encompasses paternity leave, parental leave, leave for carers, domestic violence, stress at work, as well as the more 'traditional' areas of equal opportunities. This is not only because all are crucial to equal opportunities, but because trade unions will only achieve certain objectives by campaigning for change in the wider social context. Lack of adequate affordable childcare is probably the biggest single factor inhibiting the progress of working women and it now seems incredible that at the end of World War II there were 1,300 nurseries providing places for 62,000 children. Without the political will and sustained government support, genuine improvements in childcare will be marginal. Trade unions have a vital role in campaigning in the wider political arena to improve opportunity, access, education and child support for women. Progress in the workplace is part of the whole.

13

THE APPEAL AND THE CLAIMS OF NON-DOMINANT GROUPS

Gillian Stamp

Background

The focus of this chapter is on understanding a range of discriminatory problems shared on the basis of gender, ethnic background, culture and religion and on their key elements. One of these is that, as individuals, all are members of the non-dominant group (MNDs). For example, an individual who has limited paper qualifications in an organization that sets great store by them; someone who is Hispanic or black in a predominantly Anglo-Saxon company; Caucasian in a Japanese company; female in a male-dominated organization; Roman Catholic in a Protestant organization; an engineer in a company run by accountants; Malaysian in a Chinese company; a Christian in an Islamic institution.

In any organization it is the members of the dominant group who will define the overall purpose and values, and have direct control over decision-making processes including the contribution made by junior members. Depending on circumstances, the members of the dominant group will either actively encourage the development of MNDs, or make assumptions about their capabilities that confine them to lower levels of responsibility. There will be various courses between these two extremes – of which empowerment and affirmative action are just two examples – but negotiating perceptions of individuals on the basis of their social identity is at the heart of the need for change and the problem of management.

The costs of not properly using the capabilities of people who are members of the non-dominant group are borne by both organization and individual. This chapter suggests that, especially in the case of members of non-dominant groups, to give equal attention to the individual, the organization and the relationship between them will improve efficiency, avoid unwarranted assumptions and ensure that capabilities are used to the benefit of all.

The capability of every individual can be identified and released, and the challenges presented can be paced by the organization in response to the natural growth of that capability over time. In the case of MNDs, any barriers to the expression of their full potential can be seen in the light of the organization's need for continuity, rather than as a result of discrimination on grounds of gender, culture, religion, skin colour or any other factor.

Five themes

Over the past seventeen years my colleagues and I have spent many fascinating hours listening to people talk about the way they approach their work. The purpose of these 'guided conversations' was to arrive at a view about the pace at which it would be appropriate for the person to take on more extensive responsibilities at work. We used a procedure called Career Path Appreciation (CPA) to understand as much as we could about how each person approached their work, focusing in particular on what they did when they did not and could not know what to do, in other words, on how they exercised their judgement in the face of uncertainty. The people worked in a wide variety of organizations in different parts of the world – some national, some multi-national, in economies at different stages of development, and they carried responsibility at all levels.

One of the main reasons for the widespread application of CPA as a procedure is its focus on the capacity to *make* a decision by putting something of oneself into it, rather than to *take* a decision on the basis of careful deduction from the data available. Specifically it provides a view of an individual's current capacity to exercise judgement in the face of uncertainty and a reliable prediction of how that capacity is likely to grow. The uncertainty of the current economic and social environment, and the emphasis on responsiveness to customers, places a premium on using judgement to make decisions. For this reason the capacity to exercise judgement is regarded as the essence of management and individual contributor potential. The particular relevance to MNDs is that all our research suggests that while there are differences in the capacity to exercise judgement, they cannot be attributed in any way to gender, educational attainment or ethnic background.

From the very rich and diverse material provided by the CPAs we have learned that people at work in very different settings have much more in common than one might at first suppose. And their stories have remarkable similarities around five basic themes. First, they all know – and describe in similar words or phrases in many different languages – what it is like to be '*in flow*', to feel a dynamic tension between the challenges of their work and their own capabilities with a sense of exhilaration as they cope successfully with new challenges. Second, most know what it is like to become increasingly anxious and uncertain as the complexities of the job *overwhelm* them; worry takes over from exhilaration as they are forced to gamble rather than make coherent choices. Third, many know the debilitation of being '*underwhelmed*', as exhilaration ebbs away in simply doing the same thing over and over again with no real choices to make, losing heart, spirit and skill as time goes on. Fourth, each person knows that their capability has 'a life of its own' *growing* as they grow older and constantly seeking expression in fresh challenges. And fifth, they know that the *context* in which they work is critical for the expression and reception of their capabilities.

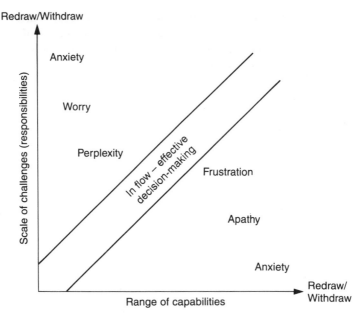

Figure 1 The experience of work
Source: Adapted from Csikszentmihalyi (1991)

The first four themes are summarized in the figures given. Figures 1 and 2 are 'snapshots' illustrating the experience at a particular point of capability and challenge. Figure 3 shows that capability grows over time and that 'flow' and effective decision making will be maintained only if challenges are aligned with that growth. The theme of context is taken up later.

Experiences of members of non-dominant groups

As mentioned above, these experiences are remarkably common across very different cultures and organizations and may be felt by the dominant group too, but the poignancy of each tends to be sharpened for MNDs.

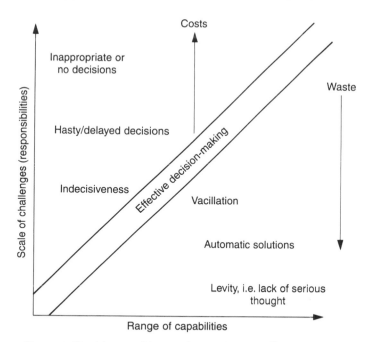

Figure 2 Decision-making and organization effectiveness
Source:Adapted from Csikszentmihalyi.

Underuse of capability

Angela is Afro-American and had been a systems analyst in the information technology division of a public utility for twelve years when we worked through a Career Path Appreciation. She talked about how she had been asked to take on extra responsibility a little early, how she had caught up as her capability grew to meet the challenges, but how, since then, her growing capability had not been recognized and affirmed in wider responsibilities despite her determined efforts. The increasing desperation of her pressure on her boss and his reactions will be all too familiar to others who have had similar experiences.

> I'd really enjoyed being head of a section. So it was great when they asked me to take on a small department – although I have to admit I was a bit pushed at first and a few

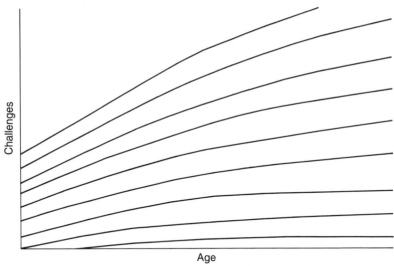

Figure 3 The growth of capability
Note: see also Jaques 1976
Source: © Elliott Jaques

things did fall through the net. But we managed to pull things around until the figures were fine and the customer complaints had dropped right off.

And then I started to get bored. I'd done it all before and nothing new looked like coming up. I felt I was ready for a move to head up a larger department but nothing came my way. Eventually I spoke to Jim [her manager] and he said 'Yes, yes, we'll try and do something.' But nothing happened and so after I'd waited a while I went to Dave [Jim's boss] and said 'Look, I'm really ready for more now. I know there were a few problems five years ago, but everything's fine now and you can see I can cope.'

He said 'Don't rush us, you have to be patient. Things have gone very well for you so far, you don't want to tempt fate by taking on more responsibilities, but we promise we'll do something as soon as we can.' So I waited for another eighteen months. I was still doing the job well but getting less and less interested in it.

By that time Jim had moved on so I went back to Dave and reminded him of his promise. This time he carried on about cut backs, flatter structures, fewer opportunities and a slower pace of advancement for everybody. This just didn't square with the fact that three men who had worked for me in the section were now managing departments. I was getting mad by this time but just didn't know how to tell him without him coming back and accusing me of being 'emotional' or 'over excitable'.

Angela's is a classic story of being overwhelmed, feeling the relief as her capability grew, and then the increasing desperation as it continued to grow and she became progressively 'underwhelmed' and pushed more and more into a corner with unspoken but clear references to her gender and her ethnic background.

Too far, too fast

Ironically, affirmative action, other equity programmes and social pressures for the rapid advancement of MNDs – as in developing economies or programmes to provide more opportunities for women – can lead to some people being overwhelmed not only by the complexities they are asked to cope with, but also by the added pressure of being a 'token'. Their experience is that instead of being able to follow a path where they would be 'in flow' in line with the intrinsic growth of their capability, they are drawn at a pace that leaves them stumbling. Whether or not they set out to do so, they are painfully aware that they are carrying with them the hopes and aspirations of other members of their group. And they know that if they fail, it is not only as themselves but as that group's representative. In short, they have become the classic token.

Bob, the expatriate general manager of a mine in a newly industrialized country in Southern Africa, very much wanted to promote Reuben, a local engineer, into a senior role as a head of function. Reuben intuitively felt that he was not ready to cope with the responsibilities of that level of work.

When Bob first brought it up I was really pleased, but deep down worried because it'd come too soon. I tried to tell him

I'd rather have a bit more experience and perhaps do a master's degree before taking the promotion, but made a complete mess of it. His first response was 'You know your problem, don't you? You've got no ambition – you just want to go on being a student for the rest of your life.'

So I let it lie for a bit, but he wouldn't let it alone and one day he called me up and said I was being 'damned awkward'. By this time he and I just couldn't communicate, and eventually he accused me of deliberately trying to sabotage the localization programme which was very important to the mine.

That was when I worked through the Career Path Appreciation. It confirmed my sense that I needed another three years or so to be really on top of the head of function role. It was a huge relief to have what I knew put into words by someone else, and it gave me a basis for going back to Bob and talking it all through more calmly. We sorted out a plan together and after that it went fine.

Reuben gained wider experience by working in another part of the group, he did not take his master's degree, and less than three years later took on the engineering division. For the first six months he was stretched to the utmost but gradually became more effective and confident.

Having looked at the first four themes and at the added poignancy of the experiences for people who are members of the non-dominant group, we turn now to the fifth theme – the context. Again, the experiences described below are not peculiar to MNDs. They are part of the considerable changes in working lives as global influences touch enterprises of all sizes all over the world. But guided conversations with MNDs make it clear that these changes affect them in ways that are different from the experiences of those who have been or still are members of the dominant group.

Paper, glass and rubber ceilings

It is perhaps in facing and finding ways through organizational barriers – often described as 'ceilings' – that MNDs have a particularly difficult task. One writer has suggested that these institutional barriers have four different kinds of impact: on the individual as he or she feels under pressure to behave in particular ways; within the group where efforts may be made to reduce inequalities and to affirm capabilities; on the standards that govern the organization as a whole and which are likely to assign higher values to certain functions; on the patterns of culture that define the images, myths, symbols and values of the organization (Giele 1978).

Paper ceilings

The image of the 'glass ceiling' – not seen until you knock your head on it – is all too well known. But glass ceilings are not the only barriers to the full realization of capability. The 'paper' ceiling – prevalent in organizations where appointment and/or promotion tends to take place on the basis of educational qualifications – rests on the assumption that capability is directly related to educational level, and thus denies opportunities to people who have not had the chance to acquire them.

This barrier can present particular difficulties for MNDs who are more likely to have had limited opportunities for educational attainment. The moves to first line manager who is usually a head of a section, first level specialist, principal specialist and departmental manager all tend to be especially tightly controlled by 'paper ceilings'.

Antonia was a clerical worker who had left school at 16, and because she lacked certain educational qualifications the organization where she worked had assumed that she could progress only to a limited extent. She was 33 and the Career Path Appreciation made it clear that her intrinsic capability had consistently been underused in her clerical roles. Although she had had a very strong sense of this and had been growing more and more depressed as time went on, she felt that without paper qualifications she had no way of convincing others of her capability. Strengthened by the evidence of the CPA, she tackled her supervisor who was very responsive and prepared to give her supervisory experience and the opportunity to study for a diploma in computer studies. Eighteen months later she was a competent and content section head.

There is evidence that the requirement for qualifications can aid women workers because the existence of formal qualifications can help to overcome prejudice. For example, a number of women have become part of top management teams in areas such as finance. However, our research suggests that they may still find themselves firmly confined to their own function and having to work very hard to have their input on general strategic decisions heard.

And MNDs who obtain qualifications may still not be promoted. This is an especially delicate issue in developing economies where much emphasis is often placed on qualifications which the individual obtains with great sacrifice but it is felt that their qualifications do not reflect their capability to exercise judgement.

For example, in Botswana the government has a policy of localization for the planned and systematic training and development of Botswana citizen employees to facilitate their accession to expatriate-held positions on a one-to-one basis.

I quote from the report of the personnel director on one particular mine.

There was a pool of people with similar qualifications, and the challenge was who should get the job first? Appointments had been made on the basis of qualifications, experience and performance in the previous job, but some individuals did not perform as expected and this gave the policy of localisation a bad name. It became evident that the major factor was that we had no means of assessing potential. As we all know, a good artisan does not necessarily make a good foreman. We needed to find a means to determine which artisan will.

Career Path Appreciation was introduced to address this issue and has been very successful in doing so. It is now also used in:

(i)   selection where CPA helps to match individual potential to the level of work to be done

(ii) in development plans – the most important way it has aided us in the localisation area is in the pacing of individuals' development such that one is always doing work that 'stretches' them sufficiently but does not 'over extend' them

(iii) identifying the potential of people who do not have qualifications but whose capability cannot be used to the full without them.

This last point links directly to the nature of capability and the importance of *making* rather than *taking* decisions in the present complex and uncertain economic environment. It gives rise to important questions; making rather than taking decisions requires a significant shift in the respective roles of knowledge, experience, skills and judgement. In taking decisions the first three are paramount with judgement playing a small, subsidiary role. In making decisions the skills, knowledge and experience become tools used to support judgement. This is not to deny their importance, but to point to the economic imperative to *make* rather than *take* decisions.

This shift has three very important implications for the development of human resources in a country like the new South Africa where many black people have had inadequate education:

1 There is an enormous untapped reservoir of capability which can be evaluated and developed regardless of educational attainment: knowledge, skills and experience can then be aligned with it.

2 Assumptions about individual capability should never be made on the basis of qualifications, or demonstrated skill alone.

3 Managers at all levels will need help in perceiving the capability of people rather than making assumptions about them on the basis of their qualifications or lack thereof; there will be an added pressure and need for support in that, for the managers, re-entry to a global economy will mean exposure to massive uncertainty and the need to reconsider their own decision making to give primacy to judgement.

Glass ceilings

Unlike paper ceilings 'glass ceilings' are not necessarily barriers that have been deliberately put in place in order to block people and deprive the organization of their capabilities. From the point of view of the organization, they are there in part to protect the continuity of certain views and attitudes that would be open to challenge if people who were not members of the dominant group were given the chance to use their capabilities to the full. Of itself this continuity is not negative, but individuals are likely to see the barriers as a deliberate attempt at control.

Our research suggests that 'glass ceilings' often seem to be in place between the level where the theme of the work is *best practice* – making sure that the processes of producing goods or providing services are as efficient and effective as possible – and the level where the theme is *strategic development* – considering what is not happening but might or needs to, as the marketplace changes.

The likely impact of an MND on best practice and procedure can be significant and valued by the organization but, to put it bluntly, his or her influence can be contained within a part of the organization subject to decisions and changes controlled elsewhere. In the case of multinationals the decisions may be made in another country and culture; from the point of view of women they may be made in male settings to which they do not have access. It may also be that members of the dominant group assume that women and other MNDs are not capable of contributing to strategic decision making.

The frustration of the glass ceiling has different effects on individuals which can be directly related to the pace of growth of their capability. People whose capability has been growing at a pace that would make them comfortable and effective when carrying responsibility for strategic development work in maturity may have a relatively smooth passage through jobs as first level specialists or section heads, and may be given limited departmental responsibilities. But as they approach the upper boundary of departmental management the doors are suddenly closed and opportunities fall away. Ironically, it may be the very same group of people who are encouraged into 'token' roles because they are seen to have potential to contribute to policy making but are not felt to be likely to raise questions about the overall strategic intent and direction of the organization.

Henrietta is a 35-year-old financial analyst working in a bank in London.

I've been here now for seven and a half years. The first six were a pretty exciting, fast-moving time with new challenges and responsibilities coming my way at just the right moments. But in the last eighteen months it's begun to dawn on me that I'm just not going to get the promotion to general manager that is the next step. I'm starting to feel that I'm stuck, but when I raise it I get something like 'Don't rush, there's plenty of time . . . they're planning to make improvements in some of the systems in your department . . . times are difficult right now for the bank . . . '. By now it's clear that these are brush-offs, and so I'll have to move on. But it's a shame because I've enjoyed it here, and have learned a lot which I know could have been of benefit to them as well as me.

Then there is another group of people whose capability is growing at a pace that would make them comfortable to work in top management in maturity. They would be ready to take responsibility for strategic development work in their early thirties and in most organizations it would be unusual even for a member of the dominant group to be given opportunity at this kind of level. But there can be an added confusion for MNDs in that, if they have this kind of potential, they may well have had a lot of attention in the form of further education, individually tailored career planning, etc. Their passage through early specialist and/or management roles and through contribution to or management of practice and procedures may have been relatively smooth (even smoothed), but as they approach the boundary between current practice and strategic development, the doors are suddenly closed.

For the individual this is a major disillusionment, they feel let down, that they are no longer trusted and that all the earlier promises have been betrayed. What the dominant group has suddenly found itself facing is the possibility that serious, well-researched questions may be posed about strategic development, about means and ends, about appropriate directions in the market, and that these questions will be asked by individuals who, on their previous showing, are not likely to be satisfied with vague responses. The very promise that these people showed has now become, if not a threat, at least thoroughly disconcerting for the members of the dominant group who have decided on strategic direction and the kinds of development that will forward it.

In the present climate, where change is the only certainty and where strategic direction has to be more a plan of navigation than a tightly constructed path to be followed, this kind of questioning is even more disturbing. The questions must be asked, and top management knows it, but it is disconcerting to hear them from people who have been members of the non-dominant group.

Rubber ceilings

The barriers that lie beyond the level of work of strategic development touch on the standards that govern the institution as a whole, on the culture that defines the images, and on stories of what the enterprise is about.

The experience of trying to penetrate those barriers was well described by a woman working in a multinational in Italy: 'It's a rubber ceiling . . . as soon as you think you've pushed it away, it closes softly around you again.' Seen through the eyes of the individual this claustrophobic experience is depressing, frustrating, very annoying, especially as it may seem as if progress has been made, suggestions and contributions to these very important issues have been heard. But if they have, they may well have been rephrased by a member of the dominant group as their 'radical' view or absorbed with a casual 'Well, we have always been aware of that and the necessary changes are in hand.'

For the members of the dominant group this may be the only way they can take in the contributions of 'strangers' who have not previously been in a position to comment on, let alone influence, such matters. In this they are acting no differently from any group with established beliefs and ways of doing things. This is the old argument of 'revolution or evolution' and clearly both are necessary if there is to be substantial change. But when MNDs understand the influences that produce different kinds of resistance, they are able to make a more informed judgement about when to revolt and when to be 'in there' contributing to the evolution.

There are now consistent pressures on dominant groups in many different enterprises to reconsider their position. Not surprisingly, this may make it even more difficult for MNDs to express their capability to the full and have it received and affirmed, in that the resistance of people under pressure is likely to be all the more determined. But many of the changes brought about by global information technology in particular are allies of those who have been without power. Instant analysis of events, trends and necessary action, once the jealously guarded preserve of dominant groups, is now available at the touch of a button directly or indirectly even to people of limited education. These changes are already helping to 'make gender work' where gender is seen as a particular case of non-dominance. And rapid communication across the world provides important lessons about MNDs in terms the dominant group understands. One particularly apposite example is the growing acceptance that micro-lending to women in developing economies has been enormously successful both in empowering them and for the commercial success of the banks involved because women are extremely reliable creditors.[1]

Information technology also supports the kind of distributed control that is coming to replace the command and control patterns of most organizations as they adapt to become more flexible in the face of uncertainty. This point is elaborated below in the discussion about ladder and nested hierarchies.

Making non-dominance work

Ten years ago thinking about the kinds of experience described above in terms of dominance and non-dominance helped to lift the debate away from gender and ethnicity and to look more objectively at the institutional barriers that organizations put in place to sustain their continuity (Giele 1978; Stamp 1986).

Career Path Appreciations since then have demonstrated that the picture is now even more complex and that the context for MNDs is full of apparently contradictory influences. On the one hand, the unilateral power of dominant groups still prevails, on the other, there is much talk of the competitive advantages of managing diversity. With yet a third hand, most organizations are trying to do both. So this leaves individuals trying to reconcile these competing claims in their own working lives without ever being quite sure which view has the greatest influence, and still subject to expectations that they will change their behaviour to 'fit' the dominant culture. Programmes for more equitable treatment have to respond to all the agendas simultaneously.

The dominant/non-dominant dichotomy remains useful because unilateral power still prevails in many work settings, but this view is under pressure as organizations are forced – by the need to be more responsive to continuous rapid change – to reconsider the meaning of power and the economic advantages of distributing it in such a way that the binary dominant/non-dominant view would no longer apply.

Charles Handy argues persuasively for federalism as a way to govern increasingly complex organizations, pointing out that this reverses a lot of traditional management thinking.

> In particular it assumes that most of the energy is out there, away from the centre, and down there, away from the top. Power is redistributed because no one person and no one group can be all-wise, all-knowing, all-competent . . . federalism is not simple. It matches complexity with complexity – the necessary variety of a global world. Federalism is in tune with the times – times that want to value and respect diversity and difference.
>
> (Handy 1992)

The ladder hierarchy

The dominant/non-dominant view remains strong not only in 'male bastions' but also, for example, in aid projects where expert knowledge is almost always privileged over the tacit knowing of people on the spot. In many businesses the realities of dominance remain in, for example, short-term employee contracts and the increasing number of women in part-time, poorly paid, non-unionized jobs.

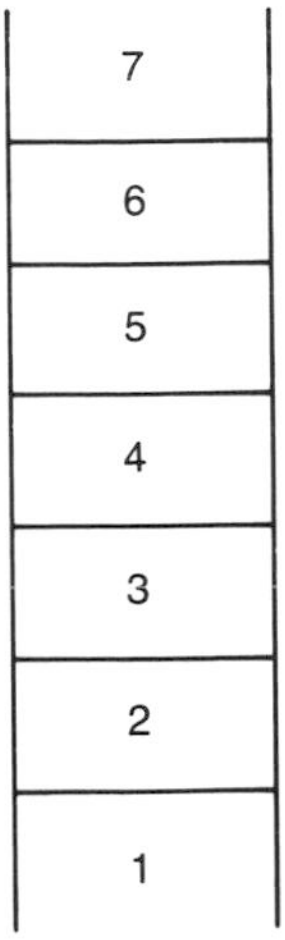

Ladder hierarchy

Figure 4

Where this kind of pattern prevails the organization is a ladder hierarchy of command and control where knowledge and control come from the top down with each step on the ladder representing increasing power and status. From the same unilateral perspective this 'propositional hierarchy' announces 'Have we got a super new product for you!' (Hampden-Turner and Trompenaars 1993) and pays little or no heed to small signals from the market, or indications from customers as to what kind of product or service they might want or prefer. As a consequence a ladder hierarchy sees little need to draw on the information and understandings generated at levels in the organization concerned with direct service to individuals or direct assembly of products where many MNDs are likely to be employed.

In similar fashion, the organization expects to control all employees and this can fall particularly hard on MNDs. The control may be autocratic, paternalistic, willing to give away some power but unsure of how to do it without losing its own; genuinely wishing to empower and distribute decision making as long as it is possible to keep a balance between autonomy and accountability.

Many of these ladder hierarchies are now making real attempts to move away from command and control and the limitations of the dominant/non-dominant view and to encourage the full participation of staff and particularly MNDs. It is significant that these attempts are driven, not by concerns for the people involved, but by economic imperatives – command and control is simply not sufficient in rapidly changing conditions. Because there is an economic imperative, this change in attitude is more likely to last than changes introduced for social or ideological reasons which tend to be reversed when economic pressures increase – training and development and equal opportunity programmes for example.

Nested hierarchies

So alongside the dominant command and control approach we now see a growing awareness of the need to distribute control in order to contain operating and capital costs, make the most of all the information available in a rapidly changing environment, and ensure a supportive operating environment for the future of the enterprise (Bohm 1980).

Awareness of this change can be seen not only in commentary on economics, development and organizations (Waring 1988; Aoki *et al.* 1990; Aktouf 1992; Chambers 1993) but also in the writing of people who have been at the top of companies in the last few years.

One example is 'Riding the Whirlwind', co-written by a former Chief Executive Officer of British Telecom (Benton and Benton 1990). In a way the title says it all, but one of the main thrusts of the book is that the essence of a turbulent market place is that no one caucus decides what should be; the market place arises from numerous forces acting at different places, at different times and coming from different origins. The authors sum up in the comment 'we have a humbler perception of our powers'.

In other words, command and control needs a rethink! And this humbler perception is leading to forms of organization more apposite to the need to make the most of what can be gleaned and learned from the environment. Instead of pushing out a new

Nested hierarchy

Figure 5

product or service, the customer is asked 'What would you like us to make? What are your specifications?' Instead of a ladder hierarchy of command and control where all information, knowledge and control come from the top down, control is distributed throughout a nested hierarchy so that the understandings and insights of each part are given due weight and can inform the whole.

As organizations modify their forms, the opportunities for and pressures on MNDs increase; the former partly as an outcome of the particular skills they are likely to have developed precisely because of their lack of power, and partly because of the recognition of the value of diversity; the latter because, as already mentioned, these changes are making very heavy demands on members of the dominant group which make it difficult for them to do things differently at the pace MNDs would like. The outcome is often an unwillingness to give members of the dominant group the benefit of the doubt and bewilderment on their part that their intentions are not appreciated. As one writer pointed out, we always judge others by their actions, but we judge ourselves by our intentions (Milner 1985).

A look at the difference between the way one level of work is done in a ladder and a nested hierarchy may help to illustrate both the difficulties for MNDs and the particular strengths they bring to the latter. Here I repeat that, in our experience, many MNDs are working in organizations that are firmly constructed on the ladder principle, most are in organizations trying to move from one to the other. Those who are working in nested hierarchies are, by definition, no longer MNDs because such a binary concept would make no sense in a setting where all views and insights are potentially economically significant. The changes in attitude required to move from command and control to distribution of control and equity of contribution are profound. The changes are happening but are hampered still by assumptions which can lead members of the erstwhile dominant group to assume that they now have no power, that all they have done in the past has been wrong and that there must be a reversal of control rather than a distribution. This can create a very difficult situation for those who have been MNDs and who are now taking on wider responsibilities in organizations and in circumstances that demand a completely different way of organizing work. The example below will help to make the point.

The work of *best practice* is to make sure that the processes of producing goods or providing services are as efficient and effective as possible. Whether this work is being done in stable or turbulent conditions, the individual managing or contributing to it must be able to *connect* to draw together a number of single instances into a continuous thread that can put limits around uncertainty by gathering events into a coherent whole. In other words, he or she needs to have a flexible grasp of everything that is going on and be able to play with it as a juggler might keep a number of balls in the air.

A member of the dominant group is more likely to make these connections in the light of the prevailing expectations of the organization and may find it more difficult to 'think outside the box' or to keep extra balls in the air. He or she may thus find it easier to function in stable conditions and have to put in considerable effort to make the changes in approach required by turbulent conditions. This can have the paradoxical effect that they both welcome and are upset by the approach of MNDs who, by virtue of their non-dominant position, are likely to have heightened sensitivity to possible change because they will have needed to anticipate anything that might increase their dependency and vulnerability. Thus, at the most extreme, a servant will be able to anticipate and adjust his behaviour to change in an employer's mood before the employer herself is aware of it.

So the MND is likely to be especially alert to tiny differences in behaviour, to be 'outer directed' and thus readier to spot emergent trends in customer need, or to be 'polyocular' – seeing a world that consists of differences rather than objects (Maruyama cited by Hampden-Turner and Trompenaars 1993). In conditions where dominance is accepted, this kind of sensitivity may actually increase the perception of dependency because it is seen as the behaviour of those without power. In turbulent conditions the kinds of skill that heighten alertness and lead to responsive and pliant behaviour take on a different meaning because they are seen to confer competitive advantage. For example, good service organizations now tap the direct experience of people at the sharp end where services are delivered in order to learn about what actually constitutes customer satisfaction rather than what top management thinks might. And organizations committed to flexible manufacture and continuous improvement can do this only by creating information, by combining articulated knowledge with the tacit understandings and knowledge of people who, in another setting, would be seen as MNDs.

So, without wishing to be flippant, there is good news and bad news. The bad news we all know and it has in many ways been compounded by recession and reactions to change. But the good news is that the economic imperative has a human face. It may be precisely the skills learned in dependency – awareness of the needs of the other, alertness to tiny indications that a situation is about to change, sensitivity to hints and possibilities – that global interdependency demands. Shall the meek inherit the earth?

Note

1 There is a diversity in experience between different countries. In the case of Bangladesh while women were formally in control of the credit it was generally their husbands or sons or other male relatives who determined how the credit was used (Goetz and Zen Gupta 1994).

14

CONCLUSION – FEMINIZATION AND NEW FORMS OF EXPLOITATION: THE CHANGING LANGUAGE OF EQUAL OPPORTUNITIES

Jenny Shaw

It is such early days for gender work and equal opportunities that any attempt at a progress report is bound to be inconclusive. There can barely be an interim, let alone a definitive assessment of where it is going. The world, certainly the world of work, is changing at such a rate that, although the purpose of this book has been to assemble experiences from the field in order to help and guide new entrants, what clearly matters is thinking about future trends and their implications for gender work. Sadly, we can say with some confidence that despite legislation outlawing unequal pay and sex discrimination employees are still stratified by gender, both horizontally and vertically. Pay rates, work conditions and promotion prospects still vary, and as fast as measures are introduced to limit or eliminate old forms of discrimination, new ones develop. Rather like a virus which mutates, gender inequality finds new niches in which to flourish and, along the way, mops up an increasing amount of energy in combating it. Like doctors dealing with a virus, those fighting gender-based inequality know that there is an 'awful lot about', but no equivalent of penicillin. Instead, what is quite often applied is inappropriate technology or sticking-plaster rhetoric.

To continue the medical metaphor, if gender inequality is like a virus, much of its treatment is like keyhole surgery. Concentrating on promoting women managers, on mentoring or on building networks seems, like keyhole surgery, a dramatic and relatively cheap way of improving performance, reducing waiting lists and contributing to social justice. But, just as keyhole surgery illuminates only a tiny area for the surgeon and leaves the bulk of the body invisible, much equal opportunities work is irrelevant to the bulk of women who are nowhere near managerial grades. The individualistic strategies advocated for potential high-fliers may be effective, but they do not touch the working conditions of the majority. Indeed, if they did, there is a good chance that they would be abandoned, for equality of opportunity, in and of itself, implies no commitment to equality.

The sociologist Frank Parkin (1979) redefined the theory of class relations in terms of two complementary but opposed strategies: 'usurpation', which was the goal and the strategy of the excluded, and 'closure', the retaliatory strategy of those who already enjoyed a certain amount of social privilege. Such terms also make sense of the stop-go shape of equal opportunities work generally. There has been a tendency to think of the backlash to feminism as somehow unique, but of course it is not. It is part of the power relations process and, as Rosabeth Kanter (1993) has shown, is bound to increase following medium-term gains. As women move beyond being a token minority within an organization and begin to pose a numerical 'threat', they are treated as threatening in all senses and the quality of personal interaction deteriorates.

As some progress is made, the challenge of gender work changes. In the next decade the immediate task is to think through strategies which apply to the majority of women, not just a small number of fast-track women. This means not treating women as a unitary category, but looking at divisions within women, as well as between men and women. The second task is to identify new forms of exploitation as they develop, and the third is to explore the enhancing or inhibiting effects of the changing language, or discourse, of equal opportunities.

To effect change at these levels demands a machinery far beyond the scope of individual equal opportunity officers. For this reason attention is often given, on superficially pragmatic grounds, to 'low tech' solutions. One such is the belief that role models are an effective stage in transforming skewed workforces and diluting the concentration of men in positions of power and influence. Presented as a necessary and sometimes even sufficient way of producing change, it is actually one of the most pernicious myths in equal opportunities work. Supposedly encouraged by the sight of others to raise their own aspirations and self-esteem, all women are meant to forge ahead. However, not only does this scenario rest on a naive view of the psychological process of identification and, indeed, envy between any two individuals, it is a version of the 'blaming the victim' approach. That is, it holds that the problem for women is their own low expectations, which could be transformed by a simple 'look-see' device. Role modelling is a non-strategy, and may even be dishonest. The visible promotion or success of a few women is both tokenistic and may even contain or limit the headway that can be made by women in general. Support for a few women in the spotlight lets individuals and firms off the hook of thinking more fundamentally and structurally about their organizations, and it encourages individuals to think that by being personally ambitious, they might be contributing to a greater social good.

New forms of exploitation

Predictions, as most people know only too well, are usually wrong. They apply to stable conditions which rarely occur in the real world, hence most social scientists are loath to make them. Nevertheless, there is a widespread belief that, even if the rate of progress varies, social change is heading in the right direction and irreversibly towards an egalitarian and less gendered society. When challenged, the most common explanation of this view is that economic growth generally produces an all-round improvement in the quality of life and, if this is not enough, the demographic time-bomb and worsening dependency ratio (i.e. the decreasing number of those in work compared with those who are retired, sick, unemployed or too young to work) will ensure it. The projected shortage of school leavers and skilled men in the 20–50 age range is advanced as the reason why employers will drop traditional prejudices against women, for it is in their interests to do so. These two trends were widely assumed to underwrite a steady improvement in women's conditions at work. Then the recessions of the late 1980s and early 1990s hit, growth was arrested and so was the anticipated improvement in women's conditions. In fact, the recessions provide a kind of test for how much commitment to equal opportunities is driven by economic conditions or changed values, i.e. the result of feminism.

Whilst no one can foresee the future with certainty, the labour market is widely held to be entering a totally new phase (Freeman and Soete 1994). Given the economic imperatives of growth, expanding markets and reducing costs, the two most common scenarios are either mass unemployment, with a small, 'lean', but highly productive labour force, or greater work intensification for all. In all except the oil-rich states further growth depends on possessing the most recent technology and a flexible labour force (Toffler 1990). This flexibility, however, can mean many things. Traditionally it has meant labour mobility and wage flexibility though increasingly it is linked to retraining, new skills and 'nimble' or 'agile' organizational change. Sometimes hailed as a boon to women, if it means flexitime at the employee's wishes it more usually means casualization, mass unemployment, weak unions, unsocial hours and general deregulation: the end, in fact, of a century of improving labour relations. Individuals lose job security and governments get to worry about who should bear the responsibility for, and the brunt of, change.

Though there is no reason to assume that women *per se* are more at risk from these labour market changes, because of their concentration in part-time work, in the least well unionized sectors and in the service sectors, their experiences may very well be paradigmatic (Mitchell 1986). As in the Third World, women have been at the cutting edge of change and borne the heaviest costs of structural adjustment policies (Moser 1989). In macro terms, the increasing proportion of women working is changing the nature of work in a fundamental way. Not just, as some have argued, because it helps drive down overall wage levels and increases differentials, but because it can lead to changes in the culture and norms of work. Many of the contributors (Valentine, Pemberton, Brown, Stamp, Burnett, Harker) to this volume have stressed how culture can aid or obstruct the progress of women, but little has been said about whether a more feminine culture is unambiguously progressive. Although not always explicit, there is a common assumption that feminized cultures are generally better cultures, more liberal, more tolerant. But, without wishing to encourage anti-feminists, progress is not straightforward. When an occupation is said to be feminized, this usually means that average pay declines, and when social policy analysts talk of the feminization of poverty, they mean that women dominate among those defined as poor. An issue so far relatively unexplored is how a more feminized culture such as one which discounts personal gain and stresses loyalty may aid the newer forms of exploitation.

In addition to their labour market location women are traditionally exploited in different ways to men, both objectively and subjectively. A consequence, therefore, of more women being formally employed is a subtle change of work norms and, we suspect, the reinforcement of certain techniques of exploitation. Of these, those that are time-based are the most critical. Again, a number of trends converge. Performance-related pay, target setting and personal contracts create secrecy and often drive individuals to make unrealistic commitments, rather like 'sealed bids' which make them hostages to fortune. Added to which, there is a cultural equivalent to the quasi-markets of the public sector. Slogans are promoted which stress the importance of 'doing more for less' though they may, in fact, provide only 'regulatory comfort' to those in the grip of what Michael Power (1994) calls the 'Audit Explosion'. The demand for accountability may encourage simulations of efficiency rather than real efficiency gains because there may be no simple measure of output. However, a tangible by-product of the increased accountability and introduction of measures such as Citizen's Charters is the increase in workers having personally to face complaints for system failures, the causes of which are largely outside of their control. A consequence of this is an intensification of anxiety as a mode of internalized control. November 1994 saw the first British case of an employer being successfully sued for failing to protect an employee against overwork and stress. Although the case concerned a man, his occupation, social work, is a largely female one, like teaching and public sector work generally, all ones where stress levels are growing. This, we suggest, is not coincidental.

Whilst most measures of time spent at work show men working longer hours than women, there are several reasons for thinking that the true picture is more complex. Certainly, adding unpaid domestic labour to paid work gives a higher overall total to women, but the long hours of women's work are also a result of their being predominantly task-oriented rather than time-oriented. The caring work that they undertake is not subject to efficiency savings from new technology or economies of scale and, as much of it is emotional work, not only is 'switching off' difficult (Hochschild 1983), but quite often it simply cannot be fitted tidily into blocks of time. Added to which, women work long hours because they are masochistic, that is, because they have an exaggerated sense of responsibility (Haug 1992) and, it can be argued, because they are prone to being unrealistic (Coward 1992).

A syndrome that is particularly characteristic of women's work is that of high responsibility and low recognition, a form of work intensification that operates at both the subjective and objective levels and is on the increase (Karasek and Theorell 1990). Although we are not used to thinking of women as leading social change, there are sound reasons for suggesting that this is exactly what is happening. It also makes sense of the somewhat paradoxical reports (Hakim 1991, 1993) that women prefer part-time work, despite their knowledge that it is insecure and poorly paid. The part-time option itself may be a chimera that women are prone to be deceived by. Part-time work appears to be a solution to overload and stress, yet what it may support more fundamentally is the unrealistic but specifically female fantasy that a woman should be able to do the emotional and other work necessary in raising a family, that is, earn money, shop and service that family, and still find self-fulfilment in work. The broad implication of this is that increasing numbers of women working itself encourages time-based forms of exploitation. In addition to the well-known differences in pay between men and women in the same jobs that has already come under legal scrutiny there needs to be a parallel concern with time differentials. Whilst recorded hours and actual hours are notoriously discrepant in some occupations, a 1994 study of the workloads of British academics carried out by the Association of University Teachers showed that male professors worked, on average, 55 hours a week whilst female professors worked 65 hours. We consider it likely that similar comparisons exist for other occupations, and that if studies were repeated they might provide evidence of an emerging form of time- and gender-based inequality.

The most popular explanations of the worldwide intensification of competition, the quickening cycle of boom and recession, the shift out of primary industries and manufacturing and into process work and services tend to be technological. However, sociologists are wary of final causes and like to ask what conditions produce technical change or innovation? Is it the sheer joy of invention, or is technological development itself need- or scarcity-driven? (Wilkinson 1973). Land, labour, capital and technology are the traditional economic variables, though time is beginning to be seen as an even more fundamental factor driving technical change in process and service based industries (Von Tunzelmann 1995). As an ultimately scarce resource, time figures in the competition between organizations and between employers and employees. Employers shed costs in any way that they can, making employees responsible for their own time by treating them as self-employed, hiring for periods which do not cover lunch or tea breaks or by re-establishing piece rates. These time-saving strategies are most acute in the labour intensive process and service industries. As women are concentrated in all these sectors they are inevitably subject to work cultures where pressure to save time through organizational change is particularly intense. Added to which, because of lower rates of unionization and a pattern of socialization which encourages accommodation, they are less well equipped to resist the negative aspects of this process. Across all occupations the total number of hours spent at work has stopped its historical decline and is for many groups rising sharply (Foner and Roediger 1989; Christopherson 1991; Edwards and Whiston 1991; Schor 1992). Although not all commentators agree that the current rise is a real reversal of the long-term decline in working hours (Gershuny 1992), there is little doubt that increases in productivity in the service sector come as much from greater time exploitation as from new technology. After all, time management is itself a minor industry.

New communications lead to 'institutions without walls' and trading around the clock. Just as place of work may become irrelevant so, too, may old-fashioned forms of work supervision. The internalization of control and responsibility for the completion of any task may seem like a return to 'piece work', but because it is a prominent feature of service and 'people work' or 'caring', it is not. Looking after babies or old people is 'on demand' and not easily confined to schedules and the association of this sort of work with women is far from accidental or contingent (Bates 1990). The segregation of women or men into certain spheres of work has often been attributed to preferences on both sides. Employers may value dexterity, pliability or whatever, whilst employees may feel 'qualified' to undertake work that appears as a continuation of their domestic roles and skills. If time is ever singled out in these sorts of explanations it is usually to suggest that women are more likely to take time off to care for their own family. But a particular orientation towards time may be one of the advantages of employing women in some occupations. Women may carry into their work a greater concern with task than time, whereas men's orientation to their work is more time-based. A longer collective experience of formal employment has left men with a stronger sense of their individual rights. Many women still think of themselves as lucky to have any job at all and, because of patterns of socialization, have a weaker sense of boundaries (Chodorow 1978). Even in the professions, where long hours are becoming universal, men are more likely to have secretaries to guard their time and the delegation of tasks recommended by time management specialists is culturally far easier for men. Thus the time-based element of increasing work intensification, like a 'willingness' to accept lower wages, is critically tied to gender.

The changing language of equal opportunities

As evidence of continued gender segregation and inequality accumulates, public perception and response to it becomes more complex. Partly because there is no accepted standard of how long socially engineered change in gender relations might be expected to take, there is no easy measure of the success or failure of any intervention. The fact that everything has not changed in the twenty-five years since second wave feminism made its debut need not be a sign of failure. Any intervention can only be judged against a sense of what it would be reasonable to expect. However, there is evidence of a backlash to feminism (Faludi 1992) and to equal opportunities more generally in the form of a ridiculing stance towards 'political correctness' (Dunant 1994). This supposed orthodoxy is largely imaginary though by over-reaction it has become a significant force and focuses our attention on how battles may be fought out at the level of discourse and language.

The legal distinction between direct and indirect discrimination is an extremely important one: it allows us to see that demands to work unreasonable hours or to travel away from home a lot are forms of indirect discrimination against women; but the process of making a case along these lines, because it involves challenging taken-for-granted assumptions, increases the risks of seeming trivial and de-legitimizing the case for equal opportunities. Equal opportunities or gender workers have often a fine line to walk. They need to emphasize that pay differentials between the sexes have remained surprisingly stable and that segregation between and even within occupations has hardly been dented, but they also need to avoid being dismissed as part of the 'culture of complaint' (Hughes 1993). In this light it is no accident that 'diversity training' rather than equal opportunities is beginning to appear in staff development programmes and personnel journals. New terms as well as new solutions have to be found for old problems if the issue is to be kept alive. But, as the discourse changes, so does the potential for effective action. Lisa Harker's chapter is a case study in point: being family-friendly is clearly better than being just woman-friendly. It is both genuinely more progressive because it does not assume that only women have family responsibilities and avoids some negative stereotypes.

Changing the vocabulary is not wholly a matter of maintaining news worthiness, it can be a reaction to backlash. Feminism still arouses fear in some quarters and a continuing problem is how not to be seen as a 'whinger'. Folding gender issues into a broader definition of equal opportunity may lead to less attention being given to anything, or it may confer legitimacy by demonstrating that the 'interest' is not partial. Which way this may go will not always be clear, but all work aimed at transforming public attention has, to some degree, to be opportunist and use a flexible vocabulary.

Gender workers need to be very sure-footed, for there are traps around every corner. Policy recommendations, as Margaret Hodge details, need to be feasible and 'go with the grain'. For example, on the day the Social Justice Commission report was published in 1994 one of its members suggested that the problem about new jobs was that when they were created they went to the wives of men who already had jobs and not to members of the no-jobs households. This could be heard, though we are sure that it was not intended, to mean that new jobs should go to men and not to women. The problem, of course, is that many of the new jobs are low-paid and part-time and most men simply will not consider them. Arguing that some jobs should go to men or to women rather than that there should always be equal opportunities can be very tricky. The case from the 'right' is that men should have first crack at jobs because men are more socially destructive than women when they are unemployed. From this perspective a greater moral hazard is avoided by paying women less than men, for low pay will deter some women from entering the labour market at all, leaving more jobs free for men. A similar, more left-wing, version argues, conversely, that it is inefficient to permit over-qualified women to clog up low-skilled jobs which do not make full use of their talents and which could be filled by some men who really could not manage any other type of employment. Although one version is obviously more in tune with equal opportunities objectives, both appeal to scenarios of static or diminishing employment which themselves form the basis of an undercurrent of reluctance to support equal opportunities.

In certain ways equal opportunities or gender work has taken over from earlier reform movements. Many of the practical features once recommended by those interested in industrial democracy, job satisfaction and job design such as flatter hierarchies or a preference for collaboration rather than consultation, are the same as those now promoted as a route to more equal opportunities. And some of the people who have spent a good part of their lives committed to making this sort of change happen can feel annoyed at what may be felt as a take-over of their ideas, their campaigns and their achievements. More importantly, whilst some problems such as sexual harassment stem directly from gender, others do not, but are rather integral features of hierarchy and power. Collectives, even feminist collectives, can produce hierarchies and personal relations every bit as oppressive to their workers as conventional workplaces.

Conclusion

A feature of the 1990s has been the attempt to show that a wider sense of social responsibility makes good business sense. Reports like those from the Royal Society of Arts (1994) or New Consumer (1993) argue that competitive pressures are pushing firms to take a more 'inclusive approach' and urge them not to be concerned exclusively with shareholders. Rather, if they are to remain competitive, they need to recognize their interdependence with other companies and the communities in which they operate. Though such reports are not directly concerned with equal opportunities, they use a similar discourse and point out that changes in individual aspirations, the rise of pressure groups and the reduction of public confidence in governments and other institutions have changed the environment in which companies exist. Organizations like Opportunity 2000 are clearly useful in showing the way, although equally clearly change via example is more limited than change in response to legislation. The story of making gender work in the UK is another version of the old agency or structure debate. Individuals really can make a difference but if their efforts are to be copied and consolidated strong legislation is necessary and, frequently, we need to look to Europe for that legislation.

Of course, the root question of 'How does gender work?' cannot be finally answered – circumstances change, work changes and gender divisions mutate to accommodate these other changes, creating a whole new slate of problems or angles on equal opportunities. In addition to the diversity that has to be understood if equal opportunities are to be managed, there is the continuing problem of deciding priorities and mediating between competing claims. Then there is backlash. As this has been the subject of several recent books we have not discussed this in detail, though several of our contributors describe problems flowing from a partial acceptance of equal opportunities, a resistance that masquerades as complacency. Nor have we dealt with the role of the press and the media although this too clearly affects how equal opportunities are managed. The 'compassion fatigue' or 'culture of contentment' is partly a media phenomenon and represents a serious threat to equal opportunity workers. It means they have to remain on their toes, adept at identifying new threats and opportunities and sophisticated in making their cases. This is a familiar message. But it should not be read as a wholly depressing one, for all the contributors to this volume demonstrate that, even in a period characterized by high unemployment and widening income differentials, progress has been made. Even the 1980s were not wholly 'dark ages' and, as Margaret Hodge points out, many of the measures introduced to a chorus of ridicule in the 1970s are now mainstream. Lastly, to repeat a point made by Helen Brown, the task ahead is to find ways of linking the potential for change in people, organizations, policies and cultures.

REFERENCES

Aktouf, O. (1992) Management and theories of organizations in the 1990s. *Academy of Management Review*, 17(3): 407–31.

Allaire, Y. and Firsirotu, M.E. (1984) Theories of organizational culture. *Organization Studies*, 5(3): 193–226.

Allcock, D. (1993) *Typecast: Unlocking Secretary Potential*. London: Industrial Society.

Aoki, M., Gustafsson, B. and Williamson, O.E. (eds) (1990) *The Firm as a Nexus of Treaties*. London: Sage Publications.

Association of University Teachers (AUT) (1993–4) *Universities Statistical Record*, vol. 1. London: AUT.

Bacchi, C. (1990a) Pregnancy, the law and the meaning of equality, in E. Meehan and S. Sevenhuijsen (eds) *Equality, Politics and Gender*. London: Sage.

Bacchi, C. (1990b) *Same Difference: Feminism and Sexual Difference*. Sydney: Allen and Unwin.

Barr, N. (1993) *The Economics of the Welfare State*, 2nd edn. London: Weidenfeld and Nicolson.

Bartholomew, R., Hibbett, A. and Sidaway, J. (1992) Lone parents and the labour market: evidence from the Labour Force Survey. *Employment Gazette*, November, pp. 559–78.

Bates, I. (1990) 'No bleeding, whining minnies . . .': the role of youth training in class and gender reproduction. *British Journal of Education and Work*, 3(2): 91–109.

Becker, G. (1957) *The Economics of Discrimination*. Chicago: University of Chicago Press.

226

References

Benton, P. and Benton, P. (1990) *Riding the Whirlwind*. Oxford: Basil Blackwell.

Berry-Lound, D. (1993) *An Employers' Guide to Eldercare: A Guide for Employers on Practical Initiatives in the Workplace to Assist Employees in Combining Work and Caring for Adults and Elderly Dependants.* Sheffield: The Host Consultancy.

Bevan, S. and Thompson, M. (1992) *Merit Pay, Performance Appraisal and Attitudes to Women's Work*, IMS Report no. 234. Brighton: Institute of Manpower Studies.

Bevan, S., Buchan, J. and Hayday, S. (1989) *Women in Hospital Pharmacy.* Brighton: Institute of Manpower Studies.

Blau, F. (1993) Gender and economic outcomes: the role of wage structure. *Labour*, 7(1): 73–92.

Bohm, D. (1980) *Wholeness and the Implicate Order*. London: Routledge and Kegan Paul.

Bourne, C. and Whitmore, J. (1993) *Race and Sex Discrimination*, 2nd edn. London: Sweet and Maxwell.

Brown, H. (1993) Managing to success. Paper given at the 'Women in Public Management' conference, Northern Ireland, 13–14 September.

Brown, H. (forthcoming) Women in higher education: equal opportunities, in H. Eggins (ed.) *Women and Leadership in Higher Education*. Buckingham: SRHE/Open University Press.

Brown, H. and Goss, S. (1993) Can you hear the sound of breaking glass? *Health Service Journal*, 23: 26–7.

Bruegel, I. (1994) Municipal feminism: relating gender and class to hierarchies, markets and networks. Paper to the ESRC Women and Welfare Group, London, April.

Bruegel, I. and Perrons, D. (1995) Where do the costs of unequal treatment for women fall?, in J. Humphries and J. Rubery (eds) *The Economics of Equal Opportunities*. Manchester: Equal Opportunities Commission.

Business in the Community (1993) *Corporate Culture and Caring: The Business Case for Family-Friendly Provision*. London: Business in the Community/Institute of Personnel Management.

Chambers, R. (1993) *Challenging the Professions*. London: Intermediate Technology Publications.

Chodorow, N. (1978) *The Reproduction of Mothering: Psychoanalysis and the Sociology of Gender*. Berkeley: University of California Press.

Christopherson, S. (1991) Trading time for consumption: the failure of working-hours reduction in the United States, in K. Hinrichs, W. Roche and C. Sirianni (eds) *Working Time in Transition. The Political Economy of Working Hours in Industrial Nations*. Philadelphia: Temple University Press.

References

Clarke, K. (1991) *Women and Training: A Review*, Research Discussion Series no. 1. Manchester: Equal Opportunities Commission.

Clarke, L. (1994) *Discrimination*. London: Institute of Personnel Management.

Clement, B. (1992) How to make opportunity knock, *Independent*, 29 April, p. 28.

Clement, B. (1993) Workplace parity between sexes will take 25 years, *Independent*, 19 January, p. 3.

Clement, B. (1994) Civil service slow to promote women, *Independent*, 26 January, p. 9.

Cockburn, C. (1991) *In the Way of Women – Men's Resistance to Sex Equality in Organisations*. London: Macmillan.

Cockburn, C. (1993) Men's stake in organizations, gender and power, in Papers from an IRRU Workshop, Warwick Papers in Industrial Relations. University of Warwick: Industrial Relations Research Unit, pp. 4–8.

Collinson, D.L., Knights, D. and Collinson, M. (1990) *Managing to Discriminate*. London: Routledge.

Commission of the European Communities (1993) *Mothers, Fathers and Employment 1985–1991*, DGV.B4 Equal Opportunities Unit. Brussels: CEC.

Commission on University Career Opportunity (CUCO) (1994) *A Report on Universities' Policies and Practices on Equal Opportunity in Employment*. London: CUCO.

Committee of Vice-Chancellors and Principals (CVCP) (1991) *Equal Opportunities in Employment in Universities*. London: CVCP.

Connell, R.W. (1987) *Gender and Power: Society, the Person and Sexual Politics*. Cambridge: Polity Press.

Coward, R. (1992) *Our Treacherous Hearts. Why Women Let Men Get Their Way*. London: Faber.

Cowe, R. (1993) Burtons cuts 2000 jobs as union attacks move to part time work, *Guardian*, 8 January, p. 20.

Cox, T. (1991) The multi-cultural organization. *Academy of Management Executive*, 5(2): 34–48.

Coyle, A. (1989) The limits of change: local government and equal opportunities for women. *Public Administration*, 67: 39–50.

Coyle, A. (1993) Gender, power and organizational change: the case of women managers, in Papers from an IRRU Workshop, Warwick Papers in Industrial Relations. University of Warwick: Industrial Relations Research Unit, pp. 14–16.

Crompton, R. (1994) Occupational trends and women's employment patterns, in R. Lindley (ed.) *Labour Market Structures and Prospects for Women*, pp. 43–53. Manchester: Equal Opportunities Commission.

References

Crompton, R. and Sanderson, K. (1994) The gendered restructuring of employment in the finance sector, in A.M. Scott (ed.) *Gender Segregation and Social Change: Men and Women in Changing Labour Markets.* Oxford: Oxford University Press.

Csikszentmihalyi, M. (1991) *Optimal Experience.* Cambridge: Cambridge University Press.

Davies, C. (1990) *The Collapse of the Conventional Career: A Model for Equal Opportunities Employment in the NHS.* London: English Nursing Board.

Davies, C. and Rosser, J. (1986) *Processes of Discrimination: A Report on a Study of Women Working in the NHS.* London: HMSO.

Deal, T. and Kennedy, A. (1988) *Corporate Cultures: The Rites and Rituals of Corporate Life.* London: Penguin.

Department of Employment (1991) Costing of the Directive on working time. London: DoE.

Department of Employment (1992) Compliance cost assessment: Directive on the entitlement to maternity leave and dismissal protection of pregnant workers and workers who have recently given birth. London: DoE.

Department of Health (1988) *Equal Opportunities for Women in the NHS,* Report of the National Steering Group. London: DoH.

Department of Health (1991) *Women Doctors and their Careers,* Report of the Joint Working Party. London: DoH.

Dunant, S. (ed.) (1994) *The War of the Words. The Political Correctness Debate.* London: Virago.

Eatwell, J., Milgate, M. and Newman P. (eds) (1989) *The New Palgrave: Social Economics.* London: Macmillan.

Edwards, P. and Whiston, C. (1991) Workers and working harder: effort and shop floor relations in the 1980s. *British Journal of Industrial Relations,* 24: 593–601.

Eisenstein, H. (1991) *Gender Shock. Practising Feminism on Two Continents.* Sydney: Allen and Unwin.

El-Faizy, M. (1994) Fair sex, fair deal, *Guardian,* 7 March, p. 10.

Ellis, E. (1988) *Sex Discrimination Law.* Aldershot: Gower.

Ellis, E. (1991) *European Sex Equality Law.* Oxford: Oxford University Press.

Employment Gazette (1992) Women and the labour market: results from the 1991 Labour Force Survey, September, pp. 433–59.

Equal Opportunities Commission (EOC) (1988) *Equal Treatment for Men and Women, Strengthening the Acts, Formal Proposals.* Manchester: Equal Opportunities Commission.

Equal Opportunities Commission (EOC) (1991) *Equality Management: Women's Employment in the NHS.* London: HMSO.

Equal Opportunities Commission (EOC) (1992) *Women and Men in Britain 1992.* London: HMSO.

Equal Opportunities Commission (EOC) (1993) *Women and Men in Britain 1993*. London: HMSO.

Equal Opportunities Commission (EOC) (1994) *Country Profile Series: Netherlands*. London: EOC.

Equal Opportunities Review (EOR) (1994) EC Social Policy Green Paper, *Equal Opportunities Review*, 53: 3–4.

Ernst, S. (1989) Gender and the phantasy of omnipotence: case study of an organisation, in B. Richards (ed.) *The Crises of the Self. Further Essays on Psychoanalysis and Politics*. London: Free Association Books.

Esping-Anderson, G. (1990) *The Three Worlds of Welfare Capitalism*. Cambridge: Polity Press.

European Values Group (1991) *The European Values Study 1981–1990*. London: Gordon Cook Foundation.

Faludi, S. (1992) *Backlash: the Undeclared War against Women*. London: Chatto and Windus.

Families and Work Institute (1993) *An Evaluation of Johnson & Johnson's Work–Family Initiative*. New York: Families and Work Institute.

Figes, K. (1994) *Because of Her Sex: The Myth of Equality for Women in Britain*. London: Macmillan.

Fina Sanglas, L. (1991) The third action programme on equal opportunities for women and men (1991-95), in *Equal Opportunities for Women and Men*, Commission of the European Communities 3. Brussels: CEC.

Finch, S. (1993) *A Practical Guide to Childcare for Personnel Managers*. London: Working for Childcare.

Folbre, N. (1994) *Who Pays for the Kids: Gender and the Structure of Constraints*. London: Routledge.

Foner, P. and Roediger. D. (1989) *Our Own Time. A History of American Labour and the Working Day*. London: Verso.

Freeman, C. and Soete, L. (1994) *Work for All or Mass Unemployment? Computerized Technical Change into the 21st Century*. London: Pinter.

Galinsky, E., Friedman, D.E. and Hernandez, C.A. (1991) *The Corporate Reference Guide to Work–Family Programs*. New York: Families and Work Institute.

General Household Survey (1992) London: HMSO.

Gershuny, J. (1992) Are we running out of time? *Futures*, 24(1): 3–22.

Giele, J. (1978) *Women and the Future*. New York: The Free Press, Collier Macmillan.

Glyn, A. and Miliband, D. (1994) *Paying for Inequality: the Economic Cost of Social Injustice*. London: Institute of Public Policy Research/Rivers Oram.

Goetz, A. and Zen Gupta, R. (1994) *Who Takes the Credit? Gender, Power and Control Over Loan Use in Rural Credit Programmes in Bangladesh*, IDS working paper no. 8. Brighton: Institute of Development Studies.

References

Goss, S. and Brown, H. (1991) *Equal Opportunities for Women in the NHS*. London: NHS Management Executive/Office for Public Management.

Green, A. (1992) Spatial aspects of the SEM scenarios, in R. Lindley (ed.) *Women's Employment: Britain in the Single European Market*. London: HMSO, pp. 33–55.

Gregg, P. and Machin, S. (1993) *Is the Glass Ceiling Cracking?: Gender Compensation Differentials and Access to Promotion Among UK Executives*, London: National Institute for Economic and Social Research Discussion Paper no. 50.

Gregg, P. and Wadsworth, J. (1994) Women, households and access to employment: who gets it and why? Paper presented to the EOC Experts Seminar on the Economics of Equal Opportunities, Wilmslow.

The Guardian (editorial) (1995) 'New Man' absent from the kitchen, 24 January, p. 8.

Hakim, C. (1981) Job segregation: trends in the 1970s. *Employment Gazette*, December, pp. 521–9.

Hakim, C. (1991) Grateful slaves and self-made women. *European Sociological Review*, 7(2): 101–21.

Hakim, C. (1992) Explaining trends in occupational segregation: the measurement, causes and consequences of the sexual division of labour. *European Sociological Review*, 8(2): 127–51.

Hakim, C. (1993) The myth of rising female employment. *Work, Employment and Society*, 7(1): 97–120.

Hallaire, J. (1986) *Part-time Employment: its Extent and Problems*. Paris: OECD.

Hammond, V. and Holton, V. (1991) *A Balanced Workforce? Achieving Cultural Change for Women: A Comparative Study*. Berkhamsted: Ashridge Management Research Group.

Hampden-Turner, C. and Trompenaars, F. (1993) *The Seven Cultures of Capitalism*. London: Piatkus.

Handy, C. (1985) *Understanding Organizations*. London: Penguin.

Handy, C. (1992) Balancing corporate power. *Harvard Business Review*, November/December: 59–72.

Handy, C. (1994) *The Empty Raincoat: Making Sense of the Future*. London: Hutchinson.

Hansard Society Commission (1990) *Women at the Top*. London: HMSO.

Harman, H. (1993) *20th Century 21st Century Woman. How Both Sexes Can Bridge the Century Gap*. London: Vermilion.

Harrison, B. and Bluestone, B. (1990) Wage polarization in the US and the flexibility debate. *Cambridge Journal of Economics*, 14: 351–73.

Harrison, R. (1972) Understanding your organization's character. *Harvard Business Review*, May/June: 119–28.

Hart, V. (1994) European rights and British citizens: the emergence and potential of constitutional politics in Britain. Unpublished paper, School of English and American Studies, University of Sussex.

Harvey, E., Blakely, J. and Tepperman, L. (1990) Toward an index of gender inequality. *Social Indicators Research*, 22: 299–317.

Haug, F. (1992) *Beyond Female Masochism*. London: Verso.

Hearn, J. (1989) *The Sexuality of the Organization*. London: Sage.

Hewitt, P. (1993a) *About Time: The Revolution in Work and Family Life*. London: Rivers Oram/IPPR.

Hewitt, P. (1993b) Flexible working: asset or cost? *Policy Studies*, 14(3): 18–28.

Hirsch, F. (1977) *The Social Limits to Growth*. London: Routledge and Kegan Paul.

Hobsbawm, E. (1981) The Forward March of Labour Halted, in M. Jacques and F. Mulhern (eds) *The Forward March of Labour Halted*. London: Verso.

Hochschild, A. (1983) *The Managed Heart: The Commercialisation of Human Feeling*. Berkeley: University of California Press.

Hofstede, G. (1980) *Culture's Consequences: International Differences in Work Related Values*. Beverley Hills CA: Sage.

Hogg, C. and Harker, L. (1992) *The Family-Friendly Employer: Examples from Europe*. London/New York: Daycare Trust/Families and Work Institute.

Hogg, C., Kozak, M. and Petrie, P. (1989) *Childcare Links: Partnership in the Community*. London: Daycare Trust.

Holtermann, S. (1992) *Investing in Young Children: Costing and Funding and Education and Daycare Service*. London: National Children's Bureau.

Holtermann, S. (1995) The costs and benefits to British employers of measures to promote equality of opportunity, in J. Humphries and J. Rubery (eds) *The Economics of Equal Opportunities*. Manchester: Equal Opportunities Commission.

Holtermann, S. and Clarke, K. (1992) *Parents, Employment Rights and Childcare*, Research Discussion Series no. 4. Manchester: Equal Opportunities Commission.

Hughes, R. (1993) *Culture of Complaint: the Fraying of America*. New York: Oxford University Press.

Humphries, J. and Rubery, J. (1992) The legacy for women's employment: integration, differentiation and polarisation, in J. Michie (ed.) *The Economic Legacy 1979–1992*. London: Academic Press.

Humphries, J. and Rubery, J. (eds) (1995) *The Economics of Equal Opportunities*. Manchester: Equal Opportunities Commission.

Hunter, L.C. and Rimmer, S. (1994) An economic exploration of the UK and Australian experiences. Paper presented to the EOC Experts Seminar on the Economics of Equal Opportunities, Wilmslow.

References

Hutton, W. (1995) *The State We're In*. London: Jonathan Cape.

International Labour Office (1992) Yearbook of Labour Statistics. London: Equal Opportunities Commission.

Jaques, E. (1976) *A General Theory of Bureaucracy*. London: Heinemann.

Jewson, N. and Mason, D. (1986) Modes of discrimination in the recruitment process: formalisation, fairness and efficiency. *Sociology*, 20(1): 43–63.

Jewson, N., Mason, D., Lambkin, C. and Taylor, F. (1992) *Ethnic Monitoring Policy and Practice: A Study of Employers' Experiences*, Department of Employment Research Paper no. 89. London: Department of Employment.

Joshi, H. and Davies, H. (1992) *Child Care and Mothers' Lifetime Earnings: Some European Contrasts*. London: Centre for Economic Policy Research.

Joshi, H. and Davies, H. (1993) Mothers' human capital and childcare in Britain. *National Institute Economic Review*, November, 50–63.

Jowell, R., Witherspoon, S. and Brook, L. (eds) (1988) *British Social Attitudes: the 5th Report*. Aldershot, Hants: Social and Community Planning Research.

Jowell, R., Witherspoon, S. and Brook, L. (eds) (1990) *British Social Attitudes: the 7th Report*. Aldershot, Hants: Social and Community Planning Research.

Kandola, R.S., Milner, D., Banerji, N.A. and Wood, R. (1991) *Equal Opportunities Can Damage Your Health. Stress Amongst Equal Opportunities Personnel*. Oxford: Pearn Kandola Downs.

Kandyotti, D. (1994) The paradoxes of masculinity: some thoughts on segregated societies, in A. Cornwall and N. Lindisfarne (eds) *Dislocating Masculinity: Comparative Ethnographies*. London: Routledge.

Kanter, R. (1990) *When Giants Learn to Dance: Mastering the Challenges of Strategy Management and Careers in the 1990s*. London: Unwin.

Kanter, R. (1993) *Men and Women of the Organization*, 2nd edn. New York: Basic Books.

Karasek, R. and Theorell, T. (1990) *Healthy Work. Stress, Productivity, and the Reconstruction of Working Life*. New York: Basic Books.

Keller, S. (1984) Social differentiation and social stratification: the special case of gender, in W. Powell and R. Robbins (eds) *Conflict and Consensus*. New York: Free Press.

Kessler, I. (1994) Performance related pay: contrasting approaches. *Industrial Relations Journal*, 25(2): 122–35.

Kiernan, K. (1992) Men and women at work and at home, in R. Jowell, L. Brook, G. Prior and B. Taylor (eds) *British Social Attitudes: the 9th Report*. Aldershot: Dartmouth.

Labour Research Department (1992) *Working Parents: Negotiating a Better Deal*. London: Labour Research Department.

Lane, C. (1993) Gender and the labour market in Europe: Britain, Germany and France compared. *Sociological Review*, 41(2): 274–301.

Le Grand, J. (1991) *Equity and Choice: An Essay in Economics and Applied Philosophy*. London: HarperCollins.

Liff, S. and Dale, K. (1994) Formal opportunity, informal barriers: black women managers within a local authority. *Work, Employment and Society*, 8(2): 177–98.

Lindley, R. (ed.) (1994) *Labour Market Structures and Prospects for Women*. Manchester: Equal Opportunities Commission.

Lipman-Blumen, J. (1976) Towards a homo-social theory of roles, in M. Blaxall and B. Reagan (eds) *Women and the Workplace: the Implications of Occupational Segregation*. Chicago: Chicago University Press.

Lister, R. (1993) *Women's Economic Dependency and Social Security*, Research Discussion Series no. 2. Manchester: Equal Opportunities Commission.

Lovering, J. (1994) Employers, the sex-typing of jobs and economic restructuring, in A.M. Scott (ed.) *Gender Segregation and Social Change: Men and Women in Changing Labour Markets*. Oxford: Oxford University Press.

Maddock, S. (1993) Barriers to women are barriers to local government. *Local Government Studies*, 19(3): 341–50.

Marshall, J. and McLean, A. (1988) *Cultures at Work*. London: Local Government Management Board.

Marshall, S. (1992) Increasing the authority of women in organizations: facing the challenge. Paper given at the Women in Public Management conference, London, 21–23 October.

Martin, J. and Roberts, C. (1984) *Women and Employment: A Lifetime Perspective*, Report of the 1980 DE/OPCS Women and Employment Survey. London: HMSO.

Maruani, M. (1992) *The Position of Women on the Labour Market, Women of Europe Supplement no. 36*. Luxembourg: Commission of the European Communities.

McRae, S. (1989) *Flexible Working Time and Family Life – A Review of Change*. London: Policy Studies Institute.

McRae, S. (1991) *Maternity Rights in Britain: The Experience of Women and Employers*. London: Policy Studies Institute.

Metcalf, H. (1990) *Retaining Women Employees: Measures to Counteract Labour Shortage*, IMS Report no. 190. Brighton: Institute of Manpower Studies.

Metcalf, H. (1992) Hidden unemployment and the labour market, in E. McLaughlin (ed.), *Understanding Unemployment: New Perspectives on Active Labour Market Policies*. London: Routledge.

Michie, J. and Wilkinson, F. (1994) The growth of unemployment in the

References

1980s, in J. Michie and J. Grieve Smith (eds) *Unemployment in Europe*. London: Academic Press.

Miliband, D. (ed.) (1994) *Social Justice: Strategies for National Renewal*, Report of the Commission for Social Justice. London: Vintage.

Miller, K. and Steele, M. (1993) Employment legislation: Thatcher and after. *Industrial Relations Journal*, 24(3): 224–35.

Milner, M. (1985) *A Life of One's Own*. London: Virago Press.

Mitchell, J. (1986) Reflections on twenty years of feminism, in J. Mitchell and A. Oakley (eds) *What is Feminism?* Oxford: Basil Blackwell.

Morris, L. (1990) *The Workings of the Household*. Cambridge: Polity Press.

Moser, C. (1989) The impact of recession and structural adjustment policies at the micro-level: low income women and their households in Guayaquil, Ecuador, in Unicef *Women, Recession and Adjustment in the Third World*. New York: Unicef.

Nadeau, J. and Sanders, S. (1991) Equal opportunities policies: the cuckoo in the nest or the goose that laid the golden egg? Problems encountered and lessons learned, in J. Batsleer, C. Cornforth, and R. Paton (eds) *Issues in Voluntary and Non-profit Management*. Wokingham: Addison-Wesley/The Open University.

National Federation of Housing Associations (NFHA) (1992) Equal opportunities in housing associations – are you doing enough? London: NFHA.

New Consumer (1993) *Good Business: Case Studies in Corporate Social Responsibility*. Bristol: SAUS.

New Earnings Survey (1993) London: Department of Employment/HMSO.

Nicolaas, G. (1995) *Cooking: Attitudes and Behaviour*. London: OPCS Social Survey Division.

Obholzer, A. and Roberts, V. (1994) (eds) *The Unconscious at Work: Individual and Organizational Stress in the Human Services*. London: Routledge.

O'Donovan, K. and Szyszczak, E. (1988) *Equality and Sex Discrimination Law*. Oxford: Basil Blackwell.

Organisation for Economic Cooperation and Development (OECD) (1994) *Women and Structural Change, New Perspectives*. Paris: OECD.

Office for Public Management (OPM) (1992) *Getting More Women to the Top: a Strategy to Increase Opportunities for Women within Housing Associations*. London: OPM.

Office for Public Management (OPM) (1994) *Getting More Women to the Top in the Housing Association Movement – a Practical Guide*. London: OPM.

O'Leary, V.E. and Mitchell, J.M. (1990) Women connecting with women: networks and mentors, in S.S. Lie and V.E. O'Leary (eds) *Storming the Tower: Women in the Academic World*. London: Kogan Page.

Opportunity 2000 (1993) *Second Year Report*. London: Opportunity 2000.

References

Ouchi, W.G. and Johnson, J.B. (1978) Types of organizational control and their relationship to emotional well being. *Administrative Science Quarterly*, 23: 292–317.

Parkin, F. (1979) *Marxism and Class Theory: a Bourgeois Critique*. London: Tavistock.

Perrons, D. (1994) Measuring equal opportunities in European employment. *Environment and Planning A*, 26(8): 1195–221.

Perrons, D. (1995) Economic strategies, welfare regimes and gender inequality in employment in the European Union. *European Urban and Regional Studies*, 2(1): 90–101.

Peters, T.J. (1988) *Thriving on Chaos*. London: Macmillan.

Peters, T.J. (1993) *Liberation Management*. London: Macmillan.

Peters, T.J. and Waterman, R.H. (1982) *In Search of Excellence*. New York: Harper and Row.

Pettigrew, A.M. (1979) On studying organizational culture. *Administrative Science Quarterly*, 24: 571–81.

Platenga, J. (1994) Part time work and equal opportunities: the case of the Netherlands. Paper presented to the EOC Experts Seminar on the Economics of Equal Opportunities, Wilmslow.

Powell, G.N. and Butterfield, A.D. (1994) Investigating the 'glass ceiling' phenomenon: an empirical study of actual promotions to top management. *Academy of Management Journal*, 37(1): 68–86.

Power, M. (1994) *The Audit Explosion*. London: Demos.

Prechal, S. and Burrows, N. (1990) *Gender Discrimination Law of the European Community*. Aldershot: Dartmouth.

Rajan, A. and van Eupen, P. (1989) *Good Practice in the Employment of Women Employees*, IMS Report no. 183. Brighton: Institute of Manpower Studies.

Rees, T. (1992) *Women and the Labour Market*. London/New York: Routledge.

Rhode, D.L. (1989) *Justice and Gender*. New York: Harvard University Press.

Roberts, R., Brunner, E., White, E. and Marmot, M. (1993) Gender differences in occupational mobility and structure of employment in the British civil service. *Social Science and Medicine*, 37(12): 1415–25.

Roos, P.A. and Reskin, B.F. (1992) Occupational desegregation in the 1970s: integration and economic equity. *Sociological Perspectives*, 35(1): 69–91.

Royal Society of Arts Inquiry (1994) *Tomorrow's Company: The Role of Business in a Changing World. Interim Report. The Case for the Inclusive Approach*. Royal Society of Arts: London.

Rubery, J. (ed.) (1988) *Women and Recession*. London: Routledge.

References

Rubery, J. (1992a) *The Economics of Equal Value*, Research Discussion Series no. 3. Manchester: Equal Opportunities Commission.

Rubery, J. (1992b) Pay, gender and the social dimension to Europe. *British Journal of Industrial Relations*, 30(4): 605–21.

Rubery, J. and Fagan, C. (1994) Occupational segregation: plus ça change . . . ?, in R. Lindley (ed.) *Labour Market Structures and Prospects for Women*. Manchester: Equal Opportunities Commission, pp. 29–42.

Rubery, J., Horrell, S. and Burchell, B. (1994) Part time work and gender inequality in the labour market, in A.M. Scott (ed.) *Gender Segregation and Social Change: Men and Women in Changing Labour Markets*. Oxford: Oxford University Press.

Schein, E.H. (1985) *Organizational Culture and Leadership*. London: Jossey Bass.

Schein, V. (1994) Power, sex and systems. *Women and Management Review*, 9(1): 4–8.

Schmitt, J. and Wadsworth, J. (1994) The rise in economic inactivity, in A. Glyn and D. Miliband (eds) *Paying for Inequality: The Cost of Social Injustice*. London: IPPR/Rivers Oram Press, pp. 114–29.

Schor, J. (1992) *The Overworked American. The Unexpected Decline of Leisure*. New York: Basic Books.

Scott, A.M. (1994) Gender segregation in the retail industry, in A.M. Scott (ed.) *Gender Segregation and Social Change: Men and Women in Changing Labour Markets*. Oxford: Oxford University Press.

Sidney, E. (1994) *Gender Audit Questionnaire*. London: Mantra Consultancy Group.

Simkin, C. and Hillage, J. (1992) *Family-Friendly Working: New Hope or Old Hype?*, IMS Report no. 224. Brighton: Institute of Manpower Studies.

Sloane, P. (1994) The gender wage differential and discrimination in the six SCELI local labour markets, in A.M. Scott, (ed.) *Gender Segregation and Social Change: Men and Women in Changing Labour Markets*. Oxford: Oxford University Press.

Smircich, L. (1983) The concept of culture and organizational analysis. Paper presented at the ICA/SCA Conference on Interpretative Approaches to Organizational Communication, Alta UT, July.

Social Trends (1995) No. 25. London: HMSO.

Stamp, G. (1986) Some observations on the career paths of women. *The Journal of Applied Behavioural Science*, 22(4): 385–96.

Sugarman, D and Straus, M. (1988) Indicators of gender equality for American states and regions. *Social Indicators Research*, 20: 229–70.

Thomas, R.R. (1990) From affirmative action to affirming diversity. *Harvard Business Review*, March/April: 107–17.

Toffler, A. (1990) *Powershift. Knowledge, Wealth and Violence and the End of the 21st Century*. New York: Bantam Books.

237

References

Trapp, R. (1994) Women slip back on the corporate ladder, *Independent*, 5 May, p. 38.

Von Tunzelmann, G.N. (1995) Time-saving technical change: the cotton industry in the English industrial revolution. *Explorations in Economic History*, November, 1–27.

Walby, S. (1988) *Gender Segregation at Work*. Milton Keynes: Open University Press.

Walby, S. (1990) *Theorizing Patriarchy*. Oxford: Blackwell.

Waring, M. (1988) *If Women Counted*. London: Macmillan.

Wharton, C. (1994) Finding time for the 'second shift': the impact of flexible work schedules on women's double days. *Gender and Society*, 8(2): 189–205.

Whitehouse, G. (1992) Legislation and labour market gender inequality: an analysis of OECD countries. *Work, Employment and Society*, 6(1): 65–86.

Whitting, G., Moore, J. and Warren, P. (1993) *Partnerships for Equality: A Review of Employers Equal Opportunities Groups*, Department of Employment Research Series no. 19. London: DoE.

Wilkinson, H. (1994) *No Turning Back: Generations and the Genderquake*. London: Demos.

Wilkinson, R.G. (1973) *Poverty and Progress*. London: Methuen.

Wilson, L. (1973) *Introduction to Social Movements*. New York: Basic Books.

Working For Childcare (1994) *Survey of Employer Sponsored Nursery Provision – Britain*. London: Working for Childcare.

Yeandle, S. (1984) *Women's Working Lives: Patterns and Strategies*. London: Tavistock Publications.

INDEX

239

Index

East Sussex Local Authority,
127–8, 159–69
Eatwell, J., 41
ECJ, *see* European Court of Justice
economics and equal opportunities,
14, 27, 32–53, 82, 210
education, 29, 36
see also higher education; training
Edwards, P., 221
eldercare, 99–100
electricity industry, 181–2
El-Faizy, M., 19
Elida Gibbs Company, 98–9
Ellis, E., 57, 63
emergency leave, 120
employment breaks, *see* career
breaks
Enderby v. Frenchay Health
Authority, 65
equal opportunities, 2, 8, 125–9,
214–25
deregulation, 72–88
economics of, 32–53
non-dominant groups, 193–213
organizational culture, 108–23
public sector, 130–8, 140–5,
159–69
role of the law, 54–71
trade unions, 178–92
voluntary sector, 138–40, 170–7
Equal Opportunities Commission
(EOC), 3, 4, 45, 46, 181
action, 63, 64, 133, 179, 184
reports, 81, 135
equal opportunities policies, 8,
72–6, 79, 132
economics, 33, 44–52
implementation, 100–5, 159–69
monitoring, 80–7, 144, 167
Equal Pay Act (1970), 15, 55, 57, 64,
181
Equal Pay Directive (75/117), 64–5
equal pay for work of equal value,
49–50, 64–6, 73, 77, 79, 83, 183
Equal Treatment Directive, 68
(75/207), 68, 69, 70
equalities audit, 118–22

equality, 15–16
of opportunity, 41–4, 50, 82–3,
215
of outcome, 13, 16, 43, 61, 82
equivalence, 16, 22, 43, 83
Ernst, S., 4
Esping-Anderson, G., 30
ethnic minority groups, 81, 148,
152, 163, 171, 199
European Court of Justice, 58–9, 62,
63, 64–8, 79, 184
European legislation, 15, 26, 73,
156, 161, 225
European Market, Single, 94
European Union (EU), 49, 63, 84,
91, 96
social policies, 14, 48, 75, 76
exploitation, 3, 8–9, 214–25

Fagan, C., 74, 75
Faludi, S., 222
family-friendly policies, 17, 27,
89–107, 119, 223
family leave, 97
family relationships, 40, 41, 57,
105–6
family responsibilities, *see* caring
family structure, 17, 89, 90–2, 179
fathers, 41, 47, 68, 91, 104, 105
paternity leave, 39, 47, 96–7
federalism, 208
feminism, 2, 3, 217, 222, 223
feminization, 214–25
Figes, Kate, 5, 143
Fina Sanglas, L., 76
Finch, S., 102
Firsirotu, M.E., 116
flexibility, 93, 172, 217
flexible working, 22, 23–4, 76, 77,
88, 136
family-friendly policies, 89, 92,
94–5, 103, 104, 119
flexiplace working, 96
Folbre, N., 8
Foner, P., 221
France, 22, 25
Freeman, C., 217

241

Index

Index

Index

Roberts, R., 29
Roberts, V., 4
Roddick, Anita, 29
Roediger, D., 221
role culture, 112, 113
role models, 104, 127, 216
role reinforcement, 40, 56
Roos, P.A., 29
Rosser, J., 135
rubber ceilings, 206–7
Rubery, J., 11, 22, 33, 50
   pay and conditions, 14, 75, 76, 77, 78, 83
   women's status, 23, 27, 41, 74, 80

sameness, *see* difference
Sanderson, K., 25, 26
Schein, E.H., 113, 115–16
Schein, V., 30
Schering AG, 95
Schmitt, J., 20, 21
Schor, J., 221
Scott, A.M., 6, 11, 25
SDA, *see* Sex Discrimination Act
selection, 136, 166
self-employment, 3, 220
service sector, 7, 213
   conditions, 20–1, 24–5, 218, 221
   growth, 2, 91, 92, 179
sex discrimination, 38, 44, 164
   legal action, 1, 4, 63, 182
Sex Discrimination Act (1975)(SDA), 15, 46, 55, 57–62, 67
sexism, 28, 190
sexual harassment, 30, 38, 58, 115, 164
Shaw, Jenny, 1–11, 19–31, 125–9, 214–25
Sheffield Hallam University, 141–2
Sidney, E., 118
Siemens AG, 97
Simkin, C., 23, 24, 93
single parents, *see* lone parents
Sloane, P., 7
Smircich, L., 110, 113
Soete, L., 217
Stamp, Gillian, 6, 123, 128, 193–213

Steele, M., 76
stereotyping, 42–3, 59, 78, 79, 89, 163
Straus, M., 85
stress, 4, 219
subcontracting, 77, 133
success, definition of, 126, 134
Sugarman, D., 85
Sweden, 39, 47
Szyszczak, E., 57

targets, 152, 165, 166, 190, 218
task culture, 112
technology, 26, 207, 217, 220
teleworking, 96
tenants' associations, 147, 149
Tepperman, L., 84
Tesco Company, 95
Thatcher, Margaret, 148–9, 151, 176
Theorell, T., 219
Third World, 27, 218
Thomas, R.R., 116, 117–18
Thompson, M., 28, 78, 79, 87–8
threat of non-dominant groups, 178, 206, 215
time exploitation, 219–22
Toffler, A., 217
trade unions, 76, 78, 127, 149, 178–92
   pay and conditions, 9, 64, 94
   training, 29, 36, 137, 168–9, 190
   access to, 93, 136, 167
   positive discrimination, 45, 46, 156
Trapp, R., 28, 30
tribunals, 1, 58, 66, 142, 181, 182
   divergent views, 15, 60, 61, 62
Trompenaars, F., 209, 213

unemployment, 20, 21, 34, 37, 49, 51, 180, 217
UNISON Trade Union, 127, 181, 182, 187–92
United States of America (USA), 20, 75, 84–5, 96, 99, 101
   equalities work, 56, 59, 61, 66, 116–17, 181

245